"There are very few academics at the cutt
who can engage with parents and practitic
language and examples which chime with .... a parent
or to work daily with other peoples' children. This careful selection
by Caroline Vollans of the letters from parents and replies of Susan
Isaacs' (known as Ursula Wise) in the 1930s editions of the much-
respected *Nursery World* magazine demonstrated her genius in
being able to do this. The book brings out the ability of Susan Isaacs
to get alongside parents and also to influence the readers of *Nursery
World* who are nannies, nurses, nursery nurses and teachers. She
helps parents and practitioners to understand the children and gives
them the possibility of acting in ways which help and comfort both
the child and themselves. Caroline Vollans notes that each letter is
thought provoking, reassuring and helpful to read. Selecting which
letters to include in the book was a challenge, but one to which she
has risen with skill and has created a well organised framework
showing the central aspects of Susan Isaacs's guidance for parents
and practitioners. I missed my stop on the tube because it was such
a thoroughly well put together book and an absorbing read."

Professor Tina Bruce *CBE, Honorary Visiting Professor in Early
Childhood at the University of Roehampton, UK*

"Susan Isaacs is one of the hidden names of child development and
education, who spent most of her adult life trying to understand
and create the most appropriate ways in which adults can help
children grow emotionally and cognitively. She was a patient and
meticulous observer of children and bringing her work back into
the public sphere is a great help for anyone wanting to understand
how children tick."

Professor Michael Rosen, *Professor of Children's Literature at
Goldsmiths, University of London, UK*

"This is an important book, providing recommendations and
answers that remain valid for many of the problems facing children
and parents today. Fearfulness, phobias, vivid fantasies; the learning

of words, nervous strain, and eating problems – these concerns of parents in the 1930s find an immediate echo in today's world. The responses and discussions that are reprinted here are commentaries made by one of the most important of the psychoanalysts who developed Freud's work in this country: they are all moreover couched in ordinary language, and they aim to join together expert insights with a down-to-earth common sense. A phrase used by Susan Isaacs in these columns grasps the central theme of this work – she aims, she says, despite the difficulties of the developing relation between parent and child, to formulate this bond in terms of a 'living relationship'. Caroline Vollans does a great service to anyone with an interest in this primary relation between parent and child."

Professor Bernard Burgoyne, *Emeritus Professor of Psychoanalysis, Middlesex University, UK*

WISE WORDS

"Harassed" writes: *"Your answers to correspondents are exceedingly clear, and when I read them I say, 'That is just the answer I should think of', though I believe I should have great difficulty when it came actually to putting it into words! However, I cannot answer my own problems, so will you please help me?" (20 August 1930)*

This much-needed collection brings together the columns of parenting adviser Ursula Wise, "agony aunt" for *The Nursery World* between 1929 and 1936, and pseudonym for the eminent educationalist and pioneering psychoanalyst Susan Isaacs.

Wise's replies, informed by theories in education, psychology and psychoanalysis, provide an insight into the development of modern, child-centred attitudes to parenting, with remarkably fresh and relevant advice. The letters are passionate, urgent, occasionally provocative, sometimes funny and always thoughtful. Topics from behaviour and temperament, anxieties and phobias, to play and education are explored and each theme is introduced and contextualised in contemporary parenting approaches.

Bringing pivotal theories from the fields of education, child psychology and psychoanalysis into dialogue, this is an essential read for early years practitioners, teachers, course leaders and those studying in the field of early years education and child psychoanalysis. The continued relevance of Isaacs' advice for modern parenting also makes this an enjoyable and informative read for parents, and it is an excellent resource for those interested in social history and the little-known contributions made by women pioneers.

Caroline Vollans gained fifteen years of experience as a primary school teacher before training in psychoanalysis and becoming a member of the Centre for Freudian Analysis and Research, UK. She now works as a school counsellor, freelance researcher and writer.

WISE WORDS

HOW SUSAN ISAACS CHANGED PARENTING

Caroline Vollans

Routledge
Taylor & Francis Group

LONDON AND NEW YORK

First published 2018
by Routledge
2 Park Square, Milton Park, Abingdon, Oxon OX14 4RN

and by Routledge
711 Third Avenue, New York, NY 10017

Routledge is an imprint of the Taylor & Francis Group, an informa business

British Library Cataloguing-in-Publication Data
A catalogue record for this book is available from the British Library

Library of Congress Cataloging-in-Publication Data
Names: Vollans, Caroline, author. | Isaacs, Susan Sutherland Fairhurst, 1885–1948.
Title: Wise words : how Susan Isaacs changed parenting / Caroline Vollans.
Description: Abingdon, Oxon ; NewYork, NY : Routledge, 2018. | Includes
    bibliographical references.
Identifiers: LCCN 2017025145| ISBN 9781138096776 (hardback) |
    ISBN 9781138096790 (pbk.) | ISBN 9781315105185 (ebook)
Subjects: LCSH: Isaacs, Susan Sutherland Fairhurst, 1885–1948—Correspondence. |
    Child rearing. | Parenting. | Child psychology. | Child development.
Classification: LCC HQ769.I8 V65 2018 | DDC 306.874—dc23
LC record available at https://lccn.loc.gov/2017025145

ISBN: 978-1-138-09677-6 (hbk)
ISBN: 978-1-138-09679-0 (pbk)
ISBN: 978-1-315-10518-5 (ebk)

Typeset in Aldus Roman and Scala
by Book Now Ltd, London
Printed and bound by CPI Group (UK) Ltd, Croydon, CR0 4YY

In memory of Kirsty Hall who brought
Susan Isaacs to my attention

CONTENTS

ACKNOWLEDGEMENTS

Thank you to:

The staff at the UCL Institute of Education archive for being so accommodating and friendly – Sarah, Becky, Jessica, Kathryn H, Kathryn M, Amy, Anthony.

Thank you to the staff at *Nursery World* for their cooperation and permission to use this material.

Michael Rosen and Bernard Burgoyne for their kind endorsements.

Leigh Wilson for sharing her considerable expertise and for liking the Ursula Wise column.

Tina Bruce for her guidance on Froebel and general wisdom.

Abigail Knight for her ongoing engagement and input.

Alexandra Langley for her tireless interest and affirmation.

Tamara Bibby for telling me, "You could write this standing on your head".

Olivia O'Sulllivan, Sue McGonigle, Anni McTavish, Michelle Strange, Liz Brooker, Glen Pike, Annie Johns and Ginny Reddick for their unique contributions.

Maisie Vollans whose spirit and academic rigour are always an inspiration.

And, most of all, to Julian Grenier – not only for his unwavering belief in this project from the start but for his remarkable insights. Thank you so, so much.

Main introduction

Susan Isaacs (1885–1948) was a prolific writer, visionary theorist and ground-breaking practitioner, yet her name goes largely unrecognised. Despite working exceptionally hard throughout her life and making lasting contributions to the theory and practice of psychology, psychoanalysis and education, Susan Isaacs has not been given her due acclaim. Indeed, Philip Graham's biography, only the second to be written, was prompted by this fact (Graham, 2009).

In the 1920s, a time when psychoanalysis was burgeoning, Isaacs was a prominent figure in the Kleinian group.[1] Later, during the Controversial Discussions,[2] she presented a rigorous exposition of the concept of unconscious phantasy – a complex idea based on the premise that the baby's instinctual bodily experiences become associated with concrete mental representations or "imagined" representations. For example, the baby's bodily feeling of hunger becomes associated with an internal malevolent object or figure that causes the discomfort of hunger. The infant then is beset by a fear of this something

---

1 Melanie Klein (1882–1960), eminent psychoanalyst whose work centred on therapeutic play techniques for children.
2 A series of debates (1942–1944) in the British Psychoanalytical Society resulting in a tripartite split – the Kleinians, the Anna Freudians and the Independent group.

that exists inside of them – hence their propensity to have a distressing time. Such a vivid phantasy life, experienced as real, gives some insight into the extent of the infant's upsets, rages and terrors. This, Isaacs's notion of unconscious phantasy,[3] is her renowned and lasting contribution to psychoanalysis.

In the field of education, Susan Isaacs was one of the pioneers of play-based learning in England. That a play-centred curriculum today is the norm in good early years settings tells us something of the power of her influence. The *Oxford Dictionary of National Biography* describes Isaacs as being "the greatest influence on British Education in the twentieth century" (Pines, 2004). Her pioneering work in child-centred and play-based education was brought to prominence through the experimental Malting House School in Cambridge (1924–1929). For Isaacs, play is a continuous experiment where children learn as little researchers, constantly opening lines of enquiry and making new discoveries. Under her leadership at Malting House, the children were given great scope and freedom to foster their individual development: the role of the teacher being to observe, guide and facilitate them through their play.

It was her approach to play both as an educationalist and a psychoanalyst that made Isaacs uniquely influential – play not only being valuable for the development of skills and knowledge, but also because of its capacity for sublimation and the diffusion of anxiety. In *Intellectual Growth of Young Children* (Isaacs, 1930) Isaacs explores how fantasy play and symbolic play are useful for the expression of feelings and mental states. This can be critical for young children in learning to acknowledge and manage their emotional being. For Isaacs, young children can tell us most about their developmental needs through the medium of play. Indeed, one of her main contributions in the field of teacher education was the importance she put upon making close observations of children at play: both for the training of and the continued professional development of teachers. Not only is this practice key to the training of teachers, but also in the training programme for child psychotherapists, educational psychologists and child psychologists: psychology being the third field of Isaacs's eminence.

Isaacs graduated from Newnham College, Cambridge with a Masters in psychology in 1913. She went on, twenty years later in

3 *Phantasy* spelt this way refers to a fantasy that is unconscious.

1933, to head up the Child Development Department at the Institute of Education.[4] Isaacs was critical of the renowned psychologist Jean Piaget, whose theories of the cognitive development of young children she found overly schematic. She thought Piaget did not pay enough attention to closely observing children at play in natural settings. She famously disagreed with him whilst they were both watching a five-year-old on his trike in the gardens of the school she ran in the 1920s, the Malting House School: contrary to Piaget's theories, the child was able to explain why his trike was not moving forward (Graham, 2009, p. 144).

Isaacs's significance in these three major fields is clear. However, as someone trained and qualified in two of these fields (primary school teaching and psychoanalysis), I can say that she was not mentioned in either of my professional trainings. Fortunately, I came across her when studying for a Masters in psychoanalysis and, later, through contact with colleagues interested in the academic strands of early years education. It seems that, over the years, Isaacs's name has been somewhat erased, though her impact certainly has not.

Notwithstanding each of these exemplary achievements, there remains a further area of Isaacs's work which was highly influential, yet is even less known. From 1929 to 1936, using the pseudonym of Ursula Wise, Isaacs wrote a weekly parenting column for *The Nursery World*,[5] where she responded to the concerns of parents and nannies; most weeks replying to two or three letters. The column, "Childhood Problems", was headlined "Ursula Wise is always pleased to answer letters from mothers about difficulties with children. All queries are answered on these pages, so please give initials or a pseudonym". Isaacs, under her pen name, replied to every correspondent's letter – including those that were not printed. Although the readers were informed in 1934 that "Ursula Wise is, in fact, a psychologist, holding the degree of MA, DSc, whose authority to advise on the difficulties of childhood is unquestioned by those who know her", the name of

4 Now called the UCL Institute of Education, ranked for each of the last three years as the world's number one education university in the QS World University Rankings by subject.
5 First published in 1925. It is now printed as *Nursery World* – omitting *The* from the title.

this agony aunt was never disclosed. It is this work, so little known about, that I am bringing to the fore in this book.

Isaacs's extensive archive at the Institute of Education contains thirty-eight folders, twenty-eight of which are devoted to this parenting column. Every column is there, just as it appeared in *The Nursery World*, as well as many of her replies in their original typed manuscript form, including her handwritten notes and annotations. As soon as one glances at the archive, her assiduous work as Ursula Wise is palpable. Perhaps significantly, in the last year of her life, she published a book, *Troubles of Children and Parents* (Isaacs, 1948a), containing a collection of these columns.[6] It seems, from this, possible to deduce that it was important to Isaacs that her work in the guise of Ursula Wise should not to be forgotten in her legacy.

In the preface to *Troubles of Children and Parents*, Isaacs tells us something about how she saw her role as Ursula Wise, her intentions and hopes. Though she shortens some of the letters, Isaacs explains her choice to reprint the original letters, rather than give a synopsis: "I felt the local colour giving the picture of the actual children and parents, and of the living relationship between them, was much more likely to make the replies helpful than any artificial summary of the questions could do" (Isaacs, 1948a, p. vi). She clearly valued the words of her correspondents. Isaacs describes, too, what she hoped to offer her readers:

> What I always tried to do in my replies to these anxious enquiries, and that I hope this book will do for its readers now, is to give parents and nurses some sense of children's normal development and at the same time a greater awareness of the reality and intensity of the child's feelings in his various relationships – how human he is, even as an infant, and how necessary it is to be aware of this if one is to treat him reasonably.
>
> (Ibid.)

Isaacs, too, makes clear the limitations of the column:

> I do not suggest that one can be as useful to parents through the medium of a letter as by means of a first-hand diagnostic interview, but there are many

---

6 This collection of letters is limited to concerns regarding the social, psychological and emotional development of children.

cases of children with urgent problems of behaviour where circumstances
do not justify or may even preclude a visit to the Child Guidance Clinic.

(Ibid.)

Wise's columns were written twenty years after Freud's hugely controversial paper on *Infantile Sexuality* (1905) which, though familiar
in intellectual and academic circles, had not infiltrated the world of
child rearing. That said, it was a time when a psychological understanding of the child was beginning to come to the fore and questions
were being asked about the behaviourists' rigid and doctrinaire methods of child rearing – this is evident in the correspondence. Having
said that, it was still the case that Truby King's behavioural methods
prevailed and continued to be the most popular reference point for
carers – a military routine of feeding, sleeping, fresh air, toileting and
keeping a good distance from the baby.[7] For King, it is all about training and conditioning the infant to fit the world, sometimes referred
to as "breaking the baby".

Wise, in absolute contrast to King's one-size-fits-all approach, pro-
poses something at the opposite end of the spectrum. Reading her
columns, it is palpable that Wise showed an unremitting understanding of both the child and parents when dealing with the majority of
concerns. Whereas King's approach was about toughening the baby
up, Wise's was about understanding and being sensitive to the development of babies and their accompanying feelings and emotional
states. Wise's role was about helping their parents get through difficulties in a way that was informed and dignified for both parents
and infant.

Wise's unique selling point is that her advice comes out of her vast
number of first-hand observations of children, knowledge and practice as an educationalist, psychologist and psychoanalyst. It is these
that she brings into dialogue in the replies to her correspondents.
Having said that, though theoretically informed, her advice comes
across as *common sense* in manner. This is perhaps the most impres-
sive feature of Wise's column – that she manages to write in a way
that is remarkably well informed, yet accessible and reader-friendly.

---

7 King's influential handbook: King, F. T. (1913) *The Feeding and Care of Baby.*
London: Macmillan and Co. Ltd.

This is surely a measure of both the calibre of her writing and her dexterity in using her knowledge and experience. It is, too, in keeping with the tenor of the column – weighty theory from an agony aunt could be off-putting to the reader, especially in an era long before the massive popularisation of psychology.

This collection of letters is grouped into themed chapters – for each chapter I have written a short introduction intended to provide background information where necessary but mainly to entice the reader to read on. I want the letters to speak for themselves and be read as they were written – for the regular readers of *The Nursery World*. This gives the column a quality that I do not want to taint by attempting to explain the psychoanalytical and educational details informing her letters – this would not only skew the nature of this work, but run the risk of deadening it.

Selecting the letters was no easy task – the omissions being the difficult part – there is something of value and interest in all of them. The letters remain in their original form: they have not been short-ened or altered in any way: the only difference being that the originals are in columns and illustrated.[8] Despite the vast social changes over the years and growth of technology and commercialisation, parents and carers of young children tend to worry about the same things as the decades pass. Many of Wise's letters have withstood the test of time and remain relevant today. Though the advice was given almost eighty years ago, it is generally adaptable for today: this is simply because the guidance is based on a sound knowledge of young chil-dren and a principled approach to their upbringing.

Wise's manner, vocabulary and turn of phrase put us in touch with her voice – it is one that is candid and full of verve yet sensitive. There is nothing sterile or clinical about her replies: she is serious, yet lively and engaging. There are, too, the voices of her correspond-ents which are fascinating in that they reflect the era and provide us with an invaluable social history. They are the voices of real women appealing for help in raising their children – as such they can be profoundly moving. The letters are beautifully written and full of personality – they can also be very entertaining.

---

8 Some of the photographs are included – in the original columns many of the photos are repeated in later editions. Interestingly, too, the photographs and illustrations often bear little correspondence to the theme of the letter.

It is, then, with great admiration and satisfaction that I have brought this project to fruition. This book is not only an attempt to bring Susan Isaacs's name and work as a parenting mentor to the fore but to make the claim that she was a significant and trail-blazing pioneer. Using the medium of an agony aunt column, Ursula Wise was the first to popularise a new and more enlightened approach to child-rearing – she was, indeed, a revolutionary figure.

The Ursula Wise column is an insightful, poignant and spirited column that is a pleasure to read.

CHAPTER ONE

Behaviour and temperament

INTRODUCTION

Wise comments that concerns about behaviour and discipline are "as old as parenting itself" – it is perhaps not surprising that the majority of letters are on this theme. A riff that runs throughout the column is Wise's attempt to draw the distinction between that behaviour that is wilful and behaviour that is part of natural development. Whatever the cause, her responses emphasise the handling of the symptoms rather than the interpretation or analysis of them.

Wise informs her readers that the links between behaviour and child development are inseparable: a child's behaviour cannot be considered without bearing this in mind. She urges her readers to become more interested and informed about this topic and at times includes recommendations of psychology books. For Wise, what is often manifested as troubling behaviour is usually an expression of normal, healthy growth and only to be expected. Her principal message to her correspondents is that there is generally nothing to be distressed about. Given sensitive and age-appropriate handling, problems should be temporary and pass over time.

Having said that, Wise understands that allowing development to take its course can be a lengthy and demanding business – she advises her readers not to be discouraged. During this time, challenging behaviours need to be responded to and managed. Careful handling, as well as dealing with the situation in hand, has the advantage of enabling the child to begin to regulate their own feelings and states. Wise reassures her correspondents that establishing reasonable and fair limits will not dull the child's spirit – for Wise, a docile child is not one to aspire to or encourage.

It is important that parents are frank and clear – the child will then feel safe in the knowledge that someone knows what they are doing. Wavering or a lack of certainty will be sensed and only serve to generate further anxiety – parental confidence is key. Wise stresses the caution that the adult must exercise when expecting a child to do what is asked of them – it must be suited to their needs at their stage of development.

Wise is dismissive of any notion of obedience as *an end in itself* and of the child complying *per se*. Indeed, she expresses her less than flattering opinions on the sort of personality that might result from this. Obedience is an educative tool of social importance and must be of use to the child later in life. It is not primarily a means of making nursery life simpler.

For Wise, discipline does not imply that one cannot be kindly and affectionate. She is adamant that there is no advantage in it being an unpleasant process: reproaching and scolding a child will only exacerbate the difficulty. Engaging in a friendly manner and encouraging their cooperation is the approach that she advocates.

Wise is stridently opposed to brutality of any kind: frightening or blaming a child will only generate further anxiety. She is zealously opposed to smacking, whatever the situation – it seriously impedes a child's development. On this theme she is entirely rigid and her tone is unusually harsh and unforgiving towards the parents. Wise has much to say on the topic – there are many letters throughout the correspondence where she asserts and reasserts her position. Though smacking is not such a pressing issue today, due to the way that thinking and the law has progressed, it was quite something at the time to advise so strongly against it and be so immutably opposed to it.

Wise goes on in Chapter 3 to elucidate the effects of physical health on children's behaviour – the effects of an upset digestive system, for example, cannot be underestimated and must be eliminated before further attention is given to the behaviour. She does not let the psychology of the situation blur common sense.

Wise, despite her advice, acknowledges throughout that no parent is a saint!

DIFFICULTIES WITH TWO-YEAR-OLDS

20 AUGUST 1930

"L.J.R." writes: "I should be so very glad of your advice regarding my daughter of two years and two months. She is an only child and extremely healthy, full of spirit, and, I am told, more than ordinarily intelligent for her age. Until recently she has been fairly easy to manage, although very self-willed and inclined to be disobedient. Now, however, when told to do anything, or told NOT to do anything, she immediately starts screaming as loudly as possible, and ends by crying bitterly. We try not to demand anything unreasonable, but she seems to delight in seeing how far she can go without being punished. I realise it is quite useless to keep on scolding and punishing, but, on the other hand, if you give in to her on a single point she immediately takes it as a sign of victory, and it is no use trying to retrieve it afterwards. She has entirely been brought up on Truby King lines, sleeps fourteen hours out of the twenty-four, never has a light in her room, or is nervous of anything. Lately, too, she keeps picking at her nails (not biting them).

I also notice that she is much more disobedient when her Granny is with us than when she is alone with either her Granny or myself, although her Granny is, if anything, more strict with her than I am, and she is thoroughly used to her, as she stays with her Granny one day and night a week. Baby is very loving and affectionate and is always extremely sorry after one of these fits, and always promises not to scream again, but immediately forgets again. She has plenty of toys, although she does not take much notice of them, and prefers to play with odds and ends and run messages about the house. I should so much like your guidance in the manner of treatment, as I do not want to break her spirit, but on the other hand, I cannot have constant screaming at the slightest correction."

Your little girl gives us another example of what has been brought out in a large number of the letters I have had recently – that is, of the way in which a child who may have been very easy and placid

and docile as a baby will often become difficult and defiant in her third year. A period of rebelliousness and temper seems to be quite a normal occurrence round about two to four years of age. In part, it must be taken as a sign of healthy development towards independence and self-reliance, and when, as seems to be the case with your little girl, there is practically no sign of nervousness or neurosis, the problem is fairly straight forward.

That is to say, there is nothing to be distressed about, although the child's behaviour may for a time cause practical difficulties and be trying to your patience. It is simply a matter of maintaining steady firmness and gentle affection towards her, and resting assured in your own mind that, given these conditions, the child will pass through this phase of difficulty, and after a year or two will settle down into a more cheerful acceptance of denials and demands.

There is no reason to think that keeping firmly to your requests and controls, provided these are reasonable, will "break her spirit". If one set out to demand mere obedience for its own sake, irrespective of whether the things one asked the child to do were really sensible and appropriate, then one might set up a feeling of helpless frustration which would either confirm the child in miserable defiance or deaden her mental life altogether. But if the things you ask her to do and not to do are always simple and clear, and really needed by the situation, and she has always the sense of your affection and understanding, she will learn to accept your demands. During the screaming fits one can only be patient, but one must not allow the child to get her own way because she screams. There is really no way by which one can stop the screaming itself, except by letting the child learn from experience that it is useless.

What you say about her being more difficult when you and her Granny are both present is again an instance of what I pointed out a few weeks ago – namely, the child's attempt to "divide and rule", which so often happens when more than one adult is in charge. This, again, is quite an ordinary characteristic of childhood, and will be left behind presently if your little girl finds that she does not gain anything by it, and is not able to win one of the grown-ups over to spoil her, against the other.

"N.C." writes: "I want to tell you how very interesting I find your articles. I have been particularly struck by this week's problem, 'Displaced'. My little boy is one year and ten months, and his sister is nine months old. He was very unhappy at her arrival, and used to try and pull her off my lap. Now he is on the whole very good to her – tries to protect her from 'bumps', shares things with her, etc. But if he is tired or hurts himself, at once he wants my exclusive attention. As I am often quite alone (I only have occasional help) this is sometimes difficult, and now he has a funny new trick. If anything goes wrong, or the slightest word of censure, he flops down and crawls. He has walked since he was ten months old, and is particularly active and sure-footed – can climb and run like a three-year-old. And, except for talking (he can only say a few words and will rarely use them) is otherwise advanced – very independent, quite clean at night and day, feeds himself very tidily and so on. This is, I suppose, because when the baby crawls we admire and praise her, and so he wants admiration too; but it is particularly trying if there are visitors. He shows off so badly with anyone who does not pay him attention. I have two or three severe friends who are full of theories as to bringing up children (they have none of their own!), and show plainly they

consider him a spoilt, cross boy. So, he keeps up a steady whimper for
their benefit, and last time threw a plate at one poor lady.

If I could put the baby down and hold him on my knee it would
be all right, but she is frightened of strangers, too, and howls at them
(though a most good-tempered, beaming person at other times). What,
I wonder, should one do for the crawling, and the tiresomeness with
strangers? Ignore it, try to prepare beforehand, – 'Be a good boy when
the ladies come won't you?' – or is that only making matters worse?
I am sure really these things will pass, but one is so anxious that no
'complexes' should be left behind, and I do think any sort of jealousy
or feeling of neglect can linger very bitterly. I think a little child wants
a great deal of love and petting (it is a most important 'vitamin', rather
apt to be neglected these 'leave them alone in the pram' days), and yet
one equally hates to see an exigent, over-clinging child."

There is no doubt that when your little boy crawls he is trying to
win the attention and praise which his baby sister gets for doing the
same thing. I do not think you can do anything about it directly, but
a great deal can be done indirectly by letting the child win praise and
admiration for the gifts appropriate to his age. The trouble springs
from his jealousy of the baby and his fear that her coming means the
loss of your love. To his mind, your nursing of the baby means that
you love her more than you love him, and his becoming a baby again
is partly an attempt to win your approval and affection. You will have
to find ways of making him feel quite sure that, although you take
the baby on your knee, you love him as much as ever and that you
admire him because he can walk and talk and climb and make things.
His need for admiration from visitors will be greater just now, while
he is in this state of jealous fear. It would be quite useless to scold him
for it, and the demand, "Be a good boy when the ladies come", cannot
mean anything real to him. If, however, you can build up in him a
sense of his being "a big boy", and let him have your full admiration
for the things he can do and the baby cannot, this will greatly support him and make him a little less dependent on rivalling the baby
as a baby.

But I confess that when I read your letter describing the situation with the visitors, I felt that it was the visitors I wanted to keep
in order rather than the child. Your little boy obviously has very
many splendid qualities, independence, cleanliness and skill, and

tenderness to the baby. It seems clear that he is really developing very well. If he were mine I should do my best to avoid exposing him to a situation in which he senses the disapproval of a group of unsympathetic adults. Children are extremely quick to sense such disapproval, and it always makes them more difficult. If you cannot avoid your severe friends being present with your children, I should try to educate them a little in child psychology beforehand. If they understand something of what the boy's behaviour means, they might be able to help instead of hindering.

TEARS AND TANTRUMS

"I feel I have most thoroughly mismanaged her", writes a mother of her daughter of three years old who has fits of tears and obstinacy

14 FEBRUARY 1934

"Perdita" writes: "Since the birth of my second baby (a boy aged fourteen months) I have taken THE NURSERY WORLD and read it from cover to cover each week. I have meant for months to write and ask your advice with regard to my elder child, Matilda, a girl of three years nine months. I feel I have most thoroughly mismanaged her. She was a greatly longed-for baby, and her father and I were delighted to welcome a little girl, which was as we had hoped. She was a very good and pretty baby. At one and three-quarter years she could say 'Ding Dong Bell' all through, and at two she knew twenty or thirty nursery rhymes at least and could count to twenty. She was from her toddler days – in walking she was rather late – rather a 'live wire', and needed lots of patience, and I think the trouble with her began at about the age of two years. I had no maid all the summer of 1932 and also moved to this house from a flat, and of course Anthony was born in the autumn. I had other troubles, too, which made me hysterical and very ill-tempered, and my adored small daughter had many thoroughly ill-tempered slappings. I look back upon that summer with horror. My baby boy is a most placid, good-tempered little fellow, and no trouble at all, but Matilda is, I fear, most unhappy (not all the time, of course). I enclose a photograph of her taken at the age of three, and you

will see that she looks quite an intelligent, charming, small person. But she has fits of extreme obstinacy, refusing to do quite necessary things. For instance, if I have to take her hand to cross a road she will stamp and scream and try to drag herself away from me. She will be given a spoon and fork for her dinner, and will wish to change the spoon for another exactly similar, and when I will not let her she screams again. I could multiply these instances a dozen times. All her displays of rage are over most trivial matters, and sometimes I have to smack her in spite of the fact that I feel it is wrong. Occasionally, she shows signs of anger with her brother, but is really attached to him.

Another thing about her is that she has, since I was out a whole day once just before Christmas, taken to wild screaming if I even venture to go up the road to the shop for half an hour without her. She throws herself on the floor and kicks and sobs until she is exhausted. I never leave her now unless I am absolutely obliged to do so. She also wakes crying every night and has to be taken into my bed. She hates to go for a walk with the maid, but prefers to stay at home with me. She had forgotten all her nursery rhymes a month or so ago, but is now beginning to learn them again. She has never cared for toys or known how to play with them, but prefers books. I am not very good at play either. Another thing I would like to mention is that since the age of fifteen months she has rolled her head from side to side in bed, making her hair a tangled mess by the morning. She still does it, and if unhappy during the day will lay her head on a chair and roll it. When she started it at fifteen months it was not, however – so far as we could see – a sign of any unhappiness. This head rolling is quite definitely inherited. It throws a light on the recent correspondence with regard to 'bumping'. I had a rather unusual childhood, and although rather stolid outwardly was often unhappy 'inside'. When I was very tiny I used to bang my head on the pillow – or the floor if I was tired. This was before I could walk, and later rolling the head took the place of it. I remember doing it up to the age of eleven or twelve years, and have often wondered if it has any significance. I can remember it used to help me to create a dream world into which I used to escape. I tell you this in case it helps at all with Matilda. The whole position bulks very largely in my mind, and I fear I am rather muddled about it. If you could help me to try to undo the wrong I've done with regard to my

*little girl I should be so very, very grateful. She is beginning to show
great interest in letters. Would you advise me to teach her to read?"*

You are probably being unnecessarily pessimistic and blaming yourself unduly about your little girl. It is, of course, a pity that you felt
so wrought up and bad tempered at the time when her difficulties
would in any case be greater, owing to the birth of her little brother.
But the photograph shows that she is still an affectionate and charming child and is likely to have considerable powers of recuperation.
You will have noticed from the other letters which have appeared
that severe difficulties of obstinacy and tantrums are quite common in children who have just been displaced by the birth of a little
rival, so that you would not be justified in putting down the whole
of Matilda's difficulties to your own irritability. The fact that her
displays of rage occur over quite trivial matters is not surprising in
itself. It often happens and is, in fact, an indication of the great efforts
the child is making not to be angry about the important things, for
example, not to be aggressive towards her brother. She can let her
strong feelings master her with regard to unimportant things, just
because they are unimportant, and this is her safety valve for her
feelings about really significant things. It is by means of this outlet
in trivial affairs that she is able to maintain her affection for her
brother. I should give her as much freedom as I possibly could in
such unimportant matters. I should, for example, let her choose her
own spoon from the beginning, let her actually put it on the table for
herself and feel free to take the one she wants. With regard to crossing the road, I would suggest to her that you would not insist upon
holding her hand, provided she would walk steadily beside you just
while you crossed the road. If she prefers to hold *your* hand (which
is a different way of doing it), or to put her hand on your skirt, or
simply walk beside you without holding your hand, that would be all
that is necessary. There is no need to force her to feel a baby, as if she
could not walk steadily over the road. Of course, if she really wanted
to dash across wildly, that would be another matter. But if you can
avoid forcing her to do something that seems to her treating her like
a baby, I should try to do so.

The anxiety she shows about you going out is a more difficult
matter, but she will grow out of this, too. It doubtless has arisen from
the difficulties of the summer that the baby brother was born. It is

wise not to leave her unnecessarily, but I would not allow your legiti-mate affairs and need for recreation to be seriously interfered with. When you have to leave her I would tell her that you understand that she is afraid you won't come back, but that you are certainly going to, and that there is nothing for her to be worried about. The fact that she is beginning to remember the nursery rhymes shows that the processes that will lead to recovery from this acute crisis are at work. I should not try to interfere with the head rolling, which has a very complicated psychological meaning. She will grow out of it, in the way you have done. It does no harm in itself, and has a definite function in maintaining the child's psychological equilibrium in her important personal relations. It would be a very good idea to help your little girl to learn to read, not by way of definite lessons, but by way of a pleasant intercourse with you. I would suggest you getting a book by Nancy Catty: "The Child at Home: His Occupations and First Lessons". This would give you many hints as to how to help her to learn to read. If you could give her a definite time each day for this sharing of interests and pleasant intercourse, it would be a great help for her. She would then feel that she has a definite relation of her own with you which the baby has not got, and one by which she was learning new things. If it was only an hour, or even half an hour a day, really her own for these pursuits with you, that would be a great advantage to her general emotional relation with you.

CAN SELF-CONTROL BE TAUGHT?

19 AUGUST 1931

"M.E.P." writes: "Can you help me to bring up my wee daugh-ter as I find great difficulty in doing this as well as I should like? I must explain fully. She is one year old, her brother is two years eight months (he is of a sweet-tempered disposition). Just lately she has become very bad tempered. Throws the food away when she has licked the butter off, and so on. Screams when I put her on the chamber very often, and always wants to be picked up. She has only two bottom teeth, and is cutting four at the top, I think. She is remarkably strong, plump and fit, and as brown as a berry. She has always had a temper from her earliest days, and she does not care for strangers. She is full of determination and is obviously 'able to *take care of herself' even at this age. She always wants to come to me as soon as I enter the room. She is, on the other hand, a very happy child, quite fearless in her bath, and splashes and kicks, not caring if she falls over or gets her eyes wet. How am I to treat her so that she grows out of this temper? I will add an important point. It is inherited. I have, and did have as a child, a terribly hot temper (soon over). My father also has it. It has been my one great sin in life, my one and only trouble. It has caused many regrets in my life, and I do not want my little baby to have such a curse in her life. I was spoilt for peace sake, as a child (and even now, I think) because my mother's heart was not strong. When the children scream, and are very naughty I get very irritable and lose my temper. I know how wrong this is, but I am anything but a perfect mother. I always read your articles and the letters of Sister Morrison[1] to try to live up to this high standard, but it is not easy. I have only a smallish home and one maid, who is far more patient than I am. They are good kiddies really, but as I see this trait in my baby I do most earnestly want to guide it rightly. I shall be so glad to hear your answer. Baby sometimes stays awake and wants to play for two or three hours in the night if she wakes, and will not lie down. She doesn't cry, only coos and talks. Now I strap her down and she goes to sleep. You will, I hope, excuse this long letter, but I am very anxious about it."*

I sympathise very much with your difficulty, as it is never easy to handle a child who has such a ready temper, especially if one feels guilty oneself over the same sort of thing. I agree too with the importance of trying to train your little girl so as to curb her temper. There is, however, only one piece of general advice to be given – that is, to be perfectly firm in not allowing the child to tyrannise over you or other people because you are afraid of her temper. If she finds that she gains advantage by her outbursts she will naturally go on indulging in them. If, however, she finds that they bring her no gain, and she does not get any privilege or consolation through her temper, she is much more likely to control it. In your own case this policy of firm control could not easily be followed because of your

---

1 Sister Morrison was a contemporary contributor to *The Nursery World* writing primarily on diet for babies and young children.

mother's delicacy, but I gather there is not the same reason in your case for indulging your little girl for the sake of peace. I know that the problem is more difficult for you because you find it hard to be both firm and patient, and children screaming can be extraordinarily trying when they are vigorous and strong. But there really is only the one way to train a child of this kind, and that is a kind, steady firmness. If one can possibly attain this, it does gradually make the child more sensible and controlled. I am sure you know this quite as well as I do. What I wonder is whether you are not worrying too much about your own temper and striving after an impossible perfection. I sometimes wonder if my remarks in these columns do suggest a standard of perfection that cannot be attained by anybody. But, after all, all I can do here is to point out the direction in which wiser handling of the child lies. I don't imagine that children need perfect parents, or that they have the right to reproach us if we are imperfect and sometimes lose our tempers and get impatient. I think you probably get a feeling of hopelessness when you see your child screaming in temper because of your own difficulties, and that makes you less able to cope with her than you would be otherwise. But there is no need to give way to your little girl for peace's sake, and so you should be able to train her gradually to greater sense and self-control.

TANTRUMS AND TEMPERS

Children grow out of these stormy phases of development if properly handled

24 SEPTEMBER 1930

"L.C." writes: "I have complete charge of three kiddies, a little girl of seven and a half, boy of five and a half, and baby girl eighteen months, who before I had taken them had been in the charge of an auntie with no experience of children. The result is, the eldest little girl is dreadfully old-fashioned, talks and acts like a person ten years older, and is given to day-dreaming to such an extent that often it takes her an hour to dress, and it is only done then to the continual repeating of 'Hurry, hurry'. Should I have occasion to leave the nursery I often come back, say in ten minutes, and find her in exactly the *same position as when I left, perhaps with a sock half on, or petticoat with one arm in, and just staring into space, and to the question: 'What are you doing, dear?' get the reply: 'I was thinking, Nannie'. The same thing happens at the table when asked to pass anything, she sits perfectly still, and when I say, 'Did you hear, dear?', the same reply: 'Yes, but I was thinking'. I have tried helping her to dress, to show how quickly it can be done and promising a treat, and also punishment, but it all seems no good. I am anxious to do the best possible for them, so will you please advise me as to where you think the trouble lies, in the child or in my treatment of her. Now for the boy, who is a boy in all ways, is possessed of a very violent temper which up to now has never been checked, the others giving into him rather than have a scene. I was warned about this, and from the start have been very firm with him. This is the sort of thing I am up against: at 6.30 I say, 'Bed-time, Peter', and then, 'I don't want to go, and I shan't'. I have tried to reason with him, but it had ended up usually with me carrying him and forcibly undressing him, to shrieks and kicks. I do not argue or talk to him while I am doing this, but just go on with it, then lay him in his bed and leave him. Often as soon as I am gone, he is quiet and asleep in ten minutes. When I come back, the same thing happens. When we are out walking he refuses to go the way I want, I go on and leave him to follow, which he does in a very dignified manner, refusing to notice or speak to his sisters and me. People congratulate me, and say how well I manage him, and that he is quite different from what he was, but I am still wondering am I doing right, as I should not like to curb his spirit or turn him into a 'mammy coddle'. But I feel that these tempers should be checked in some way."*

I think you are doing quite rightly in being firm with the boy – provided only that apart from these moments of struggle you keep your relation with him as friendly and cheerful and affectionate as possible. If you were merely stern and hard, you might well damp his spirit and dull his mind. But a steady firmness in dealing with his tantrums will be a real help, if in general you are sympathetic and actively understanding of his play and fun and constructive interests. I should by the way, always give him a few minutes' warning before bedtime and mealtime, or any other occasions when you have to interfere with his pursuits. Children always appreciate that consideration very greatly.

The little girl is a more difficult psychological problem, and one that it may well be out of your power to solve. I should try not to be too exasperated when she is slow, nor to let her see your annoyance. Can you find some way of letting her suffer the natural penalty of her slowness – finding a meal finishes and is put away for example? Sometimes this sort of penalty is much more corrective than urgings or scoldings. But very often one has to recognise one's inability to alter these temperamental handicaps in particular children and simply take comfort in the thought that they may go along with other valuable qualities which may hardly yet have begun to show. This particular fault makes things very trying for the nurse, I know, but the only practical suggestion I have to offer is to ignore it whenever you can, and otherwise to let the child suffer the natural results of slowness wherever possible.

PARENTS WHO EXPECT TOO MUCH

24 JUNE 1931

"Dominie" writes: "Here is my problem: I shall be glad of your advice upon it. I am a daily governess to a little girl of just seven. I teach her according to the P.N.E.U.² programme. She enjoys much of it and shows capacity almost equally in all subjects, but there are tears nearly every morning at some moment or other. Veronica has a happy and interesting home life. Her parents are rather old-fashioned people and, although they love the children dearly, are rather particular about manners and conduct, compared to most people nowadays. There is a rather backward younger brother and a sweet and lively baby sister. The children have a German nurse, who is kind but also very particular. Veronica comes to me for two and a half hours each morning. She will be keenly interested in the history and Bible story one day, but cry over some memory work, such as repeating a Psalm. Another day it will be some new kind

---

2 The Parents' Educational Union was founded in Bradford in 1887 by Charlotte Mason and Emeline Petrie Steinthal. It was an organisation providing support for children being home educated following the philosophy and ideas of Charlotte Mason. The word "National" was added in 1890 and so the PNEU was formed – the Parents' National Educational Union.

of sum which she cannot grasp at first. Her crying is always either when she cannot understand or do a thing perfectly straight off, or else if she gets annoyed and bored at being asked to repeat a thing several times. As you probably know, the P.N.E.U. programmes are designed to avoid over-strain. There is plenty of variety, and no lesson is longer than half an hour, most are from ten to twenty minutes. There is time for a nature walk or drill or handwork too. I have taught children of all ages and many dispositions and have never had these almost daily tears. I find it most wearing, and it must be very bad for Veronica. I would feel like giving up, but, apart from these outbursts, Veronica is such a dear, bright and affectionate child. She is in the country, and I know her parents do not want to send her to school. I always try to make her see no one expects her to do all her lessons perfectly straight off, and that mistakes don't matter so long as she is trying her best and being cheerful. I also tell her everyone has to repeat a line of music or what they are learning by heart, and I try to let her see from experience how anything she finds difficult at first soon grows quite easy if only she will be quite patient. She is so gifted, and does everything so well and easily for her age that it seems as if she can never bear to be less than perfect in her work, and that straight off. Her mother thinks it is a form of unconscious conceit, and also a weakness and softness of fibre. She and the nurse tell me that Veronica cries too easily at other times also, and is not as brave and hardy as her delicate younger brother. She is, apart from this, so sweet, loving and lovable that it does seem such a pity. What do you think about it? In other ways, she is so sensible too! I should add that Veronica has plenty of outdoor play, and that she adores her parents and delights in her baby sister. She goes to dancing class, which she much enjoys, and though she does not see many children at other times, she enjoys their society whenever it can be managed. She sees a good many grown-up friends and relatives, and is very charming and sociable with them. Veronica has excellent health, and apart from the too easy crying is a very happy child, not fussy or grumbling or spoilt in her ways. Veronica's parents and myself thoroughly like the P.N.E.U. system, and would be sorry to give it up. I am quite sure Montessori and Kindergarten teaching would not satisfy any of us, and Veronica, though enjoying handwork, also enjoys history and geography and musical work. I am sure she would miss her

*lessons. She really enjoys all but a few minutes of them! Thanking
you for your opinion, which I shall look for with hope and interest."*

I should think you are quite right in feeling that Veronica cannot
bear to be less than perfect, and that this accounts for her outbursts
when she cannot do a thing properly straight away. It is evidently
very important to her to be able to live up to the high standards
which are set for her, and she is at an age when, with a sensitive and
intelligent child, imperfections are felt very keenly. The impression
your letter gives me is that she probably doesn't have enough free
play with children of her own age, and the high standards of behaviour which are demanded of her seem never to be relaxed at all. No
matter how loving and pleasant the grown-ups around a child are,
the child does need moments of real freedom from the pressure of
their demands. These high ideals of the grown-ups for the behaviour
of a little child press particularly hard upon a child who doesn't go to
school and doesn't have plenty of play with other children, free from
the critical observation of parents and grown-ups. Veronica seems to
be able to manage her relations with parents and friends and relatives
on the whole satisfactorily, but evidently her control breaks down at
times, and particularly often when she is being expected to learn. I
understand that it must be disappointing and trying for you when
she cries morning after morning, but I think that the crying probably
springs from the inner strains of the otherwise excellent adaptation
she is making to the life around her. For this reason, I don't think you
need to be very distressed about it. I think I should perhaps let her do
rather more with her hands than perhaps you have been doing. My
own feeling is that the P.N.E.U. method doesn't leave quite enough
opportunity for the work of the hands, and that Veronica is just an
example of the children who show the effects of over-intellectual
education. If you could find some sort of handwork in which she
could enjoy real achievement, I should let her have this pleasure and
satisfaction. Moreover, I should try to adapt the programme of work
to her individual interests, and should perhaps lessen somewhat the
amount of memory work, which fails to appeal to lots of children of
seven years of age. But otherwise, I should just go on being encouraging and understanding without making a fuss about her tears. She
is pretty certain to grow out of this difficulty within the next year or
so as she gets more assurances based on real achievement.

PARENTS AND THE SMACKING OF CHILDREN

Ursula Wise gives her reasons for believing that children should not be smacked

11 JANUARY 1933

"T.D." writes: "I should be so much obliged if you could tell me your reason for saying that one should never smack a child. I have one small son, aged thirteen months, and am most anxious to bring him up in the best possible way, and to do what is right. However, I find excellent results from two short slaps, but am worried to see how against this you are. When C. will refuse to use his chamber and I know by the time which has elapsed since he last did that he must want it, I give him two slaps in the proper place and he stops kicking and screaming and at once obliges. Also, at times he will refuse to take his lunch, even though it may be one of which he is extremely fond. He turns round in his chair and looks over the back, and the only way I can make him make him take it is by slapping his hand, and he will then sit round and eat it up with apparent relish.

He very seldom cries when he is smacked. This will last a long time, and I have merely to say, 'C. do you want a smack?' and he eats properly. I don't see in what other way you can possibly teach so young a child. It is different when they are older and one can reason with them. In the same way, when he will throw his toys into the fireplace, a smack is the only thing that will stop him doing so. However, I am very anxious to hear in what way I am doing wrong by these methods, and should be much obliged for your help and advice. He is a very strong willed, determined child, but seems to bear me no grudge for the slap and seems to realise he deserved it. I am so anxious he shouldn't be spoiled, as he is a dear little chap, very happy and affectionate, and I don't often have much trouble with him. I am sure there must be some very good reason why you always advise against a smack, and should so much like to know what it is, and what other methods I should employ."

There are a great many reasons for considering that smacking a child is a very bad method of training. I should have to write a book to give you all the answers. I cannot in a short reply do more than set out the reasons dogmatically, but they rest upon the whole psychology of the growing child, and of the relation between mother and child.

In the first instance, if you use this method, you are not giving the child any training in self-control or independence, or developing that part of his character which will enable him to do the right things when there is nobody there to smack him. Secondly, you are showing yourself to him, not as a friend or person who understands the interests and activities of childhood, but as someone who inhibits them and who is cruel as he himself wants to be. You are building up in his mind an image of yourself as a person who administers pain, which will be ineffaceable. The child does not forget that he has been slapped by his mother when he is older, or when he is a grown-up man. There is no way of wiping that memory out, and it does not seem to the child that there are good reasons for your smacking, even if it seems so to you. As a matter of fact, the reasons for smacking are not really good ones. But I know that you have done it thinking that they were. These reasons, however, have no meaning at all to the child. All he knows is that "Here is somebody who hurts my hand when I don't feel like doing something". And that experience of actual pain, and pain given from his mother, will make him want to be equally cruel to other people, perhaps his wife and children. You are setting up a train of impulses in him, the end of which you cannot possibly foresee, and it may be something very different from what you desire. He may appear to bear you no grudge, but there is no reason for thinking this is really true. He knows that you will smack him again if he shows his feelings to you. You are becoming a person to whom the child must not show his real feelings. You are preventing him, therefore, from being able to show really important feelings later in life, when he may greatly need the help of understanding.

Thirdly, it is not necessary to smack children. It is quite possible to train them to be clean by other methods. Really skilled educators never dream of smacking children. Such treatment is, for example, unheard of in nursery schools or in really good nurseries. The fact that your little boy will do what you want, now that you have trained him on the method of slaps, is no evidence that you could not have done without it, or that there are not deeper injuries below the surface of his mind. It is a great humiliation to a child, even a child of thirteen months, to be smacked, and one that most of them never forget. You have evidently built up in him a strong sense of guilt by this method, and it is that that you are drawing upon when you say "he seems to realise he deserved it". But there is no need for a child as young as this to feel guilty about natural activities. It is, for example, quite unnatural for a child of his age to sit at the meal table and get on steadily through the meal without any form of play or movement, just as if he were a grown-up. I do strongly suggest that your standards of behaviour for a child of thirteen months are not quite normal, and that you are ruling the boy by your high demands, enforced by this slapping, in a way that will really have bad effects on his future development. You are treating him as if he were a little machine, instead of a growing, real person, who could learn to co-operate and develop real skills through his love of you. You may be laying the foundations of a serious neurosis.

I have stated some of the reasons why I am against smacking as frankly and seriously as I think you wanted me to do. But the real point to realise is that smacking is unnecessary, and that positive methods of real patient training are the ones that repay both mother and child.

OLD-FASHIONED OR MODERN METHODS?

15 JANUARY 1930

"Student" writes: *"I have been very interested in some of the articles that have appeared one or twice lately in 'Over the Teacups'*[3] *about 'old-fashioned' methods and 'old-fashioned' nurses. I should very much like to know what you think of this — are they really better than the modern ways? Some of the writers seem to think that children are happier under nurses with old-fashioned ways. Do you think that this can be so? I've not had much experience myself, and never yet had full responsibility for any children, so I don't know what to think. But I'm very anxious to learn the best ways of dealing with them, and should awfully like to hear your views about this."*

I'm very glad you wrote about this, because I, too, was very interested in the discussion you refer to; and it is a far-reaching and important question.

What I wanted to say to the correspondents when I read their letters was, "But why lump everything together in this way, and talk about 'old-fashioned' and 'modern' as if either of these was *altogether* good or bad, and as if we were obliged to take *all* of one or all of the other?" If it be true that old-fashioned ways made children so happy and easy, it seems strange that anyone should ever have questioned them, doesn't it? Perhaps they were good in some respects and not in others. Is it possible to look at things in more detail, and find out *which* of the ways of the old-fashioned nurse were the ones that made little children content and easy to manage, and which of the newer methods really are an improvement?

One great quality of the old-fashioned nurse *at her best* was that she knew so well what she wanted in the way of good behaviour, and never doubted that she would get it; and so she did get it. Her views of what little children should be like were clear and simple, and she had definite and clear methods of getting them to be so. Now, if she happened to be mean and despotic (at her worst) the children were ruled with a rod of iron and their lives were closed-in and narrow. But if,

---

3 "Over the Teacups" is a contemporaneous column of reader-to-reader correspondence in *The Nursery World*.

in addition, to being firm she had a mild temper and broad, sensible ideas of good behaviour, then the children were indeed happy in having her; for they always knew what was expected of them, and what would happen if they didn't do it. They were not bewildered by being treated in one way to-day and another way to-morrow. They were helped to be good by the calm belief of their nurse that *of course* they would be – because that was the way all ordinary little children behaved, apart from exceptional moments. She was so sure of them and of herself and of the way to behave to them that her calm and content were passed on to them, and it was easy for them to know what she wanted.

Now, few mothers and nurses to-day are so clear-minded. They are not nearly so sure what they want for their children. This is partly because of changing ideas in a larger world outside the nursery, and partly because people have begun to realise that the idyllic picture of the old-fashioned nurse at her best did not always hold good, and that along with her good qualities there were often found to be big gaps in her knowledge, filled up with chunks of mere prejudice. And so people began to ask more questions, and to inquire more deeply into the real truths of child nature, what it is like, and what it needs for the most satisfactory growth. And since scientific methods of feeding and clothing the baby were turning out so infinitely better than the old ways based on tradition and rule of thumb, it began to seem likely that this might be true of social training too.

But, of course, the breakdown of belief in old-fashioned ways of punishment and such notions of good behaviour as that "children should be seen and not heard" has gone on much faster than the spread of the scientific knowledge that must take its place. Hence so many nurses and mothers really don't know what it is best to do, what good behaviour in little children is, and how to bring it about. And, of course, children are less happy in these circumstances. They are as lost and confused as the grown-ups themselves.

The only remedy for this is the serious study of child psychology and of methods based on child psychology. We have to try to bring back the old calm surety; and, to find it, our feet must be firmly placed in sound knowledge.

An expert in the treatment of emotional troubles and disturbances of behaviour in little children said to me recently, "What little children most need in their nurses and mothers is affection, stability and spontaneity". And of these qualities the stability and the spontaneity spring very largely from a sure knowledge of what is good for our children and the best ways of handling them.

THE PARENTS' PART

Child training is not just a matter of demanding obedience. Friendly co-operation and understanding are more important

2 DECEMBER 1931

"Worried" writes: *"I really am frightfully worried about my small son, aged five and a half, and feel that you better than anyone can advise me. He has been always a nervy, highly strung boy owing (the doctor said) to delayed circumcision, and backward in walking and helping himself (he was two before he walked, and twenty-two months before he crawled), but not in talking and intelligence. He is a fine, well-developed boy. He has a baby sister of two years, but started his naughty ways before her arrival, so I do not think it can be jealousy. I have always insisted on obedience, and he knows it, but on being told or asked to do things at once answers, 'No, I won't'. Also, when one makes a simple statement such as, 'It is raining', he immediately says, 'No, it's not'.*

But it is his attitude to his little sister that worries me most. I cannot make him remember he is older or instil the smallest bit of the protective attitude into him. He wants to be treated and to have everything she has, and takes anything from her, often hitting her or knocking her over until I am really scared to leave then together. I may say that she sticks up for herself well, but there is three-and-a-half years' difference. When talked to he is all affection and promises at once never to do it again, but not five minutes elapses before he is as bad as ever. He goes to a proper boys' college and loves it, and appears to get on well with his lessons, but will not run about and rough it with the other boys. He likes them, but is afraid of being hurt and knocked over. He eats well, but plays about and will not behave at meals. He also sleeps the clock round, so I do not think there can be much wrong with his health.

He does not care for punishments in the least – in fact I cannot punish him. If I send him up to his bedroom he cries up the stairs, but calmly lies down and goes to sleep. If I deprive him of sweets he says, 'Oh well, I shall be a good boy and have some to-morrow'. He cries very easily at the least thing. I should also be grateful for suggestions for useful and instructive toys for both children. They have engines and horses and cuddly toys, but seem tired of them all."

I wonder if the whole trouble with your little boy doesn't perhaps spring from the fact that you have thought of the problem too exclusively in terms of training and not enough in terms of friendly co-operation? I don't feel sure that this is the source of the trouble, but I do rather get the impression from the way you put the problem that it perhaps may be so. That is to say, from very early days the boy has perhaps had chiefly the sense that grown-ups were people who said, "You must obey", "You must do this", "You must not do that", "You must be kind", and so on, and never had the chance to find out that they could be chums and friends who understood the point of view of a child of two or three or four years. For instance, with regard to the question of his behaviour to his little sister, when a bigger boy hits and pushes in that way it is very disturbing and very exasperating, but I do seriously wonder whether there has not been too much effort to *instil* a protective attitude into him, to talk, or scold, or reproach him into feeling tender towards her. If I am wrong in thinking this I am sure you will forgive me, as, of course, I can only be of use if I say quite frankly what my impression is.

When a child does feel jealous and hostile to a younger child in this way it really never is any use to make them *promise* to be better, as such promises cannot be kept unless they spring from a real feeling of affection inside. I should therefore be inclined to avoid trying to make the child promise to be kind. I should, of course, do everything I could to prevent his hitting her or knocking her over, and if he did that I should not hesitate to send him to his room in the way you do. But neither should I feel unhappy about his lying down and going to sleep. It is very much more troublesome when a child reacts violently to being sent to his room, either by storms of rage or by hysterical crying. The whole point when he has been unkind to his sister, is to show your disapproval of his behaviour in a way that he can understand without doing anything severe or cruel to him, and being sent to his room has this meaning to him even if he *does* lie down and go to sleep. Nor can I see anything to be troubled about in what he says when you deprive him of sweets: "I shall be a good boy and have some to-morrow". It is much better that he should feel this belief in his own power "to be good and have some to-morrow" than that he should fall into despair and misery.

All these "punishments" are most effective when they are just simply clear understandable expressions of our wishes, not so severe that they really plunge the child into unhappiness. But these negative things, taking away sweets and so on, are not really the chief means of educating the child into pleasant social ways. They are only minor and occasional instruments, and the real education comes from the child's constant experience of grown-ups' sense and reliability, consideration and understanding. In any case, the child has to be allowed time to grow into a sociable and considerate person. I think you will find that if you can be quietly firm about his unkindness to his little sister without trying to make him feel that he is very bad, and if you can constantly treat him in a way that takes for granted that he *will* be more sensible and agreeable, he is likely to improve. I wonder whether he doesn't have some feeling that the little sister is more favoured by you or by his father? It is very important to make sure of even justice and affection.

With regard to his contradiction of such a statement as "It is raining", the best way to deal with it is not to treat it as a mere contradiction or challenge to authority, but to refer the child to the actual fact under discussion, e.g., to say cheerfully, "Would you like to go and see and tell me whether it *is* raining or not?" Very often a challenging attitude in a child comes about from the sense that grown-ups always decide everything and never expect a little child to have any voice or ideas of his own. With regard to toys for the two children, you would find a detailed list of toys for these ages in "Health and Education in the Nursery", by V. M. Bennett and Susan Isaacs, published by Routledge.

WISE PARENTS

16 APRIL 1930

"R.S.L" writes: "*I should be so grateful if you would advise me on how best to deal with my charge, a fine, sturdy boy of nearly four, the youngest of a family of five. He is full of spirits and energy, most intelligent, and interested in everything around him, and of a really lovable disposition. What is troubling us is that lately he has developed a most horrible love of hitting out at us, one and all. Not, apparently, out of spite, but just for sheer love of punching, and incidentally, I suppose, to see what we should do about it. I see that you sometimes advocate taking no notice of similar habits, and when they are ignored they will be discontinued. In our case it is quite feasible for the adults, but drives his two sisters of six and eight years nearly to distraction, especially when they are occupied with something he cannot do.*

He has plenty of occupations and toys, but sometimes nothing will satisfy him but to rush round the room giving sly slaps and digs, and he can hit very hard, too. I am quite concerned that hitting back does no good whatsoever, and such things as standing him in the corner, holding his hands, or sitting him on a chair may make him repentant for a few minutes, but it soon starts all over again. We have thought about getting him a punch ball, but have come to the conclusion that he would not get any satisfaction out of that, as he evidently wants us to retaliate in some way. Can you think of any way on which we can check this most undesirable trait in an otherwise sweet child?"

From the facts you give me, e.g., your impression that the boy does not hit out in spite, nor in a fit of uncontrollable temper, but largely because he enjoys it, and wants to see what will happen, it is very safe to say that this impulse is a temporary phase in development. If well-handled now it will pass away as he grows and finds more varied ways of self-expression, especially as he has a generally lovable disposition. It is a form of boyish self-assertion not at all uncommon in vigorous children at about that age. But it is one that has to be dealt with. I should never advise "taking no notice" of one child biting another or hitting a grown-up. That is quite different from his crying and screaming, or from mere angry *words*. It would be quite forced and unnatural not to take any notice of his hitting, especially as he does it so hard! I should always say, very clearly and firmly, "Please, don't do that", and hold his hands to prevent it, if necessary. I should not say this in a scolding or reproachful way, but make it a straightforward and matter-of-fact demand. I would even refuse to let him be in the same room as his sisters if he annoyed and frightened them in this way.

But I would give him plenty of other opportunity for vigorous bodily movements and rough-and-tumble games with other boys.

The punch ball would be a good thing. I have found it very useful and amusing with vigorous boys, even so young. And a pair of boxing gloves might be helpful, too, if you or the boy's father, or some sensible older boy could be persuaded to box with him sometimes. If you could turn his "punching" into a game, that would be very satisfactory. A real, but good-humoured, set-to every now and then, either with you or an older boy, would be an excellent safety-valve, and make it easier for him to contain the impulse at ordinary times.

Such a child needs even more free *outdoor* play, running about, digging, jumping, ball-throwing, etc., in fact, all movements of the larger joints than the ordinary boy. And, preferably, play with other boys. If you could arrange things along these lines, you would find the wish to hit out at his sisters or at you would be shown less and less frequently, as his skill and confidence in free bodily movements grow; but it is well to remember that the change will not come about all at once with any methods. Don't be discouraged if it takes a little time.

YOU MUST OBEY

Is your particular problem dealt with this week?

20 NOVEMBER 1929

Last week we were prompted by the question of a father to discuss the problem of training children in responsibility. This week I have had a number of letters from parents about a problem as old as parenting itself – that of how to get children to obey us. This is really the reverse side of last week's questions. We pointed out then that the ways of the nursery need to bear some relation to what will be asked of our children later in social life. And this applies here also. It would clearly be a mistake to train our children in ways of behaviour that would unfit them for the demands of the larger world, no matter how easy that made life in the nursery itself. And yet, of course, they aren't *yet* responsible beings, and we can't treat them as if they were. What we ask of them has to be suited to their needs and powers at each stage as they grow. We should probably all agree about this in a general way; the problem is to see quite clearly what *is* the best thing at each stage.

Now, there can't really be any question as to whether or not the little child should be asked to obey us, in some things and for some purposes. The call for obedience, as and when it is needed, is part of the biological responsibility of the parent. It does not need to be justified. And it has its roots deep in the nature of the little child himself. Obedience comes quite naturally to him, if we ask for it in the right way. But it is not an end in itself. It is a *means* of education, not a final purpose. The problem really is one of *what* we shall ask children to do, or say they must not do; and of *how* we give our commands and prohibitions.

Many people's difficulties come from not being clear about these things beforehand. If we are muddled in our own minds about why we want obedience, and when and how we want it, we are very likely to ask for it when it isn't really valuable; or to demand it in such a way that we actually stir contrariness or obstinacy. Or else our own uncertainties get passed on to the children, and they never really know whether we mean what we say or not. And so we are liable to get into a vicious circle of scolding, and nagging by nurse or parent, and of defiance and "answering back" (to use the words of one correspondent) by the children. When once this sort of mutual habit is set up, it is not easy to break. But sometimes it would help a little if we made a determined effort to get quite clear in our own minds what it is all about, and how and why and when we ask those things which the children have got into the way of disobeying.

In the first place, when we say that the child "should obey", we obviously don't mean that he should never do anything without being told, and never have any way of his own. Nor that we really want him to be docile to our mere whim and fancy. That would be sacrificing the whole of his future to our present convenience, and would make him a useless sort of a person. What we surely imply when we say that he should obey us is that our particular demands are reasonable and just, and that obeying them will be really good for him. But are we sure that we are making no mistake about this?

Grown-ups very often *have* asked children to do what was bad for them, as, for instance, when we used to make tiny children "sew a fine seam" with fine thread. We believed then that we were educating them; but later on we came to see that in fact we were just damaging their eyes, health and tempers.

Are we sure that as parents or nurses we are not making any mistakes of that kind? Do we ask our children to do *only* what is really suitable for them at their age and stage of development? That is the first thing to think about. The second is the *way* in which we ask for obedience.

Do we remember, for instance, when making our requests, how much less a sense of past and future the young child has, and how much more he lives in the immediate present than we do? If we remember this, we shall also remember how much more urgent his desires are than ours, and how much sharper a disappointment or a denial is to him than to us. And since he is necessarily given up more completely to anything in which he is interested without thought of time and place, it means much more to him than to us when we have to interrupt what he is doing because we want him to come to dinner or to go out for a walk. If we remember this we shall not wantonly and suddenly cut across his interests, but shall give him a little notice, so that he has time to take in the request. If when he is in the middle of an absorbing game, and we have to call him to come to a meal, we can give him a few minutes' warning, "In ten minutes it will be dinner-time", he is much more likely to come cheerfully and readily than if we tell him only at the very moment we want him to come, and expect him to do it on the instant. We ourselves hate to be suddenly interrupted when we are reading or talking to a friend. The child hates it, too. And he appreciates our consideration very keenly. Such consideration can quite well go along with firmness about the request when it is actually made – and this, too, the child appreciates.

Again, having made sure we are asking the right thing, do we take it for granted in a cheerful voice and friendly manner that he will do what we wish? Or do we show him by a doubtful or fretful tone that we are rather expecting him to grumble or defy us? If we ourselves are calm and friendly in our demands, he is more likely to agree, and to do what we want in the same friendly and cheerful way. But we *can* only be calm and confident when we are really sure that what we are asking is reasonable.

CHAPTER TWO

Play, occupations and education

INTRODUCTION

"Play is the breath of life" is Ursula Wise's mantra. In response to the many letters on how best to educate one's child, her principal and consistent message is to offer a wide range of play opportunities.

Foregrounded by Froebel (1782–1852), Wise is an advocate of the *occupations*. For Froebel, play is not a random series of doing or actions, but is based on the provision of a range of materials that give rise to skills. The *occupations* focus on real, physical, practical skills of dexterity that provide the child with power and the ability to invent as well as develop their creativity. The four Froebelian areas of occupations appear as a thread throughout the correspondence – those using solid materials (wool, beeswax, clay, mud, wood, sand, snow); those using surface materials (painting, paper folding, cutting and designing, cardboard work); those based on using the line (threading games, knitting, crochet, weaving, embroidery, slat weaving, interlacing, braiding) and those based on materials using the point (perforating paper, bean work, pea work).

As well as promoting Froebel, Wise too refers to the *Montessori method*. Montessori stresses the development of a child's own initiative and natural abilities through exploring and using apparatus. Montessori did not advocate symbolic or "make believe" play – she was closer to the notion of play as occupation, believing that the repetition of activities enables their consolidation. Wise reflects these ideas in her promotion of activities that involve exploration, manipulations, order and recurrence.

Wise's emphasis is primarily that early teaching should include very little formal work or *lessons* – such work should never replace play. She warns, too, against the perils of having too high expectations. Wise is keenly engaged in the developments of nursery education, expressing her opinion that psychologists should have an input. She points her readers towards relevant psychology books and psychological research: understanding the child was at the heart of all that Isaacs did, and part of her mission as Ursula Wise was to transmit to her readers the importance of this.

Wise cites research from Stanford University about learning to read and, indeed, engages with the *synthetic phonics*[1] discussion – though current, it is not a new debate. She responds to her correspondents' queries about the best way to teach reading – it was at a time when various new methods were being introduced. Going on the level of details in these questions, it looks like the correspondents had gleaned something about the areas of expertise of their undisclosed agony aunt. They seem to be working on the premise that they are dealing with an authority on early education and psychology.

For Wise, the education of the "whole child" is essential – the physical and physiological must not be neglected or considered to be of secondary importance. One letter in the archive (26 January, 1930)[2] refers to "The Twelve Essentials" competition in *The Nursery World* of which Wise was the judge. Readers had been asked to come up with the twelve most important aspects of being a mother for everyday life. Wise's judgement is most revealing of her priorities – she explains that the person who won second prize failed to win the first because she had not included some biology and physiology – otherwise, this entry would have won.

---

1 Synthetic phonics is a way of teaching children to read. In the beginning, children are taught the sounds that individual letters make – for example, that the letter *m* sounds like *mmm* (not *em*). Then they are taught to blend, or *synthesise* the sounds together to read a word – for example, saying the sounds *h-a-t* to read *hat*.

2 The letter referred to is not printed in this collection.

Not only was Wise concerned with instructing the child in the physical and physiological, but in using and employing the body. The necessity for physical occupations and plenty of open-air play comes up regularly – they are invaluable to the child's health and development. One of her bolder sounding pieces of advice is that of "finding useful ways of letting them enjoy the pleasures of destruction".

Included in play is social interaction and companionship. She was writing her column at a time when parents and children were not so mobile and easily connected as today. Wise examines the question of children playing alone and the appropriateness of solitude for young children. One of her correspondents describes a baby group formed by a collection of mothers – Wise is delighted by this and endorses it wholeheartedly.

PLAY IS THE BREATH OF LIFE

... to the young child, says Ursula Wise

25 MAY 1932

"Harassed" writes: *"Your answers to correspondents are exceedingly clear, and when I read them I say, 'That is just the answer I should think of', though I believe I should have great difficulty when it came actually to putting it into words! However, I cannot answer my own problems, so will you please help me? I have three children – two girls, aged five and four years, and a boy, two years three months. We are living in the country, and since January I have taught the two eldest first lessons (Montessori) myself; but also since Christmas I have had to dispense with a nurse and only have a local general servant to sleep in. As the maid has only occasionally to put the children to bed and take them out, the responsibility of discipline is mine, and they have all gone from bad to worse – shame on me, I know, but I can give no explanation. They are young, but they were much better behaved than at present. At meals they fidget, eat with wrong tools, etc., and, worst of all, they are hopelessly disobedient. They could dress themselves entirely, and, of course, can now, but do not. Sometimes the eldest will say she does 'not want to go out' with the maid, and, most irritating of all, she will dance and play about whilst you are telling her to go upstairs and take off her things. I am sure the eldest is the*

cause of the other two behaving as they do. Now, can you suggest the best method to deal with the disobedience? Smacking, of course, is taboo, but sometimes I leave the children to undress themselves (I mean take off coat, gloves, etc.), and when I come back they are just as they were, falling all over the place, and they cry and grizzle if I tell them they should have taken their things off and that the youngest has been downstairs for a long time. Can you also help me revise my routine to fit two hours' lessons and still have the maximum of fresh air? – 8 a.m., breakfast (fine mornings they go out before breakfast in garden); play in garden; 10.30, lessons; 12, dinner; 1 p.m., rest till 2.30; 3 p.m., walk; tea, 5 p.m.; bed, 6 p.m.

I have an awful time as the little boy will not stay in his pen as he used to (unless he has something very interesting), and then it is hopeless continuing lessons. I am hoping you will suggest some unusual but amusing toys for him, or would you advise keeping the children in in the afternoon for lessons while he is out for his walk? It is a problem with three, and especially when they have become unruly. What I want to know is what tactics to pursue, so that I may stick to it. It is quite useless 'talking', I am sure, and I loathe the idea of smacking or seeing a child cringe back whenever I approach."

I don't find it easy to know just what to say in reply to your letter, because I get the sense that the difficulty arises more (if you will allow me to say so) from your general attitude to the children and the problem of educating them than from any specific thing which is done or not done. You don't really tell me anything about the way in which you actually handle the children's contrariness and unwillingness, but indirectly your letter implies that you do "tell them to go and take their things off", etc. That is to say, your relation with them is essentially one of giving commands and expecting obedience, of teaching definite lessons and expecting the children to learn. It seems to me possible that two of the most essential ingredients in a successful relation with little children are altogether left out, namely the feeling of co-operation, you and they doing things *together*, and the atmosphere of play, you and they *enjoying* the things you do together. Now, if I am right in this, in thinking that you have conceived the whole question of the children's education entirely as a matter of discipline, obedience, and lessons, then that is the key to your present difficulties. Play is the breath of life to children of these years, and if one can build up the sense of real co-operation, of doing things with mother, and of mother's entering into the children's play, then many of these questions of obedience simply do not arise. A great many of the wisest educators of little children never think of the children's learning in these early years as "lessons" at all. The best Montessori teachers don't really think of the children's activities as set lessons, but as ways of helping the children do what they naturally seek to learn and enjoy doing. If I were faced with your problem myself I should be inclined to put aside all formal teaching material and all idea of set lessons for the next few months, at any rate during the summer. Instead of these I would approach the time that I had actually to spend with the children as a time when they and I could do pleasurable things – painting, drawing, threading beads, digging in the garden, modelling with clay, looking at pictures, laying the meal-table, washing the crockery and dusters, telling stories, singing songs, dancing, playing ball and going for walks. If incidentally the children took pleasure in learning to count or playing games with reading material, well and good, but I should consider it far more important to be building up the right relation of co-operation and delight in mutual activity, and giving the children the sense that you are interested in their interests – jumping and running and shouting and looking at the birds and flowers – whatever it be, than in learning any sort of formal set lesson. You will forgive my frankness. This is how the problem presents itself to me, and I should very much like to be able to help you through the present exasperating situation. I do really feel that to drive hard on the present lines of telling the children what to do and having set lessons will only bring further dissatisfaction and annoyance. With regard to playthings for the smaller child, you would find a list of these as well as for older children in "Health and Education in the Nursery", by Bennett and Isaacs (Routledge, 6s.).

OPEN AIR PLAY

5 FEBRUARY 1930

"C.W." writes: *"I should be so much obliged for advice about my small daughter, aged four. I am anxious to know whether or not it would be advisable to send her to a kindergarten next term. I have*

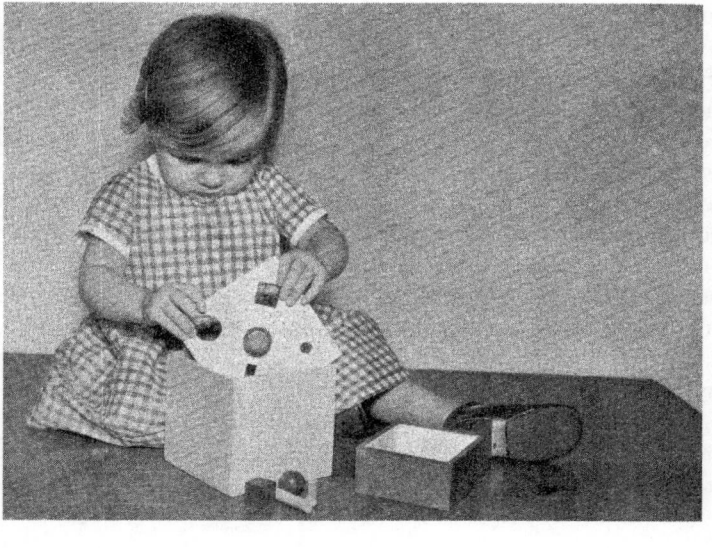

found one near home, but it takes children from nine to twelve every morning, and is not keen on shorter times. G. has always been a difficult child, sleeps badly and wakens crying in the night. She is better since we moved into the country here. She is a self-conscious child, and gets very tired at the dancing class. I can't make up my mind whether this kind of child is better doing more with other children, or whether another six months in the country – we live on a farm, with hens and dogs and rabbits and cats, etc. – would be better. There are two other little girls on the farm, exactly her age, to play with. Should I give her lessons myself? She has a strong tendency to say in the hour supposed to be given to 'work', 'Oh, I'm tired; I would rather look at books'; and I feel this may be due to the lack of the right thing to do. The youngest child at the kindergarten is, I think, five years."

Before deciding whether you send her to the kindergarten or not, I should, if I were you, find out two things. First, just how big the difference in age is between your little girl and the next youngest child there. If it is not more than a few months, and the other child is not of a large, very vigorous or domineering type, it would not matter very much. But if the difference is, say a year, and the other child is very well advanced or a strong personality, then it would not be very good. Secondly, how much active open-air play does the school allow? If the children there are mostly sitting indoors, then the farm life and free play with the two other girls at home would certainly be better. If she had no other children to play with, the kindergarten would be better for her. But if you can arrange for her to spend her mornings regularly with the other two, watching the animals, running and jumping and climbing, exploring the fields and the farm, that should be a very good life for her. I would not, however, advise anything in the nature of "set lessons" at her age and with her "liability" to nervous fatigue. You can help her best by giving her the right sort of conditions for play and things to play with, and by sharing her fun in games and interests. I think that you would find that some of the books I have suggested to other readers recently would be very helpful in your problem, too.

THE NEED FOR EXERCISE

8 JANUARY 1930

"K.A." (India) inquires: "I wonder if you would be good enough to give me the names and authors of one or two books on child psychology which you would advise me to get? My little girl is just two years old, and I am very anxious to do the best for her in spite of living in an out-of-the-way part of India, where she is unable to have other children to play with. She is a very healthy child, full of life. I have brought her up strictly on Truby King methods with good results. I have THE NURSERY WORLD sent to me every week, and your articles on 'Childhood Problems' I find very interesting. I am anxious not to spoil my little girl, for her own sake, but at the same time, let her enjoy the wonderful years of baby-hood to the full."

I am glad to hear that you find these articles useful, and I shall be glad to answer any particular questions at any time, but as you are preparing yourself beforehand for any problems that may arise as your little girl grows older, you will probably be able to deal with them as they come. The fortunate children *are* those whose parents think about things beforehand, and gather all the knowledge they can of how to meet each new need of growth as it comes along. If you are keeping your little girl with you in India during the next year or two, and want any further information about material for play or for handicrafts, or for learning to read and write, I shall be very glad to let you have it. There are so many delightful and *educative* things for young children to do, if only one knows them. In last week's issue I gave a short list of useful and inexpensive books, but in case you have not this by you I will repeat it here:

1   "Educate your child", by H. McKay (Oxford Press, 2s. 6d.)
2   "The Nursery Years", by Susan Isaacs (Routledge, 6d.)
3   "The Psychology of the Free Child", by C.M. Meredith (Constable)
4   "Dr. Montessori's Own Hand-book" (Heinemann).

"D.L. (Anerley)" asks: *"My little boy is four years old next March, and for some months he has been very difficult to manage, and as he gets still more difficult as the weeks go by, I feel that probably I am not treating him the best way. So would you please tell me the names of one or two inexpensive books on general training? Why is he so destructive? I'm sure he hasn't a breakable toy left or a picture-book whole. I have followed various suggestions. I give him newspapers to do as he likes with, and he has his own scissors, for one thing."*

Many children, especially boys, do tend to become very destructive about this age. There are several things to remember in trying to deal with it. First of all, it is an undoubted fact that a certain amount of destructiveness is quite normal and healthy in these years. The quick, explosive action of knocking things down or breaking them is so much easier to the untrained muscles of the young child. It is a definite relief to him, faced as he is with all the complicated business of learning control of his body and of his social behaviour. Some form of destructive action *must* be provided for vigorous children. It is an error to imagine that they can *all the time* be making the effort of handling things in just the right way or of building things up. The problem thus becomes one of finding useful ways of letting them enjoy the pleasures of destruction. The scissors and newspapers which you have already given to your boy are certainly excellent, but not enough for him. They would not be enough in themselves for any healthily growing young child, for the simple reason that they use only the smaller muscles of the fingers and wrist. And what children need so much in these years is plenty of the larger swinging movements of arm and shoulder and hip. If they don't have enough of these, children will always show signs of nervous tension and be restless and difficult.

I would therefore strongly suggest that you look into this, and see whether your boy is getting enough free exercise of his limbs and larger joints in throwing, running, jumping and climbing. Has he got room to do these things? If not in your garden, perhaps there is a common or open space nearby where he could play with other children in these ways. Then, again, perhaps you could think of things for him to do that would satisfy his destructive impulses and yet be useful. For instance, digging in the garden with a trowel or strong spade is very satisfactory; or helping to break up lumps of coal for the fire, or pieces of old crockery for putting at the bottom of plant pots; sawing logs, or learning to knock nails into a lump of wood.

The nails should be broad-headed and the hammer a suitable size and strong. Toy hammers and spades are useless for destructive children. I do hope you will try some of these suggestions, and let me know how the boy goes on.

SHOULD THEY PLAY ALONE?

Self-sufficiency on the one hand or a wish for someone to play with on the other are matters of temperament

13 MAY 1931

My first correspondent this week, "J.H.", raises two very interesting and important problems. The second of these, namely, the question of whether children ought to play alone, is also raised in the letter from "C.U.F.", who writes about it in "Over the Teacups" this week. I will deal with the first half of "J.H.'s" letter first and then take the second half together with "C.U.F.'s" letter.

"*J.H.*" writes: "*In your answer to my letter, published in the Christmas Number of THE NURSERY WORLD, you were kind enough to say that you would like to hear again about my son, who is now two years old. Most of the toys you suggested he got for Christmas, and they have almost all been very successful, especially the Noah's Ark. He plays with a much larger variety of toys now, and in a greater variety of ways, but he still insists on almost all his games being of a definitely educational nature, though he enjoys occasionally a romp with a ball or something similar. He likes short verses read to him if the words are pointed out as they are read, and he has recently begun to pick out one or two words that he knows well in verses that are read often. His talking is coming gradually; he now picks up and remembers words very easily, and occasionally puts them together in short phrases. He is still backward in talking, but he is certainly improving. His picking out of words when read to has made me wonder about the 'Look and Say'[3] method of teaching reading. Of course, it will be some time before we personally are directly concerned, but the fact that my son, before he was two, had begun to recognise words seems to indicate that it is a quick and natural way of learning to read. I understand, however, that it is very new, and I should be interested to know whether the results in after years have yet been tested. Are children who have been taught in this way quick and accurate in reading and spelling? And are they not more likely to be defeated by an unfamiliar word than children taught in other ways? There has been nothing in THE NURSERY WORLD about kindergarten education, except an occasional answer to a letter, and I should think a series of articles would be very interesting.*"

I have on several occasions described in some detail possible ways of using the "Look and Say" method in the nursery. The method is very far from new. It is, indeed, far older than phonic and phonetic methods. In fact, someone said to me privately the other day how amused she was to find me advocating this method, since it *was* such

---

3 The "Look and Say" approach is based on children learning to recognise whole words rather than individual letters, groups of letters or phonemes. The words are written on cards and shown repeatedly to the child until they can recognise words fluently. The word cards are used to construct sentences for the child to read, and give context to the word.

an old one! As a widely used method in England, however, it could be said to be new again, as there was a period in schools when it was almost completely displaced by various types of synthetic method, i.e. building up either from letters or sounds.[4] It is, however, becoming increasingly valued here, and in Belgium, Germany and America has never been displaced to any considerable extent. There is thus a far greater body of evidence in favour of its value than there could be in favour of the alphabetic or phonic methods. The weight of opinion in its favour is, however, not only that of practical teachers (always excepting, of course, the Montessorians who have used all sorts of methods), but also that of general psychologists who have analysed in various ways the actual processes of reading and of learning to read.

Interestingly enough, the post brought me this very morning an important monograph from Stanford University in America, describing a very careful experimental study of this actual problem. In this study a number of children, bright and ordinary and dull, between three and five years of age, were taught to read by a special method based upon the whole word. The results were extremely satisfactory, and the details fit in with this general view that the word and the sentence are the natural units for children in learning to read, not the letter or individual sounds.

The way in which "J.H.'s" little boy is picking out words that he has heard several times is certainly evidence that it is a quick and natural way. As regards the question of unfamiliar words at a later stage, there are a number of teachers who like to combine some attention to individual sounds and letters at a later stage with the whole-word method, but there are others who don't find that this is necessary, and consider that children taught naturally by the whole-word method spell quite as well later on, and can deal with unfamiliar words just as effectively.

"J.H." continues: *"Another thing with which you dealt in your answer to me, and again more recently, was the question of leaving a child alone to play. Obviously, it would be extremely bad for a child to have no companionship at all, but it seems to me that if he has companions for a large part of the time, a short time alone can only do him good, especially in a comparatively well-to-do home, where*

4   See footnote 1 for a brief definition of "synthetic phonics".

he has a mother and nurse devoting almost all their attention and energy to him, thereby providing a good deal of mental stimulus. A child of two has a day of about nine or ten waking hours. During that time he is constantly having new impressions thrust on him and new accomplishments suggested to him, either consciously or unconsciously, on the part of his companions. In other words, his mind is being constantly stimulated except in sleep. No grown-up could stand so much mental stimulation; those who really use their minds almost always need a quiet time alone, and those who live constantly with companions usually cease to use their minds for useful purposes. Surely this would apply to a child too. An hour or so to try over his new ideas and achievements by himself will encourage habits of concentration and thought, and tend to fix his knowledge firmly in his mind. It will also help to prevent his growing up into that deplorable type of person of whom we hear so many complaints nowadays, who is never peacefully happy, but must be always having a so-called good time. You say, too, that most children who enjoy playing alone are either dull and unintelligent or asocial. Of course, my own experience is limited to my own child, and I hesitate to say that he is intelligent, as I know that all mothers think that their children are unusually intelligent. But the qualities that seem to strike other people most are just in great busy-ness and concentration. He is usually completely absorbed in something, trying to puzzle out how it works, or trying to improve his skill. And, secondly, his strong sense of humour and his insistence that everybody present must appreciate the joke, too. In most ways he seems to be up to the normal standards of accomplishment, and in some he is beyond it. Although he is quite happy playing alone, he is always pleased if someone joins him, and anxious to show what he has been doing. So I do not think, in spite of the slowness in learning to talk, that he is less sociable than most children. He has a very good memory for people. During the last six months he has had about an hour alone daily, with occasional visits from us and an hour and a half at least to play with a grown-up – almost always myself – besides the usual companionship of walks, meals, dressing, etc., which seem to entail a lot of conversation with his nurse."

"C.U.F." writes: "*I always read your pages in* THE NURSERY WORLD *with profound interest and admiration. Your remarks about children playing alone have, however, frankly, amazed me, and it would be extremely interesting to hear the grounds for your views, as your opinion is certainly to be respected. I enclose a copy of a letter I have written to 'Over the Teacups', and do hope that you will give us more details of your belief."*

I am very glad "C.U.F." has put this question and asked me to make myself more clear. Probably there are other people who may have misunderstood me or felt they would like to know my reasons. First of all, I don't mean to suggest that it is never desirable for little children to play alone. I fully agree that it is *desirable* that they should have the *opportunity* of occupying themselves quietly alone from time to time. It is a good thing in itself for both grown-ups and children not to be altogether dependent upon the presence of other people for content or interest. So, I would never deprive a child of the chance to play by himself, and, on the whole, I should be pleased if a child would be content to do so as an occasional thing. But that is very different from saying that *every* child "ought" to play alone, whether he wants to or not, and for a certain part of every day, right through the years of toddlerhood. It is this rigid idea for which there is no justification. To begin with, children differ very much in their temperaments, even from the cradle. What is easy and natural for one child, may not be good or possible for another. Any idea of virtue or method of training which is built upon a rigid pattern for all children is certain to create more difficulties than it solves. Nor does this cut across what I am always saying about the value of a regular routine. A regular routine is absolutely essential as a background for a child's life, but, of course, it is more important in things like mealtimes and bed-times and bath-times and training in cleanliness than in such a question as this. Here *regular* must not mean *rigid*. A child may be happy to play alone one day and not the next. I would always give him the opportunity, but I would never consider that he was naughty if he preferred to be with his mother or nurse on some days, or even if he were of such a temperament that he always preferred to be with someone else. Secondly, with some children it is not even a question of "temperament", but of positive fears of being left alone. As some of the letters to me dealing with this have shown, there are lots of children who are really terrified if they are left alone, or who, at any rate, feel so strongly the need for companionship that enforced solitude makes it impossible for them to interest themselves or to make their play happy and valuable. I should, therefore, think it most undesirable to compel such children to play alone, or even to suggest in any way that it was "naughty" not to want to do so. What I would do would be, as early as possible, to arrange for other little children to play with them so that they could become more independent of the grown-ups.

My own general impression is undoubtedly that far more children between the age of one year and four prefer to play with others or with a grown-up than to be alone, though, of course, there are quite a number who, like "J.H.'s" little boy, will play happily alone. When they will it is fortunate, but it is neither a universal characteristic of the age nor a virtue that should be sternly enforced.

Thirdly, with regard to "C.U.F.'s" point about the modern methods of training infants so that they lie quietly awake for long periods. This, of course, I agree is of the greatest value for health and development, and nothing I say about not enforcing *toddlers* to be alone applies to children under, say, one year. But the problem for children who can walk and talk, who have become actively interested in people, and whose social development and curiosity about the world are rapidly developing, is quite a different one from that of the infant. Just as their diet changes and needs to change, so their needs of *mental* development change. I have known several children whose development has been definitely held up by enforced solitude. On the other hand, of course, I agree it would be a great mistake to be constantly stimulating them by talking to them, telling them stories, persuading them to play at this or that, or teaching them. But the presence of an adult is not necessarily stimulating. This depends, naturally, on the adult and on the way she behaves. Very many of the children described in the letters to me seem to need the actual presence of a grown-up who can be busy about her own work, or sewing, or reading, while the child occupies himself with his own pursuits. If we just quietly respond to anything the child says to us or asks of us, there is no risk of over-stimulation. But he is certainly over-stimulated by his imaginative terrors or tempers if we force him to stay alone against his real needs or the natural trend of his temperament. As against these fears and phantasies the presence of an adult may be actually soothing. I hope my correspondents will feel that I have made the issues a little clearer now.

THE NURSERY SCHOOL

6 JUNE 1934

"Enquiring" writes: *"I have only been taking THE NURSERY WORLD for a month or so, and I do not know whether you have yet dealt with the nursery school – its advantages and disadvantages. I should be glad to know your opinions on these schools as a whole. My little daughter is aged one year, ten and a half months, and I have decided to send her daily to a nursery school in the summer. We live in a flat, and shall continue to do so for some years yet; the garden is not a particularly exciting one for a child to play in, and I feel that she will have more scope if she goes to school. She is very active, walked early, talks very little, although always 'chattering' in her own way; is a bad and faddy eater – always impatient to get down from her chair and to get on with the next thing in this interesting world; is very independent and insists on feeding herself, and doing other odd jobs. So far we have had no trouble with 'potting' or with my leaving her occasionally. For the last six weeks she has been dry from six until getting up time, and asks for the 'po-po' regularly during the day, and likes to fetch it herself; she does not mind my leaving her when I have to go out. She will call for 'Mama' at bed time, and if she falls down. For the first twelve months of her life I was out a lot and had a nurse for her; and now I look after her myself. I think she would be better away from me at times, as I know my limitations as a 'perfect mother'! I was nineteen when she was born and had, and still have, a quick temper – sometimes it is just temper, and sometimes it is nerves, as I am very nervous of many things! She is nervous of coalmen, dustmen and any sudden noise, such as a band playing in the street, or a cup breaking in front of her. I took her to a hairdresser's twice, but she was frantic with fear at the baby electric 'dryer,' and I can never take her now.*

We were looking forward to providing her with a companion for her second birthday, but a miscarriage unfortunately took away that hope. Now, however soon a brother or sister arrives, she will be almost three, and I should like have to have companions before then. There are no children here, and getting to any of my friends with babies means a day's outing and plenty of arrangements beforehand. I do not claim that she is in any way more advanced and intelligent than most children – though naturally I sometimes think so – but looking at her from a detached point of view – if it is ever possible to do that with one's own children – I can see that she has the makings of a good, and lovable character in her. Do you think it will help or hinder her to go to the nursery school? I can see a lot of advantages for her, but I may have the wrong viewpoint – I am only anxious to help her as much as possible, without being fussy. I should hate to see her changed a great deal, and turned out to a set pattern, while she is still so pliable. What do you think? I might add that she will go to a convent when she is about four and a half – quite a big one – as a day scholar only, and probably a boarding school at about ten years of age. I think your answers to mothers and nannies are most interesting and helpful."

When one tries to speak about the advantages and disadvantages of the nursery school one always has to ask first of all what the age of the child is who is being considered. Experience shows that the nursery school for the child over three is extremely helpful, always assuming of course that it is a well-run one, with a good attitude on the part of the grown-ups and plenty of the right playthings and methods. With a child under three, however, there is more to be said on the contrary side, and the demands that one makes of the nursery school are more rigorous. Children under three are so dependent on the love and care of a grown-up. They need so much to have constant personal contact with one grown-up with whom they feel secure, that if they go to the nursery school, it must be one that has only a very small group of children of this age, and with plenty of adults to the number of children. I would never send a two-year-old to a nursery school unless there were at least three adults to, say, ten or twelve children of this age. I am, of course, speaking of children who have a good home, not of children whose mothers have in any case to go out to work, or where the home is bad in some other way.[5] I am

---

5 Isaacs reflects the widespread view of her era that working mothers were responsible for "bad homes". Indeed, even the 1967 "Plowden Report", which strongly
promoted a more liberal and child-centred vision of education, states that "some
mothers who are not obliged to work may work full-time, regardless of their
children's welfare. It is no business of the educational service to encourage these
mothers to do so" (HMSO, 1967, p. 127).

considering only children such as yours, where the decision has to be made, not out of necessity, but out of choice. If there are enough adults in the group in the nursery school, so that every child can feel there is someone to whom he can turn and with whom he can be constantly in touch as a friendly and helpful person, then two or three hours of a nursery school every day are very helpful, even for the two-year-old. Children of this age do love to play in the company of other little children, provided there is an adult always close in the background; and such play in the company of other children helps gradually to wean a child from this complete dependence on the grown-up. The only child in the home is deprived of this opportunity. The benefits of being with other children for even a part of the day for children of this age are shown in many different ways. For instance, difficulties in feeding often get less or disappear altogether in the nursery school, even with children who have been quite a problem at home. The sight of other little children eating in an unconcerned way with enjoyment is far more helpful to the child who is reluctant to eat than any persuasions or commands that we give them. The moments of happy play together, with a variety of materials, are a great social education in themselves, as well as a great pleasure. Another advantage of the nursery school is that so many of the things which help the child's development at this age, for example climbing apparatus, space enough to run round in, large building bricks, and so on, can so much more easily be provided for a group of children than by each mother in her own home. All the little ceremonials of self-helpfulness, such as helping to lay the table for a meal, and to serve it in turn, are much enjoyed by children, even at three years. It is very easy for the nursery school, too, to provide toilet arrangements of the right size – arrangements so that the little children can learn to wash themselves or their dolls' garments, etc., very easily. I don't think that the really well run nursery school has any disadvantages even for the two-year-old, but it does need to be not merely well equipped and spaced, but in the hands of sensible women who can adapt the routine to each little child's need – watching to see, for example, when a child is getting over-tired and settling him down to some quiet occupation in a quiet, friendly way. It is often surprising how children of two to five will blossom out, both in body and mind, in vigour and friendliness and jolliness, when they have a few hours of each day in companionship with other children in a really well-chosen environment. The answer to your question is thus not an absolute one that the nursery school as such is a good thing, but that the well-run nursery school has very great benefits to offer, even to the child from a good home. Under these conditions there is not the slightest risk that the child will be forced into a uniform pattern. That, of course, would be very undesirable even with the older children and quite harmful with the little ones.

Now in the case of your own little girl it does seem to me that she is rather young to go to a nursery school in the summer. If there is a nursery school near you, then the best plan would be to let her have an occasional bout there, but not yet to make any regular arrangement for her to spend the full nursery school day there. You could increase the length of time in the autumn and, if she were perfectly happy and you were satisfied that the methods were good, she could even begin to take up regular school life then. In a well-run group there are ample opportunities for quiet rest and sleep. But I should certainly enquire about all these details before I made any decision.

OCCUPATIONS FOR THE THREE-YEAR-OLD

2 MAY 1934

"Nodrog" writes: "I shall be very grateful for advice from you about hand-work for my little son. He is three and a half years old and seems ordinarily intelligent and is generally happy and contented. My two elder children are at school in Scotland, so Alastair (here in India) now has to depend more on his own resources for amusement. During the hot weather, roughly from April 1st till October 31st, he has to be indoors from 9.00 a.m. to 5 p.m., and I think that this year he will probably be glad of a definite occupation for a part of some mornings anyway. During the cold months we go into camp and are constantly on the move, so that any very large and elaborate toys, etc., are out of the question. In Karachi he has a large blackboard and coloured chalks, a frame of coloured beads, and beads for threading. He is learning to cut out pictures with blunted scissors, and he enjoys doing simple picture puzzles. He makes crude attempts at drawing and asks me to draw things for him; unfortunately, I cannot draw at all. Do you think it is wise to let him have his paint-box yet? My experience with small children is that they just mess up the paint-box if left to

*themselves, and yet at three and a half they are too small to be taught
how to use paints properly. Plasticine I have thought of, but I found
that with my other two children it was only messed about with until
after they were five years old. They took a delight in mixing all the
colours together and making balls, and I doubt whether any useful
purpose was served. Perhaps I was to blame as I am not at all skilful
with my fingers. Is basket-weaving too advanced for Alastair yet?
Are books of instruction on paper-folding obtainable? Another thing
that Alastair is very fond of doing is listening to the gramophone, and
he tries to sing the tunes he hears. I shall be very glad if you can tell
me of any records of children's hymns and nursery rhymes. The only
ones I have been able to find have such high-pitched, difficult tunes
that no small child could attempt to sing them. Pianos in Karachi are
a great luxury, the excessive dampness is very bad for them. When
mentioning any sort of hand-work, will you please let me know an
address in London where necessary materials and instructions can
be obtained, also prices, in case I am not able to get them in India."*

It is very wise to try to find satisfying occupations for your little boy
now that he is left to himself, as they are certainly the main solution
to the problem of a child who has no playmates. I suppose that the
time when you go into camp and are moving about is a more enjoyable one for the boy, as there must be a greater variety of things to
see and do. If your hot weather home is regularly in Karachi it would
be worth your while getting one or two things for use indoors that
would give your boy the type of large activity which children of his
age so much need: for example, something to climb on and jump
off, such as a low stepladder or a firmly placed box with a plank that
he could run up and balance on. It is such a mistake to think of the
child's occupations at this age simply as something to use his fingers
and keep him quiet, sitting still. He does need plenty of opportunity
for large movements of the whole body and of the larger joints. Fine
use of the fingers has only a limited value at his age. The blackboard
and chalks are, of course, very valuable, because they satisfy the need
for large arm movements as well as the child's joy in colour. With
regard to painting, I quite agree that the ordinary small paint box
with small blocks of paint is no good for little children. They have
not yet the fine co-ordinations necessary for using such a thing to
advantage. But that does not mean that they do not need and cannot

gain great value from some other form of painting. What they need are large sheets of paper; ordinary kitchen paper will do quite well, and large brushes with jars of liquid paint with which they can make bold strokes and patterns or pictures. Children, while little older than your boy, sometimes produce most delightful designs and striking representations of trains and people if they have the right material and are allowed to use it freely. One of the best arrangements is that adopted in several schools for little children that I have seen at work: a dozen or so sheets of kitchen paper – perhaps twelve by eighteen inches in size – are hung upon two brass hooks, the hooks simply being pushed through the paper on a drawing board which is stood up against the wall at a slight slope. If the board is tall enough the child can sit on a low chair to use it, otherwise he is quite happy to kneel on a cushion on the floor. Poster colour paint, thinned out beforehand in a jam jar, will go quite a long way in use, and a jar of this stood on the floor beside the child with a large paint brush will keep him happy for an hour on end. These materials do not cost much, and will give great satisfaction and make it possible for him to produce things that are artistically valuable.

It is true that little children under five are only able to make balls with plasticine and mix the balls together, but then that is quite a valuable thing for them to do. That is the normal activity of their age, which gives them great emotional satisfaction and develops the fingers themselves in a way that leads on to being able to produce objects which seem interesting to us. There is no better occupation for children between four and five than free modelling in plasticine. The use of plasticine whether or not the child can produce something that is aesthetically interesting to us, has a very soothing effect upon the children's feelings. When I had a school of my own, I used to find one of the best ways of quietening a group of children who had become rather excited and boisterous, perhaps when they had to stay indoors on a wet day, was to bring out the plasticine and let them begin to use it in a quite free way. It is the children who have been allowed to mix it and roll it and do what they like with it under five years that who become so clever in modelling elaborate engines and ships and people with it later on.

Basket weaving is certainly much too difficult for a boy of three and a half. Paper folding might interest the boy up to a point, provided it is not done in any formal way. Newspaper for making hats and Red

Indian costumes, etc., is always useful. Catalogues of motor car firms or some of the general stores would be attractive to your boy if he could cut out pictures with scissors. I would suggest that you take the most valuable publication, "Child Education", a monthly journal published at 1s. by Evans Bros., Montague House, Russell Square, London, W.C.1. It has the most delightful pictures for cutting out, as well as a great many suggestions that would be useful to you in your situation. I would suggest your writing for particulars of handicraft material to Dryad, Ltd., 22, Bloomsbury Street, London, W.C.1., Paul and Marjorie Abbatt, Ltd., 29, Tavistock Square, W.C.1., and Lady Verney's Whimsy Market, 15, Ennismore Gardens Mews, S.W.7.

EARLY TEACHING

Children learn best through their everyday interests

30 JULY 1930

This week I want to deal with the remaining questions in the letter from "M.S." (in S. Africa) whose first problem I discussed last week. The rest of her letter runs:

"(1) Could you give me an idea of what a small boy between the ages of two and four ought to be doing, and the materials I should provide for him? He has the usual dolls and animals and big toys to push and drag, and a sand heap and building blocks. He plays really well by himself, but I think this is really because his intellectual needs are being satisfied! I thought of getting the blocks and sticks you mentioned in one article (from Asen, Geneva). They charge 28 francs for Box C – I suppose that is about £1 6s. Is this the set you spoke of? And do you consider these better than 'Pick-a-Bricks' or 'Tinker Toy'? We are rather hard up and I don't want to buy anything that will not give lasting pleasure. I was awfully disappointed with the Montessori Apparatus – the only pieces of apparatus my children really took to were the two simpler sets of cylinders. Peter mastered these at eighteen months and shows no further interest in them now. Occasionally they play with the insets, and the three- and four-year-olds can manage all the easier shapes, but show no 'impulse to repeat', while they seem to realise the polygons are beyond them and do not attempt them. So, having been disappointed once in 'educative' material, I am anxious to make quite sure, before buying any other toys of this type, whether they will give lasting pleasure.

(2) Could you give me some idea of what my three- and four-year-old girls might be doing in the way of elementary science? And would any of the 'Asen' material help them with kindergarten geometry? The elder plays counting games involving addition and subtraction, with numbers up to ten, with great enjoyment, and does a good deal of informal nature study when we are gardening and on our walks, and has several pets which she takes pleasure in watching and feeding; and, of course, we answer her questions about birth as they arise; but I feel I might also be stimulating an interest in the inorganic side of nature. Do you think a young child could be interested in this sort of thing, and do you know of a book about crystals and rainbows, the properties of water, and so on? The children do lots of work with scissors, paste, and so on, and sew, and draw with crayons, and use hammer and nails in an elementary way; and we are plentifully supplied with good children's literature (Kipling, Milne, Hugh Lofting, Fyleman, etc.), and we are beginning the study of geography with stories of children from other lands; but on the science side I am very weak.

(3) Do you think it good to teach young children history? I feel that to my children, who have never seen England, a history of England would be quite unprofitable. Tabitha (the four-year-old) likes to hear about the cave-men, and loved Kipling's 'Cat that walked by himself'; and I intend reading her some time 'The Cave Twins,' by Lucy Fitch Perkins; but what is the most profitable way to proceed after this?"

There is one respect in which the *Asen* blocks and sticks I have mentioned are better than "Tinker Toy", and that is the larger size of the blocks. The parts of "Tinker Toy" are rather smaller than they should be for a child under four, making too much demand on the fingers, and not enough on the larger wrist movements. Nevertheless, I am very doubtful whether the *Asen* material would be worth the cost to anyone who had only a limited amount to spend on playthings for a family of children. I should be inclined to spend the same money on a variety of larger material for helping physical development – a climbing frame, light ladders, sliding boards, and so on, and on a wide variety of shapes and sizes of blocks for building. Children in England are now able to have quite large building blocks (even bigger than "real" bricks), which are nevertheless quite light and safe for tinies to handle because they are hollow. They are really boxes that don't open. With a generous supply of these the children can build quite large play-houses to sit in and make-believe to their hearts' content. Especially if they have a rug and a cushion or two, and, as I have so often suggested, some old pans and kitchen utensils. I don't know whether you could get such blocks made in your part of the world. Probably old cigar boxes could be fastened up securely to serve as building blocks by a strip of firm adhesive tape along the edge.

"Tinker Toy" and "Pick-a-Bricks" might well be given later on. A more valuable part of the *Asen* material consists of the large coloured wooden balls, which can be threaded on a set of upright wires, holding from one to ten of the balls. The loose balls also can be threaded by the children on raffia, making different patterns with number series of the different colours. But it might be possible to make this material more cheaply by buying the largest wooded beads one could get, and colouring them oneself.

You don't mention plasticine or any modelling material among the play-things your little boy has. Two years is, of course, rather young for it, but many children of three and a half will enjoy a large lump of plasticine, and make simple things with it. Sand and water are better general playthings, it is true, again because they use the larger movements of the body.

If your boy has all the toys and constructive material you mention, together with gardening and pet animals and walks and stories, I don't think any more "educative" material in the narrower sense is really needed. If he mastered the Montessori cylinders (as the more intelligent children generally do) at eighteen months, they would, of course have no further interest for him. My own experience is that the intelligent children do *not* have the "impulse to repeat" once the problem is mastered. In a strict Montessori school they are made to repeat, by the subtle pressure of suggestion, and by not being allowed to make-believe with the material. If left to themselves, however, they simply use the cylinders and blocks for making trains and towers and motor cars.

But the fact that the children don't want to go on playing with the geometrical insets in the routine way all the time does not mean that the insets have not any educational value. I have found that they have a great deal, even though the children don't *often* look at them, and the advanced material is very useful for later work in geometry and arithmetic, as, e.g., in the study of fractions and of equal areas. I think the insets and some of the advanced sets would be worth having for a family of four. But the "sense training" material is not necessary and not worth the cost. And I have found Dr Jessie White's number rods more useful than the Montessori rods. You would find many further useful suggestions in Dr White's catalogue of number material, which can be obtained from 46, Great Russell Street, London, W.C.1.

A great deal of interesting work in elementary "science" can be done with quite young children. But it is both sounder and safer to think of it rather as the child's interest in the everyday facts of the world around him than as "science". Intelligent children, even those of two and three and four years of age, are most interested in things like soap and soap-suds, cooking and cleaning and washing, where the water comes from in the pipes, and where it goes to, the drains and the light, the garden bonfire, the rain and sun and wind, trains and engines, motors and aeroplanes. If children are met with respect and understanding they will ask endless questions about these things.

In these early years it is best not to try to give set lessons on any of these everyday facts, but rather to meet the children's interest as it arises and as things happen. But in order to be able to help the children to answer their questions and to make use of their opportunities in the everyday events of cooking and cleaning and watching the rain and sun, one does, of course, need to have knowledge oneself of the scientific facts that are involved in these ordinary events. And for this you would find very useful the little book by H. McKay, "Experiments in Science" (Oxford Press, 1s. 6d.). In his other book, too, which I have often recommended, "Educate Your Child", McKay notes a number of simple experiments which young children can do. A larger and more ambitious book, which you might find valuable as your children grow older, is "Experimental Science", by A.F. Collins (Appleton, 6s.). And in two or three years' time your girls would probably enjoy having "Men Who Found Out" (by Annabel Williams-Ellis) read to them. This is a beautifully written account of some of the great scientific discoveries, and children love it.

I would hardly teach history as such to children so young as these. But very presently they would be ready for *the history of everyday things*, which links up with their "scientific" interest in the things around them, and with the history of everyday things one naturally works backwards from the present, instead of trying to start from a remote and unreal past which has no concrete meaning for the child. The psychological study of children's sense of time has shown how feeble that sense is in young children, and how slowly it develops even in later childhood. From to-day and yesterday and last week the definite "past" stretches only a little way back, and soon loses itself in a mist of vague words. When, therefore, we try to give young children stories involving a great stretch of time, with many wide events of peoples and nations and kings and wars and parliaments, all these things get quite jumbled up together in a meaningless mass, with no proper sequence of relation.

When, however, children become interested in trains and aeroplanes and motor-cars and buses and see the more "old-fashioned" and more "modern" kinds, they easily appreciate their history. All little children I know are very interested in comparing, for instance, Stephenson's first engine and the early "Rocket" with the engines of last year and to-day. They love to set the picture of an early bicycle beside a modern "road racer" and a "motor bike", and talk of the difference in their speed and convenience and the way they are made. And this can lead on to the general history of means of

transport – carts and chariots, horses and camels, steamers and sail-
ing ships, and the earliest boats of Egypt and Mesopotamia.

One can deal in the same way with houses and streets, with clothing and utensils and implements. And all this links up so readily with
their geography. History and geography can, in fact, hardly be taken
apart in these early stages. You would have to adapt this method to
the particular conditions in which your family lives. Perhaps they
don't have much contact with trains and cars and aeroplanes; but I
imagine there must be many points of vivid interest for them in the
actual things they have around them, and every bit of real experience
can be used as a starting point.

You would find the B.B.C. pamphlets of Broadcasts to Schools
most useful and suggestive. They can be obtained regularly for a few
shillings a year.

HANDICRAFT PLAY

"E.W.G." writes: *"I shall be so much obliged if you will advise me on
material for play and handicrafts, and for learning to read and write,
for a girl child of four and a half years; and where to get same."*

19 FEBRUARY 1930

Since you wrote your letter, my reply to "E.H." in the issue of
January 29th has appeared, and I daresay you will have read that,
since it dealt with play material for a child of the same age as
yours. In it I outlined the general point of view which should guide
us in choosing play things; I will add some further detailed suggestions here.

Most children of four and a half or so love modelling with plasticine, glitter-wax or real potter's clay. This last is a little more difficult
and messy to use than the other two, so that it should come later; but
with it children can make permanent things – plates, dishes, bowls,
vases, etc. – either large ones for gifts or to use in their own rooms, or
small ones for the doll's house. Another thing much enjoyed by little
children, and very useful for gifts, is the painting of plain wooden
bowls, beads, egg-cups, and so on, with special paint suitable for use
on white wood. Then many pleasant things can be made with coarse

brown canvas, stitches in coarse coloured thread or wool. I have in my possession several bags of different sizes, made for me by a group of little children of about your child's age. One of these was made by a boy of five, who, after, he had sewn the edges together, said: "Now I am going to put the prettiness on", and sewed some coloured wooden beads on one side in a charming design. These bags and cases were made entirely by the children themselves; the stitches are large and uneven, but the general effect very pleasing – and the bags are still in use for keeping my own sewing materials in, although they were made four years ago.

Little girls also love making jumpers and skirts and aprons, night-dress cases, curtains, and so on, with cheap, thin, coloured muslin, sewn with coarse, coloured thread. Then mats for the nursery meal-table can be made by wrapping coloured raffia or coarse wool over flat cardboard discs with a hole in the centre. And there are all the delights of drawing with coloured chalks on a wall blackboard. Or on large sheets of brown wrapping paper, or buff kitchen paper; and of painting with *large* brushes and liquid water-colour. Children so small as this cannot manage the solid blocks of paint in the usual boxes really satisfactorily. It is much better to give them jars of liquid paint all ready to use, which can be bought as "show-card colours" from an artist's colour shop. Large sheets of brown paper or of rough kitchen paper can be made into books by folding and fastening them together with coarse "Sylko" thread sewn through and tied. The children can then paste into these books coloured pictures cut out from drapers', motor-car or fancy goods catalogues, or from old magazines.

The modelling materials, canvas, beads, wooden articles and paint, raffia, etc., can all be got from the Dryad Handicraft Co., Leicester, or from the Educational Supply Association, New Oxford St, W.1.

The most important thing to keep in mind in helping children of this age to use the various handicraft materials is that we should measure achievement by *their* standards, not by ours. The impulse that leads little children to be content with large and uneven stitches is a perfectly sound one, since their eyes and fingers and nerves are not yet ripe for fine work. Neatness and precision will come later; in these early years it is spontaneity, colour, variety of interest, and the making of real, however simple, things that bring happiness and growth.

As regards reading and writing materials, again the first thing to be remembered is that *all* such material must be quite large for little children. Small print and small pictures, fine pencils or crayons should be banned entirely. Ordinary chalks, carpenter's pencils and thick crayons in wood may be provided for use on large surfaces of board or paper – surfaces so large that they call out arm movements rather than finger movements. Writing should, of course, follow on plenty of spontaneous drawing, not come before it.

In teaching reading there are two main sorts of method: the one which starts with whole simple words, names of things or actions, or with simple sentences; and the one which starts from the artificial elements of words – letters and syllables. General opinion among skilled teachers is undoubtedly in favour of the first way, since that is the *living* way. It makes a natural transition from the spoken word to the written, and it always has real meaning for the children. When the child has learnt the look of a number of words he becomes interested in the letters and the separate sounds they make; so that after the earliest stages one uses the "analytic" method as well, breaking the words up into parts and learning how they fit together. But, to begin with, carefully chosen whole words and simple sentences are the best. There are many ways of bringing these in. For instance, labels can be pinned onto all ordinary objects in the nursery – door, wall, window, fire, cup, jug, hat, mat, toy, cat, toy dog, and so on. On a wet day a game can be made of mixing these labels up and sorting them out again. Or pictures can be cut out, of things and people, and pasted in a large home-made book, with large, clearly printed labels underneath – man, can, woman, baby, etc. Or the pictures can be put into a box, with the labels in another, and the game will be to sort them out properly.

Then simple commands can be printed on loose sheets for another game – *shut the door, pick up a pin, sit on the mat, go out, etc., etc.* The child will enjoy playing this game either with you or with other children, and most children learn many words very easily in this way.

After plenty of varied experience in these methods one or two suitable books can presently be given. Again the print must be large and clear and the matter interesting and alive. You would find the New Beacon Readers very good, and quite suitable as the next step after the games I have suggested. They can be obtained at any bookseller's.

UNSOCIABILITY

... in a little girl of three years is the subject of one of this week's letters and how to deal with it is explained

3 AUGUST 1932

"C.M." writes: "I should be so pleased if you could help me with my present difficulty. I have charge of a little girl aged three years two months. She is rather nervous and highly strung and only a week ago had a convulsion. This is the second one she has had, the last one being caused by teething over a year ago, but this time I find no cause. The doctor said it might be a touch of the sun but I have been rather careful with her and her daily duty has been very regular. I am telling you this first so that you can advise me on the next subject. My difficulty is this. Jill is terrified of other small children. Whenever we happen to meet any and they come to shake hands or be friendly she will begin to sob most pitifully. I know she cannot possibly help this, but what is one to do about it? She is very sweet natured and sweet tempered, etc. We sometimes meet a little friend, but as soon as Jill sees her (if she happens to be a hundred yards away) she will begin sobbing. When I take her on the beach to play *with this little friend she will sit down on the sands near me and not move the whole time I stay. There will be an occasional sob and sigh and afterwards the only thing she will say is, 'Will we be seeing any-body today, Nanny?' or this, 'Will Elizabeth be down on the beach?' and she will fret and worry the whole day. So I have stopped seeing this little friend, but we do occasionally see one another in the street, when Jill will start sobbing before we are anywhere near. I asked her why she did not like E., and she said it was because her hair was always untidy (E. has a fringe and auburn hair). I took her to tea one day, and there was another little boy of the same age there also. Jill was quite alright (perhaps a little nervous), but the little boy became rough, pushing Jill down. She was very upset, and since then has a horror of other children. As we live in the country where there are no little friends we thought it would be nice if we met some here. But it is only making Jill unhappy, and I think she will grow out of it in time without us forcing her. After this convulsion she is rather peevish and cries very quickly over the slightest thing. To-day we met E., but Jill is just the same (sobbing, etc.). Do you not think it more advisable to keep Jill away from small children until she is older? Do you think she became upset about meeting E., thus causing the convulsion? She has a very good appetite for a small child of her age and weighs two stone twelve ounces, sleeps well, but is very quickly upset. I have been with Jill four months. Before me she had a very kind old nanny, who stayed two and a half years, and then a young nurse, who was very strict and most unkind. She stayed three months."*

The fear of other children which your little girl shows is quite unusually strong, and I should think it very likely that the convulsion she had just recently was connected with her fright about meeting the other child. In the circumstances, I should be inclined to follow the line of not forcing her to meet other children. It is thought by some doctors who have a wide experience of psychological difficulties in children that there is a type of convulsion which is definitely caused by such states of anxiety as your little girl shows, and it sounds to me as if she were a case of this. Now, if so, it does mean that her jealousy of other children and consequent fear of them is too great for her to deal with, and that her health would suffer very severely if she were, at any rate just now, constantly thrown into this state of terror. She is at an age when such jealousies are at their most acute phase, even in normal children, and in a year or two she may have got over the difficulty to a sufficient extent to enable her to meet other children without such extreme distress as brings on a convulsion. You would be fully justified in protecting your child against this for the present as far as you possibly can. You will not, of course, be able to avoid her meeting other children all together. It was very unfortunate that the boy pushed the child down on an occasion that might otherwise have led to a lessening of the general difficulty. It is quite possible that you only have to be patient for a year or two and the worst trouble will pass.

COMPANIONSHIP

Very rare fifty years ago in the days of large families, the problem of finding a companion of his own age for the toddler is one which the mother of today has to solve

7 JANUARY 1931

The following letter will interest a number of my correspondents who have to deal with the problem of finding companionship for their little children.

"D.G.H." writes: "*I was so interested in the letter from E.G., as my circumstances are almost exactly the same (except that I took my Froebel certificate in 1924 and my nurse has obtained her M.T.S. Certificate). It may interest E.G. and other readers to know how we have tackled the problem. We have become – as it were – partners and started a 'crèche'. I have advertised – setting forth our qualifications – and offered to take charge of children of any age up to seven. At the moment we have one 'out-patient', the son of my weekly 'help', who is Nurse's special care. He is only four months, and is examined weekly and given diet sheets, etc. Then we have Jean, aged sixteen months, who is brought to my flat at 9 and fetched at 5 every day. My own son is aged eighteen months, and they get on splendidly together. We hope to have three older ones for proper first lessons (I have a lot of Dr White's apparatus) and one other, baby or toddler. It is great fun, and we (i.e., Nurse and I) feel that we are not wasting our training but are gaining very valuable experience. Incidentally, we are also making some pocket money and being a real boon to busy parents. I have a nursery and garden, and am only two minutes from the sea (Hove). I do wish we could co-operate with E.G."*

It seems to me an excellent thing when this sort of arrangement can be made, but it is, of course, much the best when either her mother or her helper has had a definite training for the work. In your own case, you and your nurse cover the ground most excellently between you, the physical hygiene and the educational care.

I think this really might be one of the solutions of the problem of providing satisfactory conditions for the children of a modern small family. I am always hearing from parents (both my correspondents in these columns and elsewhere) how difficult they find it to ensure companionship for the toddlers, or good school conditions for the four- and five-year-olds. And I often suggest what seems to me one of the best ways out of the difficulty, viz., that several mothers of little children living near each other should club together, letting their children meet for two or three hours' play each morning, either in someone's suitable large room that can be well equipped, or even at each home in turn; and they or their nurses taking turns themselves at being in charge while the children play. Even if none of the mothers or nurses has had a special training, this would be worthwhile. It would be infinitely better for the children than being taken out for solitary walks or rides in the pram. And especially so if there was a good garden available, with a sandpit and room for a climbing cage of the kind I have described. Mothers who clubbed together in this way would be able to get a much greater variety of suitable playthings, too, and all the helps to physical growth that children need in these years.

But where one or more of the mothers concerned has been trained for work with little children, then the gain can be very great indeed. And, for that matter, why shouldn't young mothers and new wives *take* a training for this sort of purpose?

CHAPTER THREE

Fears, phantasies and phobias

INTRODUCTION

Working on the Kleinian premise that all young children contain primitive anger and rage, Wise is rarely taken aback by her correspondents' descriptions of toddler behaviour. A young child's innate deep fears and phantasies often result in trying behaviour: rages, screaming, destructiveness, the creation of inexplicable phobias, and similar. Wise offers reassurances that such terrors are common in two- to five-year-olds and not necessarily based on real events or dangers – it is, quite simply, part of human childhood and to be expected in the normal run of things. Her advice to parents and nurses is to try to feel less anxious about it and assume that it will pass over time – in itself, this will help to alleviate the child's anxiety. Given sensitive handling, the child will learn to regulate and manage their terrifying phantasies.

During this period, which Wise accepts can be lengthy and very testing on parents and nurses, the child needs sympathy without fuss or over-attentiveness, and comfort not cruelty or punishment. Wise advises parents to talk through the child's fears with them, showing that they too are not afraid. Occasionally her letters are coloured with possible elucidations of the phantasy or fear – that said, however, she is most careful to state that a valid explanation is not possible without knowing a lot more about the child and their specific circumstances. Generally, she does not interpret isolated symptoms – she is clear that many further details would be needed for a valid interpretation.

Physiological upsets that might induce night-time and other terrors are something to which Wise gives primary importance. Throughout her correspondence she offers the names of specialists who could help with such circumstances. Though Wise touches on some aspects of psychology, she does not let her psychological or psychoanalytical sensibility obstruct her from firstly attending to the everyday and ordinary physical childhood upsets, of which there can be many.

Though Wise considers most problems to be ones that will pass in due course, she acknowledges, too, that there are cases that have a more complex psychological component and require specific attention. She does not attempt to unravel or advise on these problems on the page – this is beyond the reaches of her column.

Wise is particularly interesting on the subject of those terrors that she considers to be real – when an actual event seems to lead to a nervousness. She is clear that the trigger does not have to be a major occurrence, and that the same incident may traumatise one child and not another; trauma is not standardised. The child must always be seen in terms of their unique particularity with their own sensitivities – she writes particularly compassionately about this in "Nervous children".

Included in this chapter are Wise's words of advice regarding a child's cruelty to his kitten, separation difficulties, and very young children attending nursery. She also highlights the potential benefits of a change of routine and the need to be reasonable and kind as well as firm and consistent in the face of young children's fears.

FEAR AND FANTASIES

A little boy's fear of being left on his own is a problem discussed this week

18 MARCH 1931

"HOPEFUL" writes: "I shall be glad of your advice re my small son, aged fifteen months. From four to ten and a half months I never had *a soiled napkin; then at that age we took him away on holiday. From the first day he changed completely – refused to use a chamber, but stiffened and screamed every time he was held out.[1] He waited till I had put a napkin on, then wet or soiled it, and has done so now for four and a half months, though I have always held him out as matter of routine. Then he suddenly developed a habit of screaming and yelling when I left him for a minute. When I go back to him I find that he has made himself sick. As I do all my own work and am very busy, I cannot take him all over the house. He has plenty of toys, dogs, pussies, bricks, tins with lids, and balls, but seems to get bored. Sometimes even when I am with him he begins to whine and fret, no matter how I try to amuse him. Even out in his pram in the afternoons he will begin to behave like this, for no reason. I feel I know nothing about children and that I can't be treating him properly. He has Sister Morrison's diet, and is normal weight, has fourteen teeth and two eye teeth coming, sleeps in a room alone – has thirteen hours at night and from eleven to one in the mornings. He was such a happy, good, contented wee chap till that holiday; but I feel there must be some deeper explanation than that a change of surroundings should so completely alter a child. I dread shopping, as the minute I leave him to go into a shop he begins to yell and scream, and everyone comes up and tries to soothe him. He has never been frightened any time he was left alone. I try not to be cross with him, but after days and weeks of it I feel something must be done. The doctor says he's all right, though he suspects adenoids. Would this affect him so deeply? Doctor also says adenoids are normal in a child of his age; if so, I feel it's a peculiar thing for a disease to be normal. I shall be so glad if you will help me."*

This is a very difficult problem, and I am not surprised that you find it so trying and puzzling. It does rather look as if something had happened on that holiday which stirred fears and jealousies and rages, making the boy both defiant and afraid to let you go out of his sight. It is clear that he is passing through an emotional crisis of some sort. I am sure you are right in feeling that a *mere* change of surroundings

---

1 Being "held out" was the toilet-training practice of holding the infant over the potty at regular intervals from a very young age (around three months).

could not so alter his behaviour; but it is quite possible that the difficulty springs not from any real external happening so much as from his own imaginings and feelings. It may not be due to anything you could well have helped. His screaming when you leave him is probably partly the outcome of rage, but also of fear that you might not come back again *because* of his rage. The only possible thing for you to do is to go on being patient and firm and gentle, remembering that the child's inner difficulties are very great, but that, given a calm and consistent treatment, he is very likely to win through them before very long. I don't think you can hope to make him happy and contented in a few weeks. Difficulties of this kind inevitably take time. You must have noticed in the letters in my columns how frequently quite placid babies become difficult during their second and third year. With your little boy the difficulty has begun rather early and rather suddenly, but in its essence is like those frequently recurring stormy phases of the toddler period. If you can feel less anxious and desperate yourself you will be more likely to help him, and perhaps the assurance that he is sure to pass through this difficult phase, provided you can keep calm and steady, will help to lessen your distress.

THE FIRST SHORTCOMINGS

6 AUGUST 1930

"F.A.S.A." writes: *"Having read all your good advice to mothers and nurses in THE NURSERY WORLD for the last few months I am at last faced with a problem myself, and am wondering what you would advise me for my present predicament. My baby girl is just nineteen months old, and up to a week ago has thoroughly enjoyed having her bath at bed-time. In fact, there was always a little crying when she had to come out of the water. Then suddenly, without any apparent reason whatever, she has quite refused to be put in the bath. She stiffens out and screams as if terrified. I have tried all ways, cajoling, smacking, bribing, but she will not sit – or even stand up – in the water. The funny part about it is that she helps in her little way to get the bath (a rubber one on a stand) ready: she carries the soap and sponge, etc., and seems quite thrilled like she always did, until the time to put her in. She will even play in the water with her hands up to the elbow until I am ready.*

I have wondered if the water was too hot last time she had a proper bath. I seem to remember her suddenly wanting to get out when half way through, but there was no scene like I have had since. She will paddle in the sea up to her knees and does not seem afraid. To-night I even went so far as to put on her rubber paddling shoes to see if she would put her feet in the bath, but she screamed just as much as ever. I do hope you can advise me what to do, as it is terrible for a child to turn so against having a bath. She is a perfectly amenable child in every respect, so I don't think it is mere perversity. Thanking you in anticipation."

Your little girl's sudden refusal to be put in the bath is clearly due to some deep fear of the kind that we call a *phobia*. There may, of course, have been some frightening experience, but from your description it would seem rather that her trouble is neurotic, and has little to do with actual experience, but springs from one of those deep, over-powering phantasies which arise in the minds of little children. Although to us these phobias seem so irrational and inexplicable, they are intensely real to the child herself. They are not easy to handle, especially when they take the form that gives rise to such practical difficulties as this fear of the bath necessarily does. If you had been nearer London I should have wanted to urge you to consult a psychologist, as it would have been an excellent thing to tackle the difficulty in this early period of development. All these neurotic troubles are so much more easily dealt with in the first two or three years. A sudden phobia such as this does indicate some deep-seated trouble, but if it had been possible for you to arrange for psychological treatment some time during the next year or two a favourable psychological development could be made certain.

If this cannot be arranged, however, the question is one of dealing with the particular difficulty yourself in the way most likely to help and least likely to fix the fear in some form, or to cause further mental distress to the child. Remembering that such a phobia cannot be treated as mere wilfulness, it is undoubtedly best not to try to force the child into doing what she is afraid of doing. I should go quite gently with her for some considerable time, letting her help to get the bath ready if she will, encouraging her to play with the water, and from time to time playfully suggesting that she should get into the bath. But I should never force her to do so, nor argue about it, nor even do much coaxing, at any rate for some time. After all, to get right into the bath is not absolutely essential for cleanliness, and sponging would satisfy all the essential demands of hygiene. It is, of course, more bother, but one has to set against this inconvenience the far more important consideration of the best way of helping the child to grow out of her fear.

I hope very much that you will find that this sort of gentle method will help the child over the difficulty, and that you will let me know how she goes on. If it should be possible to bring her to London later on I should be glad to suggest a suitable consultant.

THOSE EARLY FEARS

Some hints on overcoming such early fear of babyhood as the dread of bath-time

3 SEPTEMBER 1930

"M.D.A." writes a letter that will be of interest not only to my previous correspondents, "F.A.S.A." and "J.", who raised the particular problems dealt with,[2] but to other people who may have the same

---

2 "J."'s letter is not printed in this selection. "F.A.S.A.'s" letter is "The first shortcomings".

sort of difficulty in a lesser degree. What "M.D.A." says emphasises the importance of avoiding things which cause fright in a very young child, and shows the very great value of delicate and patient handling if it should occur. She says:

"I do not know whether you would think it worthwhile to hand on to your correspondent 'F.A.S.A.' the following experiences of mine. Twice with my son and once with my daughter I have had the same sudden development of an intense dislike to the bath. In each case it was fairly clearly due to a fright. My son at about ten months, when first sitting up alone in the bath, slipped and fell under the water. After this he behaved very much as 'F.A.S.A.' describes. Again, at about a year he pulled up the plug (as he had often done before), but got his heel caught in the pipe. The same trouble followed. My baby daughter, aged seven months, started a similar fear a few weeks ago. I am not quite certain what the fright was due to, but think it was swallowing a lot of water when 'swimming' on her stomach supported by my hands. In every case the trouble was soon got over by changing the method of bathing and adopting very gentle methods generally. In my little boy's case I washed him standing up after the first fright, as he chiefly objected to sitting down. The next time I did not bath him at all for a few days after his fright, as he chiefly objected to sitting down. The next time I did not bath him at all for a few days after his fear became obvious, and after that I only put a very little water in the bath. With the baby, I cured her not by laying her flat in the water, as I had been accustomed to do, but dipping her in feet first, and letting her jump up and down and play on my knee before and after dipping her. I suppose that such natural fears might develop into 'phobias' if improperly handled, but they seem usually to be dispelled by time and gentle reasonable methods. In 'F.A.S.A.'s' case, might not the complete change to the ordinary bath, with not much water in it be effective? I am surprised that more people do not use the big bath. The babies delight in first lying on their backs and kicking, supported only by a hand under the neck, and then in 'swimming' with two hands under the chest. They make proper swimming movements, especially with the legs and feet, from about five or six months. Again, in your article of August 6th I see a case rather similar to mine. My little boy always woke at about 4.30 a.m., in spite of every effort. Finally, I

gave up the struggle and always fed him then, and he used to go to sleep, and sleep until a reasonable hour, and have his next feed at the correct hour. For 'J.'s' consolation. I may say that soon after being weaned, at ten months, he rapidly improved."

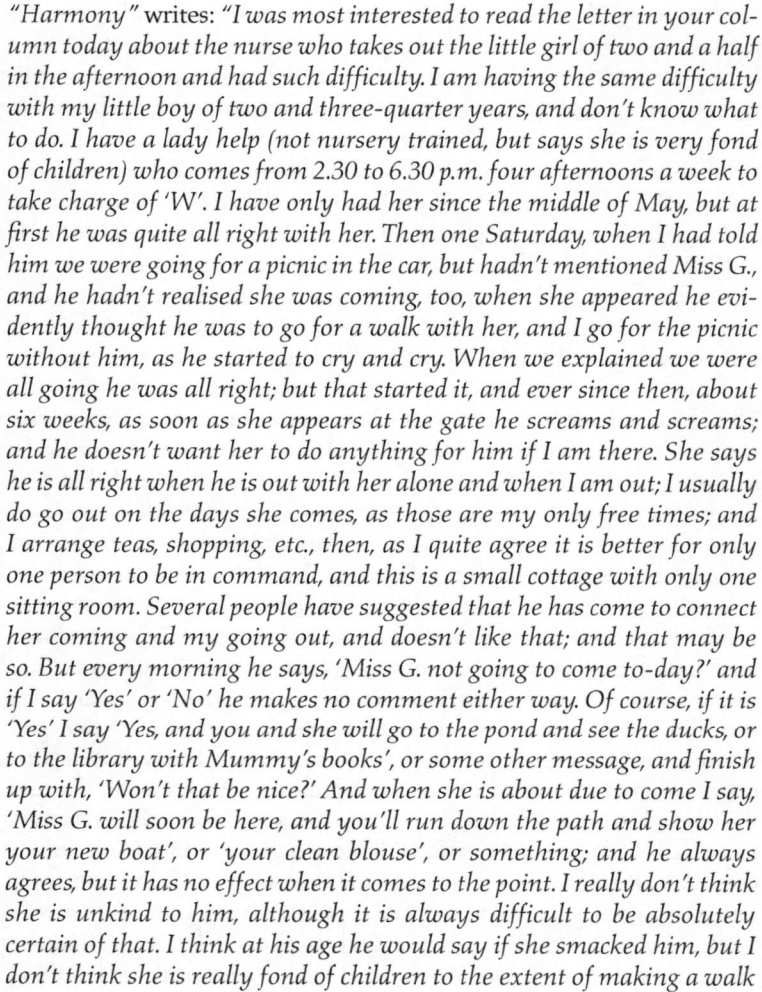

"*Harmony*" writes: "*I was most interested to read the letter in your column today about the nurse who takes out the little girl of two and a half in the afternoon and had such difficulty. I am having the same difficulty with my little boy of two and three-quarter years, and don't know what to do. I have a lady help (not nursery trained, but says she is very fond of children) who comes from 2.30 to 6.30 p.m. four afternoons a week to take charge of 'W'. I have only had her since the middle of May, but at first he was quite all right with her. Then one Saturday, when I had told him we were going for a picnic in the car, but hadn't mentioned Miss G., and he hadn't realised she was coming, too, when she appeared he evidently thought he was to go for a walk with her, and I go for the picnic without him, as he started to cry and cry. When we explained we were all going he was all right; but that started it, and ever since then, about six weeks, as soon as she appears at the gate he screams and screams; and he doesn't want her to do anything for him if I am there. She says he is all right when he is out with her alone and when I am out; I usually do go out on the days she comes, as those are my only free times; and I arrange teas, shopping, etc., then, as I quite agree it is better for only one person to be in command, and this is a small cottage with only one sitting room. Several people have suggested that he has come to connect her coming and my going out, and doesn't like that; and that may be so. But every morning he says, 'Miss G. not going to come to-day?' and if I say 'Yes' or 'No' he makes no comment either way. Of course, if it is 'Yes' I say 'Yes, and you and she will go to the pond and see the ducks, or to the library with Mummy's books', or some other message, and finish up with, 'Won't that be nice?' And when she is about due to come I say, 'Miss G. will soon be here, and you'll run down the path and show her your new boat', or 'your clean blouse', or something; and he always agrees, but it has no effect when it comes to the point. I really don't think she is unkind to him, although it is always difficult to be absolutely certain of that. I think at his age he would say if she smacked him, but I don't think she is really fond of children to the extent of making a walk*

interesting for them or taking a sympathetic interest in their play. I don't expect her to amuse him all the time. I never do, but I am always ready to admire his efforts or to suggest something else to add to his game. He is very advanced for his age and his grandmother is always urging him on and making him match colours, and sort things out, and count out four things and five things, etc., and that tends to make him nervy. Naturally, I squash it when I can, but that is a great difficulty I have to contend with, too. Ordinarily he is very happy and contented with me, but I know it isn't good for him to be always with me. But he will stay with my mother (not the grandmother mentioned above) without me quite happily, and go off for walks with any of the maids quite happily. What do you advise me to do about Miss G? Should I get another lady-help, or do you think it would be just the same thing over again? We are going away off and on until the end of September; he will only be here three weeks until then; but instead of getting better it has been getting gradually worse. Before this he has always gone out in the afternoon with our maid, who, of course, lived in the house and was always there; but now we are in a smaller home with no maid, only a char' and this lady-help. If you could help me I should be grateful."

This is the sort of problem on which it is quite difficult to give advice without knowing both the boy and the lady herself. It seems unlikely that she would be really unkind to the boy, and most probable that his dislike springs from a general distaste for anyone who takes him away from you, unless they have something really satisfactory to offer in the way of companionship. A really skilful woman would be able to handle him so as to make him enjoy his excursions with her and look forward to them eagerly. But the fact that she has not succeeded in doing this does not mean that she is unkind, nor even that she is stupid and unsympathetic. It may be that the boy gives her a specially difficult problem, needing someone particularly wise and resourceful. Or it may simply be that she is a comparatively dull and un-understanding companion. One cannot tell without knowing her and the boy. It is thus hardly possible for me to say whether it would be better to make a change or to go on with her and give her the chance to win the boy's affection and interest, for I cannot assess the situation accurately enough. If I were you I should certainly review the question very carefully, talking it over with her, and trying to get to know just how she does deal with the boy. You might be able to suggest ways of handling him that would ease things a little. And on the basis of her response to your tactful and friendly suggestions you should be able to judge how far she is adaptable, and whether she is interested enough in the problem itself to be willing to try new ways and varied appeals. One thing I am wondering about – whether it might not be better to leave her to deal with the boy altogether when she is there – to check his rudeness and petulance in her own way. It is just possible that it might be wiser, since part of the boy's objection to her may be that her presence leads to reproof from you. But I cannot say whether or not this would be really better – I only suggest it as a possibility to be kept in mind.

NERVOUS CHILDREN

12 FEBRUARY 1930

"Reason" asks: "I wonder if you would deal with this problem. I have a son, aged seven, who has a dread and hatred of anything grotesque or unnatural, and until he KNOWS HOW IT WORKS he is terrified. After the first time and the explanation he can see it again unmoved. At his first pantomime, this winter, he minded nothing but the hurly-burly scene where chairs disappeared through walls etc.; while other children screamed with laughter he was greatly distressed. At his one annual cinema he was enthralled by a motor car race in which the car ran crowds of people down, etc., but he could not endure 'Mickey the Mouse' and his unnatural antics. Yesterday at a party he saw his first Punch and Judy show; he grew graver and graver, burst into tears, and said, 'I hate it; I hate it!' His kind hostess suggested that he should go away and play with the trains; but I felt this was running away from, not conquering, his fear. I told him to remain in the room, but not to look if he didn't wish to. He pulled himself together and did this, and later I told him to come and share my chair, and, with my arm round him, watch the rest of the dolls being worked by a man in a box. He did this, and towards the end was laughing gaily. It is ALWAYS unnatural, grotesquely humorous things that terrify him. He is a child who goes off miles alone on his cycle, and will go out to tea at a strange house, alone, happily. He has never been afraid of the dark, and is the sensitive, trustworthy, conscientious type of child. He had a very keen perception of beauty – a

*beautiful sky, beautiful words, colour, fine scenery. Has this any-
thing to do with his sheer dread of grotesque ugliness? And why
is he not only disgusted but AFRAID of unnatural ugliness, when
99 children out of 100 see it as humorous? I should be intensely
grateful to known the cause and cure. Turning away from it does
not help, surely, since it would have to be faced later."*

This is an extremely interesting problem, and to unravel it fully
would take us very deep indeed into child psychology, much further
than space will allow. But I want to touch on one or two points of
psychology which may help in the practical handling of the boy's fear.
In the first place, it is clear that with a boy who is in general so coura-
geous and well-poised these grotesque things must touch off some
extraordinarily sensitive place within him, or he would not fall so far
below his usual standards of control and courage. These things that
are supposed to be dead or inanimate, but that yet have a sort of magi-
cal life or power of an unnatural, mechanical kind, evidently stir up
some very deep and hidden fantasies in the boy's mind belonging to
the earliest period of mental development in infancy. In those earliest
days of all, when the infant lies helplessly at the mercy of a strange
and powerful world, and things happen without his being able to control or understand them, there is far more fear of imaginary things,
even with a well-cared for and tenderly treated baby, than most of
us ever realise. But slowly the child comes to know what is real and
what is not real, and to feel trust and comfort in the love of those big
grown-ups who are so all-powerful and yet so kind, and his fears die
away and he feels safe in the real world as he comes to know it with
eye and ear and moving fingers. With some children, however, these
infantile terrors of unimaginable things, belonging to the time when
they did not know what was real and what not, linger on behind the
brave face they put on things. And if a child is shown cleverly con-
trived imitations of life and reality that are yet only mechanical, these
break down again, for the moment, the barrier between the real and
the unreal, and so open all the floodgates of imagination and terror.
Then *anything* might be true! For the ugliness means (in the young
child's mind) *badness*, anger, cruelty. The child will not be able to put
all of this into words. It will not be clear even in his own mind. He will
not so much *think* it as *feel* it, and that is why he cannot at first deal
with it. Less sensitive children do not dread this mixture of reality and

unreality so much. Indeed, the very fun for them and most of us lies in knowing that it is all pretence. Punch does not really hurt Judy and the baby; he is not *really* alive. Everything is really quite safe – and we feel all the safer for having pretended not to be!

But with your boy and some others these things get below the surface and stir those "old, unhappy, far-off things" of infancy. When a child *is* sensitive in this way it is best to avoid occasions of this kind, so far as this can be done without making him singular. But when occasions come along without your choice, as at the party, I think your method of dealing with the trouble is certainly the right one. He has shown that with your comradeship and the help of the explanation (which works, of course, by taking the magic and *unreality* out of the affair) he can get over the first shock. I think you did just the right thing in getting him to stay in the room and look at it while sharing your chair. But I should not press him too far. And the important thing is to avoid scolding or reproach. Do not hint that it is a social or moral misbehaviour. Just let him see that you can enjoy it yourself, and give him the support of the explanation and of your calm confidence that he also will not be afraid when he understands it. This is the only way to help him to grow out of the difficulty. As he gets older he is extremely likely, with the character you have described, to learn to control the show of fear; and as understanding grows the fear itself will lessen. But I think it is very likely that he will always keep a fundamental sensitivity to these things, and never be able to take the pleasures in them that some do. But what does that matter? The less sensitive ones may not have his delight in other forms of pleasure.

A LITTLE GIRL WHO IS AFRAID TO LEAVE HER MOTHER

... is the subject of one of this week's letters answered by Ursula Wise

4 JULY 1934

"E.T." writes: *"I have a little girl aged two years and nine months, whom I have looked after myself since birth. She is normal and healthy and seems to be quite intelligent. I feel she is a trifle lonely and in need of the companionship of other children of her own age. She is extremely friendly with everyone and gets on well with other children. The difficulty is, she can't bear me out of her sight, which is natural, I suppose. I took her to a little nursery school near here during the autumn term of last year, when she was only just two. The mistress was extremely kind and sympathetic and allowed me to stay for the morning. As long as I was there, Jennifer thoroughly enjoyed it, but as soon as I tried to leave the room she clung to me, and finally the mistress decided it would be wiser to wait until she was older. Jennifer was still then in the process of cutting her back teeth. I am wondering if you consider it is better for Jennifer, in the long run, to make her go in spite of her probably screaming most of the morning, or whether I should wait a little longer, until I can make her understand that if I leave her, it is only for a short time and not necessarily for ever. I have had to leave her, once or twice lately, in the charge of a former maid while I went to the dentist. She cried when I went out but was apparently happy during the time I was away. But now if I mention that this maid is coming Jennifer becomes very anxious and says: 'Don't want to see Violet, Mummy stay?' I can so well remember hating being left alone at parties when I was a small girl, that I can fully sympathise with Jennifer, but at the same time, I realise that it is very helpful later on if one has made friends and learnt to play and hold one's own at an early age; and also in Jennifer's case, I think it would benefit her health to have some playmates regularly each day. Most people tell me that I shouldn't take any notice if she cries to begin with, and that she would stop directly I got out of sight. I do feel, however, it is rather an ordeal for a child who isn't used to being parted from her mother, and I should be grateful for your advice on how to start Jennifer going to a nursery school in the wisest and happiest way possible."*

It would certainly be unwise to force a little girl of two to go to a nursery school if she did not enjoy it. Since you wrote to me you have probably read the article I wrote a week or two ago on the question of the nursery school for the very young child. Perhaps that has already been of some help towards your decision. If the child were five or six years of age, then the advice that you should take no notice of her crying, and that it would stop as soon as you were out of sight, would be true and sound. Children of four or five can get over the loss of the mother by their friendship with other children, and I have many a time observed that a four-year-old who cries as if his heart would break in the moment of leaving his mother, would stop and turn quite happily to other people and occupations as soon as she had actually gone. But certainly that does not often happen to the two-year-old. At two, and even at three with many children, the need for a special grown-up, and above all for the mother or familiar nurse, is very strong, and the child goes all to pieces emotionally if she cannot have this normal centre for her feelings of trust and affection. Some two-year-olds are able to feel friendliness and trust in other grown-ups too, so that they can leave the mother quite happily for short periods, and gain real benefit from the play with other children in nursery school. But I would never advise forcing a reluctant two-year-old to part from the mother and to stay in school if she showed great fear and unwillingness. The child's anxiety about parting from you is shown in the way she speaks about the coming of the maid. I should leave the question of the nursery school for a time, perhaps until next summer, and meanwhile have as many children as you can to play with your little daughter in your own house and garden, especially if you could arrange to have the children whom she will probably meet when she does go to the nursery school. Then you could begin, after next Easter, taking her for an hour in the morning, and staying with her, even for some weeks. Another year makes such an enormous difference to development at this age. It is more than likely that she will find great pleasure in the school next summer, and be able to part from you far more readily. It might then do no harm to leave her, after a time, even if she did scream, letting her get the experience that you did come back to her as you had promised, and at the time you promised. But at present she is too young to be able to learn that lesson against overwhelming feelings.

IMAGINATIVE FEARS

A mother writes this week about her little girl of three years old who cries bitterly and clings to her whenever she has to leave her with her nurse or go out for an hour or two

4 NOVEMBER 1931

"April" writes: *"May I once again ask for your help? Veronica is an only child, aged three and a quarter, and we live in the tropics where*

it is necessary to remain indoors between 8 a.m. and 5 p.m. Veronica has little friends of her own age and seems as care-free and happy as any of them, but when I have to go out there is always a scene. Veronica has an English nurse of whom she is very fond, and I cannot understand the tears. For example, nurse and I often go out together with Veronica after tea. It is very hot to push the pram alone and at this altitude, and Veronica cannot manage to walk without a pram. If I know I am going out to see friends at 7 p.m. (it is the custom here to visit at that hour) I say to nurse and to Veronica, 'I am going to Mrs. So-and-So this evening'. At the time it produces no comment, but on our return home Veronica will not leave me while I change, and at the moment of my departure there is always trouble. Veronica, with tears streaming down her face and clinging hard to me, beseeches me not to leave her. I have to go, and I leave her, weeping bitterly in nurse's charge. She tries to keep herself awake until my return, which is often not till 9 o'clock. If I go to her then and assure her I am not going out again, she will fall asleep quite happily. This does not only happen at night. I sometimes have to meet the train which comes in at mid-day. It is far too hot for Veronica to go out, and unless I can slip out without her knowing there is always a tearful scene. She makes huge efforts at self-control, and often says good-bye in a 'choky' voice and gives us a wan smile. Nurse tells me, however, that tears return after I have gone until she gets interested in some toy or book. I find this very distressing, but I try not to show it. The only thing that will comfort her is my handkerchief, which she takes from me when I go and keeps it tightly clutched in her hand until I return. As far as I know nothing has happened to scare her during my absence. I have never left her with native servants. When visiting other people's houses, she will go off quite happily alone with nurse, so I cannot think she objects to nurse personally. The other evening while we were out a friend of mine called me to her house to see some new material she had from England. There was a tearful scene; Veronica screamed, 'Don't leave me alone with nannie. Don't leave me.' I left her, but my friend was quite upset. She thought that nurse must be unkind. I am sure this is not the case as Veronica seems devoted to her without a murmur. Do you think that nurse is really nervous of being left alone and has communicated her fear to Veronica? She always says she does not mind."

It is very distressing when a little child shows these unaccountable tears and fears. They *may* be due to some actual happening, but it is quite possible that they are emotional, due to thoughts and phantasies in the child's mind that have very little to do with reality. It may, for instance be that when you go out she fears that you will never come back again, whereas when she herself goes out this fear naturally does not arise. I think it probably is something like this. If the nervousness arose from your nurse's fear of being left alone I think you would have seen the signs of that. I hardly think this explanation a probable one. It seems to me much more likely that Veronica really fears, as lots of little children do, that mother will never come back again when she leaves the house. Now as to treatments, I don't think you can do more than you are already doing, being gentle and understanding about the fear, but perfectly firm when you have to go out. It would not do to let all your comings and goings be controlled by Veronica's fears. The trouble is pretty sure to get less as she grows older. It is not like leaving her quite alone, as in the problems sometimes put to me by other mothers with regard to leaving their children alone in the night. She has her nurse there, of whom she is fond, and who seems to understand how to interest her in other things. So I don't think you need to distress yourself unduly about the difficulty, painful though it is to see such genuine fear and grief. The general happy conditions of her life will help her to grow out of the special trouble.

CHILDREN'S PHANTASIES

A little boy whose vivid phantasies needed his Mother's co-operation and absorb over-much of her time is the first problem dealt with this week

3 APRIL 1935

"B.C." writes: *"I have had THE NURSERY WORLD ever since my little boy was born four years ago now and have used a lot of your advice given to other people. Now I want to ask your advice about my own personal problem. D., who is four and a quarter, has a phase just now, when he wants always to be something else instead of himself. He wants to be an animal mostly, but sometimes he wants to be his little sister (eighteen months) or else a cousin, and I have to take an*

appropriate part. If he is a horse, I have to be the farmer driving him to market, or of he is a lion, tiger, elephant or bear I have to be the mummy lion, tiger, etc., if we are wild animals, or else the keeper if he is a Zoo animal. Other times he wishes to act any story he has heard, such as Moses in the Bulrushes, Cinderella, Three Bears, etc. He takes one part and I take the rest with appropriate gestures and inflections of the voice. He makes up his part quite well out of his head and we enjoy it very much, but my trouble is he wants to do it all day long. He much prefers to be with me than my nurse-help or the maid, and wants to be playing this game while I'm cooking, doing housework and out for the morning walk. I sometimes wonder if people think he is funny in the head when they see him going along so solemnly making the faces he thinks a horse or cow should make and pretending to eat his oats and drink water. He does not seem content to walk along and watch all the people and the traffic. My nurse-help says he does not do it so much with her in the afternoons and yet is just as happy. I should like his brain to develop well in this respect but find it very trying to run a busy doctor's house and answer all his demands. If I say I am busy and must do writing or thinking by myself there are often tears. Should I then show I am cross or ignore them altogether and leave him to it? He is very affectionate and lovable and I hate to hurt his feelings, but I haven't, I am afraid, a very placid nature and I have to keep very strict control over myself to stop from flaring out sometimes. He is terribly full of life and energetic and rather inclined to be rough with his little sister who is not a cry-baby. I also have to remonstrate with him over his kitten. Is it wrong to be constantly telling a child 'don't do that', 'don't do this'? My mother, who had five children and seems to have been successful in bringing us up, says that one's day is spent in saying 'don't' when one is with children. D. hasn't been spanked for months and is quite reasonably obedient. But I can't stand by and see him be unkind to his sister and the kitten. My husband says he must go through a phase of cruelty. Which is the right way to tackle it? Make the punishment fit the crime, or just try to point out how unkind it is or is there another method one can use? I find it rather exhausting being a farmer or a kangaroo all day long. On the other hand, I used to write fairy stories and illustrate them myself when a girl, never published of course, just a sort of natural outlet; and my father although a doctor, has had pictures in the Academy and used to compose songs and music for amateur

*operatics. If D. is to have any talent in any of these directions I want
to help not hinder him."*

It can be very tiring when a child demands that one should enter so
freely and continuously into his own vivid phantasies, and you would
surely be quite justified in limiting the extent to which you do this,
on the grounds of your own fatigue and convenience. That is to say,
there is no more reason why one should let a child tyrannise over
one in this respect than in any other. But it is certainly a help to him
that you should enter into his play whenever you can do so without
getting exasperated and distracted by it. When you have to refuse
him because you have other things to do, I should say so quietly and
firmly. Give him the reasons and then keep to what you have said,
without taking too much notice of his tears and protests. He has to
learn that the world does not exist only for him, and that you have
your responsibilities to his father as well, and something of your own
life to lead. He may not find it easy to accept this just now, but he will
gradually come to realise that he cannot have you to play with him all
the time. A child so much more readily accepts this, however, when it
is not a denial of his needs but only a limitation of the sort that we are
all subject to. With regard to the rough treatment of the kitten, your
husband is surely right in saying that boys must go through a phase
when they are liable to be brutal to helpless animals. But the fact that
the tendency is there is no reason for letting it work unhampered.
I would neither punish him not torment him in return, on the one
hand, nor reproach too much on the other. But I would definitely and
firmly say that I was not going to let him hurt the kitten. He could
play with it as much as he liked provided he did not actually hurt it.

TOO SENSITIVE

*One of the problems with which Miss Wise deals this week is
that of a highly strung little boy who is frightened by laughter
and loud noises*

18 JUNE 1930

"E.H." says: *"I am writing to ask you to help me with my little charge of
nearly one year old, a Truby King baby, healthy, happy and contented.*

He seems to be very sensitive. Often if his mummy and I laugh suddenly over a joke, he sobs broken-heartedly. Today I met a friend, and she spoke to him and then laughed, and he was awfully upset.

During our walks together he made a comical face, and we both chuckled, and again he was very upset. Also, he seems to take a dislike to some people and cries directly they speak to him. He is an affectionate little soul, and when he really knows anyone well, he is very friendly indeed. So far I have kept him rather quiet, as when he was smaller, seeing a lot of people bewildered him and often robbed him of his sleep. He loves children, but has not mixed with many so far. When he is upset re laughing I distract his attention, but do not make much fuss about it at all. Would you advise him to see more people, or mix with other children? I hope to stay a little while with him soon where two other children are living, one of two and a half and one of five years old. He is a very light sleeper, and if it happens to rain while he is sleeping in the garden, and I put the hood up and mack on, he wakes up directly. When he was younger he 'jumped' a great deal at any rather loud noise. His vocabulary consists of dada, mamma and nanna; that is all. But he is very intelligent and observant, and has always loved the trees, and now loves pretty coloured flowers, and watches the birds flying; and when quite tiny watched

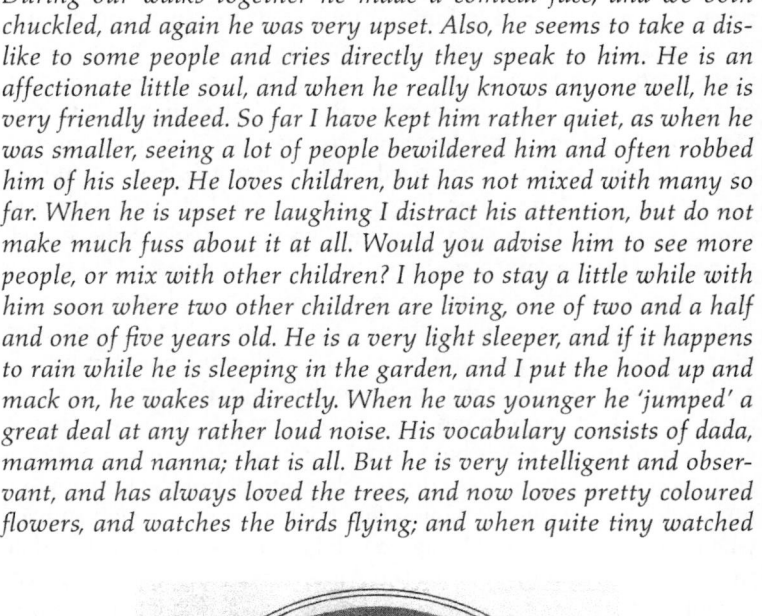

*shadows on the wall, or flies crawling around. He sleeps from 6.30
p.m. to 5.30 a.m., plays about contentedly until he goes in his pram at
8.00 a.m., and plays until his feed, and then sleeps in the garden from
10.30 until 12.30 or 1 p.m. I take him for a walk in the afternoon, but
do not know many people; but he is so interested in passers-by and
anything moving, and is quite happy. His mummy is rather shy, and
does not like meeting a lot of strangers. I do want baby to grow up
into a little man, so hope you can help me over these problems."*

I am glad you put this problem to me, for it is certainly one that needs
careful handling. Your little charge is obviously very sensitive, and
would suffer very severely if the people around him were thoughtless
or rough about this trouble. There is no reason why he should not grow
up quite manly and sensible, but just for the present he needs to be
treated with gentle consideration with regard to the particular form of
his nervous fears. To be afraid when people laugh is not a very common
form of fear, but I have known other cases. Only a few days ago a friend
of mine who is a child psychologist told me that she herself suffered
from the same fear when she was a baby. Her parents were, of course,
very puzzled by such an irrational sort of behaviour, and the way they
dealt with it was to "try to laugh her out of it". Her mother said, "Come
along, let's *all* laugh at her" – without any thought of teasing or cruelty,
of course, but just with the idea of showing her that there was "nothing
to be afraid of" and making her sensible. And the treatment *seemed* to
cure the difficulty, because it drove the child to hide her fears entirely,
and so led the mother to think no fears were there. But in fact the child
suffered very acutely, and it was years before she got over her hidden
terror when grown-ups laughed, particularly if they had rather loud
voices. And this, of course, made social life more difficult for her.
    It may very well be that the open mouth and the teeth showing
more plainly than usual starts up some instinctive fear of an attack,
as if from an animal. The fact that the fear is so silly and groundless
to our minds does not give it any less hold over the mind of a baby,
whose emotions are as yet so much more powerful than his sense or
knowledge. And until his experience of grown-ups is more sure, until
he *knows* more securely that mother and nurse are wholly kind and
gentle, and grows to know how baseless his fears are, the only way
we can help him is to avoid the situation. If you and his mummy
go quite gently with him for some time, remembering not to laugh

heartily or loudly in his presence, except perhaps when he himself has begun the laughter, and so is in a mood to understand it, and even then being ready to stop if he shows signs of alarm, he is pretty sure to grow out of the difficulty as he gets older. And I am sure you are right not to make any fuss when he is afraid, but just to calm and reassure him. The society of other children should really help him; he is likely to find the laughter of other children less terrifying than that of grown-ups. But on the whole I think you are right in keeping him fairly quiet for the present, and accustoming him to playmates gradually. I should be very interested to hear how he has gone on with the little children you are going to stay with.

EARLY CHILDHOOD

Some of the problems which are worrying to mothers and toddlers are dealt with in this article

4 MARCH 1931

"N.T.M." writes: "*I should be very grateful if you could help me with my little girl. She is just five and a half years, and started*

morning school last September. Almost every night within one hour of being put quite happily to bed she awakens screaming, and I immediately go to her, and for some six minutes she cries and talks in a rambling way and doesn't realise I am there. Suddenly she says, 'Night, night, Mummy', and she then sleeps until morning, knowing nothing of this awakening. I was advised to let her 'cry it out', which I did, but after many nights of not going to her she was still no better, I have tried diet and keeping her up later – a warm drink on going to bed, and someone in her room – I have changed her bedroom, all to no purpose. This has been happening since she was fifteen or sixteen months old, and, although I am told she will grow out of it, I am most anxious to find its cause. She is a happy little girl, and is apparently afraid of nothing. My latest experiment has been glucose, and perhaps I ought to wait a little longer for better results. I cannot remember any fright she may have had one hour after being put to bed, and she will not have a light in her room, although the landing light shines into her room. One thing, she will have her bedroom door open, but apart from this she never worries about bedtime in any way. I should be so glad to have your advice."

This certainly appears to be a case of "night terrors", not of wilfulness. If it were a mere wish to get attention and care she would not talk in the rambling way you describe, nor would she suddenly say, "Night, night, Mummy", and go to sleep. It seems to me clear that the trouble is one of genuine fright springing from one of these deep phantasies which so many little children have, and which bear little or no relation to real happenings. The long persistence of the trouble is, however, rather uncommon. With so many children the attack lasts longer on each occasion and disturbs the sleep more, but may not persist over such stretch of years. Your little girl's is a milder but more chronic form than many children show. I think it is very likely that she will grow out of it within the next year or two, as by the time they are six or seven most children seem able to master these terrifying phantasies. But I should certainly not leave her "to cry it out". This method, useful with cases of mere wilfulness and desire for tyranny, would be really cruel in the case of a genuine night terror. The child really needs comfort of your voice and presence.

The glucose may help towards an improvement, as it has been found to do in very many cases.

THE FEARS OF CHILDHOOD

23 MARCH 1932

"Doubtful" writes: *"Would you be so kind as to tell me through the medium of THE NURSERY WORLD how I should deal with my little girl's fear of cows. She is aged four and a half and a normal and, I am thankful to say, particularly healthy child. Her fear arose after the following incident. She was walking a very little way in front of her nurse in a narrow steep-sided road with no footpath. Some cows with a cowman came out of a footpath leading into the road. All except one turned in the opposite direction to which the nurse and my child were going. However, one cow ran down to the side of the road on which the child was walking and towards her in quite a harmless way, but the child was frightened, quite naturally, I think. She now does not like to walk down a footpath with me with cows in the fields on either side (hedges between the path and the fields). She does not want to go into a field with cows in it, even if it is a large one and the cows well away on the other side. Should I insist on her facing up to the fear, but sympathetically holding her hand, only not allowing her to avoid cows? I wonder if she is too young to follow such a course. On the other hand, if she never sees any she will not realise what ordinary and harmless animals cows are, and the longer the fear gets fixed in her mind the deeper it may take hold. She is not a nervy child, and the 'fear' does not worry her at any other times by bad dreams or in any way. I myself am afraid of cows and horses, having had a fall from a pony at the age of ten. I so want her as she grows up to be able to walk through a field with cows in it quite naturally like most normal people, as, of course, one knows they are harmless. But that knowledge always fights in my mind with an unreasonable but strong suspicion about the cow's goodwill towards me and my defencelessness against its horns, so I do not want my little girl to grow up with this feeling. I give her a quarter of an hour's 'reading' every morning. She can match up about sixty words and pictures, knows all the letters easily, and has some idea of the connection between letters and the sounds.*

Whom are the 'Beacon Readers' published by? Should I begin her with 'Beacon Reader' No. 1?

It is not at all surprising that your little girl is frightened of cows after that experience. The animal must look so immense to a tiny child, quite different from what it does to us. If I were you I would go very carefully in trying to insist upon her facing up to the fear. I would use common-sense with regard to the situation in which I did insist on that. I would not, for example, force her to pass a cow in a narrow lane. On the other hand, I would more readily be firm about her going down the path when there is a hedge between the path and the fields. That is a situation which, with help, she can learn to recognise as a safe one. The other, that of passing close to a cow in a narrow enclosed space, would be too terrifying for her just yet. But if you use your judgement about the occasions when it would be wise to walk past them with the help of your hand I think you should be able to bring her out of the fear in time.

The "Beacon Readers" are published by Ginn and Co., Ltd. You could start her on Book 1, but it would be as well to have the introductory books also.

CHAPTER FOUR

Sleeping

INTRODUCTION

Going on the plethora of letters on the subject, it can safely be said that sleeping or, more accurately, not sleeping is a leading concern for Wise's readers. Many of the letters in this chapter overlap with those on fear and phobias – the themes being inherently similar. In her usual style, Wise does not elaborate any theoretical explanations of night terrors and anxieties, but accepts that they happen and are only to be expected in many children. Whether provoked by a real and identifiable occurrence or not, she offers practical advice about how to manage them – what to do and what not to do.

As always, Wise encourages carers to *understand* the child's problem – this is the most likely route to a solution. One of the main uses she makes of her column is to draw links between what she is told about the child's experience and the possible reasons for them having problems at bed time. She is particularly candid with one correspondent who considers the child to show vice – Wise points out that this is not the case, but an expression of anxiety. At times, it can read as though some of the connections she makes are obvious, but it is worth remembering that it was at a time without extensive media coverage of child rearing and the psychological impact of real events, such as post traumatic stress disorder[1] and separation anxiety. Another reason for this, too, might be that it is an ageless phenomenon that one is less inclined to see the strikingly "obvious" when it comes to one's own children.

While advocating that it is best to avoid getting into "bad habits" at bed time, Wise too appreciates that it does happen and goes on to deal with the situation as it is. She does not limit the column to her own suggestions; she also gives space to parents and nurses who want to offer advice to each other, using a pseudonym or initials in a way which will be familiar to anyone who has visited the parenting website *mumsnet*.

Presumably, she considers hands-on experience to be an invaluable support and facilitates the sharing of this. She also refers to receiving second letters from parents and how she uses such feedback to inform her future advice. Wise is clearly not egotistically concerned with hers being the only sagacious voice.

Throughout this selection, Wise, in her usual style, recommends her readers to keep things as simple as possible. Do not complicate life unduly: if it fits with your lifestyle to get dinner over with and then put the baby to sleep, then do just that. Her message is clear – there are very few hard and fast rules, so do not add pressure to what can already be a tricky time of day. That is not to say, however, that there is not a place for some "nevers" in her advice. The child's welfare is always at the heart of what she says, whatever it takes.

The selection here includes what might be a reference to Wise's growing influence: a correspondent refers to her child as a *Nursery World baby*. While the *Truby King baby* was a commonplace term, found dotted throughout the letters, this coinage is a first. Wise, despite seven years of correspondence that frequently refer to King's practices, never directly criticises him. This tells us something about the graciousness of her style. She is, however, not reticent in her condemnation of treating babies as *machines* – this is the nearest she gets.

Wise takes on what seems to have been two of the biggest questions of the day: those of smacking and leaving a baby to cry itself

---

1 Now referred to as PTSD.

to sleep. Curiously, though Wise is opposed to smacking throughout the entire correspondence, she says that she wouldn't go so far as to say that smacking is *never* justified. However, she does not consider it justifiable in any one of the letters. Similarly, she never gives examples of situations when it might be appropriate. Wise is consistently opposed to leaving a baby to scream, commenting on its un-wisdom and the detrimental effects on the child's future mental health.

Though most bedtime concerns tend to revolve around a lack of sleep, Wise, perhaps typically, considers the individuality of the child and that there is not a norm to aim for when it comes to the amount of hours they need to sleep.

Unusually, Wise, in this selection, reveals something of her personal irritation and lack of tolerance with young children!

GOING TO BED

Two little girls who make trouble at bed-time are the subject of two of this week's letters answered by Ursula Wise

JULY 11 1934

"Bothered" writes: *"I always read with interest your advice to mothers whose children make a fuss when they are put to bed, but it doesn't seem to apply to my Philippa, aged two and a half, with whom, I fear, it is now sheer vice. Until four months ago I had sole charge of her and a healthier, happier, more virtuous baby was not to be found in every way. Since four months ago I am obliged to be out all day at work, and only return home after she is in bed. I have a mother's help who is admirable in every way, but I found soon after she arrived that Philippa was taking to screaming after she was put to bed. On cross-examination I found that the girl had been reading to her after she was in bed, and I realised that she discovered for the first time that it was possible for entertainment to occur after bed-time as well as before. Since then there has been no peace until she falls asleep exhausted, much too late (she starts going to bed at 6). She employs every wile to solicit attention – her 'pottie', a handkerchief, a drink, a book, a sweet, all her toys, etc. After each excursion there is perhaps a minute's peace and then the yells of pure rage begin again. I find it shattering*

after a hard day's work, as it's always accompanied by 'I want to see Mummy'. I have tried firmness (I admit it makes me extraordinarily angry – not with the child, but at all my good training having been undone in a single night), which is useless, cajolery, bribes, reasoning, all of which last about one minute. It is sheer vice, because when taxed to know why she makes this fuss she sobs, 'I'm so dull', or 'I want to talk'. By 9 o'clock one obviously can't go on amusing her or holding earnest conversations with a little girl who ought to have been asleep two and a half hours ago. What steps should I take to have my model child restored to me? It is actuated by sheer boredom. It isn't that her days aren't full enough. She goes to an excellent nursery school from 9 til 12, then sleeps, sometimes two and a half hours due to insufficient sleep at night, then out in the park all the afternoon after lunch, and then the girl is very good at playing with her and she joins with other children. She is an amazingly cheerful and philosophical child – the principal of the nursery school says she is the most self-possessed child she ever came across. It is so unnatural to her to be so unreasonably naughty, and I wish I knew either complex or cure."

I wonder if it has not occurred to you what a tremendous change in the life of a child just over two it must be when the mother, who has had sole charge of her, and had a happy, successful relation with her, suddenly begins to be out all day and only returns after the child is in bed? Would it not be a most surprising thing if such a complete change in the setting of her life did not have a considerable effect upon the child's feelings? Would it not have that sort of effect with us grown-ups if a sudden thing of this kind happened, the reason for which one could not possibly understand: if the most important person in one's environment – whom one loved and upon whom one depended – were suddenly to disappear day by day. There is in fact no experience in adult life, except the death of a dearly loved person, which can possibly correspond in its immensity and bewilderment with this experience your little girl has had. What you call vice is an intense anxiety due to the major loss and bewilderment the child has experienced. It is hard on you that the child should feel so much need of you after you return home in the evening, but it would be highly unnatural and undesirable for normal development if she did not do so. Her saying she is "so dull" and she "wants to talk" are her ways of expressing the intense need for some reassurance that your disappearance during the day does not mean loss of love. She must be starving for affectionate companionship from you. If you could realise this and let the child have an hour of friendly talk with you when you return home, telling little stories, talking about the events of the day, holding your hand and feeling you were still loving and interested in her, you would find she would soon begin to fall asleep happy and contentedly. One can no more starve a child of the natural satisfaction of her love for her mother in this sudden way than one could of her actual food. Her day-time arrangements sound as good as they can be. It is her relation with you that needs radical reflection on your part. You would find your own peace of mind greatly increased if you could recognise this real need of the child, and that it is her love for you that caused this behaviour, and you would be able to enjoy the rest of your evening in peace.

I constantly get second letters from mothers, which space will not allow me to quote, who have acted on my suggestion that it is better to recognise the child's need for special comfort when going to sleep, and give it quietly and calmly. These mothers tell me that when they have acted upon this advice the need for the presence of the mother at bed-time soon passes, sometimes even within two or three weeks, and the child learns to fall asleep contentedly. I am sure you would find that this was so with your little girl, or that she found herself able to be contented with ten or fifteen minutes of your presence after you came home. It is in any case too much to expect that a child whose mother has been out all day should be able to settle to sleep without having seen her!

GOING TO SLEEP

It is a natural impulse to comfort a child when he wakes crying, and it is wrong that he should be left to scream, says Ursula Wise

29 MAY 1935

"H.E." writes: "I was very interested (and relieved) to read your reply to 'D.G.M.' in this week's NURSERY WORLD on the question of whether or not to stay with a child who cries when being put to bed. Perhaps my experience on this matter may help 'D.G.M.' with the little girl. I have very recently brought my small son, aged 2 years 3 months, home from

*India. When we were abroad he was a model of goodness at going to
sleep alone, and I felt very pleased with myself, but, alas, on board ship
he started to show distress on being left in the cabin at night, and real-
ising how frightening a large ship with its strange noises must be to a
small child, I stayed with him until he fell asleep, usually 20 minutes to
half an hour. I thought all would be well again when we got home, and
was a little disappointed to find he still disliked being left, so I continued
to stay in or near his room until he was sound asleep. I did not actually
sit with him or talk to him, but generally found something quiet to do
in my room which leads into his, and if he called me I replied quietly:
'Mummy is here – now go to sleep', and he soon dropped off quite happily. After one or two weeks, I found I could go downstairs as soon as
Richard was in bed, and in three weeks' time my Mother could put him
to bed and he never even asked for me. I wondered to begin with if I was
doing the right thing in staying with the child, as people said I should
get him into a bad habit, but I think it is an easier, quicker and less
nerve-racking cure for all concerned than allowing a child to scream
itself to sleep. We are now staying with my in-laws, and once again
Richard seems to need me at bed-time, so I stay outside his room and
read or knit and answer him quietly if he calls out. The time I have to
remain there is gradually becoming less, thank goodness, but I try not
to get impatient, or to let him know that it is annoying for me. It was
due to recollections of my own childhood that I adopted this method,
which I am so relieved to see you advocate. With the best intentions in
the world on the part of my mother, she allowed me to scream myself
to sleep, until I got into such a state of nerves and fright that it was
a very long time (in fact until I slept in a room at school with other
girls) before I could fall asleep in a contented frame of mind. I think
on the whole Richard is a good child, as since he was 10 months old he
has never been allowed to remain in one place longer than five months,
and he has survived the many changes wonderfully well. Do you consider it bad for a child to be continually unsettled in this way, or do you
think it helps to make them adaptable? Owing to my husband's work in
India we have to be on the move a good deal. He is a very normal, not
highly strung, affectionate and quite intelligent little boy; he talks well
and distinctly, and is observant. I shall be taking him back to India in
September for probably 18 months or so, and I should be most grateful
for your advice. I expect he will soon be picking out numbers and letters,
and though of course I shall make no attempt at teaching for a long*

time, I wonder what is the best method of helping him to be interested in all he sees. Are large wooden letters and figures to be used more as playthings than anything any good in making him familiar with them, and what about paints and chalks? When would he be old enough to require these? It is difficult to get things in India, so I would like to take out with me anything you think might help him. He is simply crazy over anything mechanical at present, aeroplanes, motors, trains, and especially ships (his Daddy is a sailor so perhaps that accounts for it) and his favourite books seem to be motor magazines! He is a happy, energetic, good-tempered little boy, friendly as a rule with strangers, and not difficult to manage, though, of course, we have our ups and downs over the usual childish troubles, but we try and surmount them as they crop up by not fussing too much, and by remaining fairly calm and unconcerned. I find this difficult as I am rather impatient, but also find now that I am conquering this fault in myself because of the boy. I find your articles extremely interesting and helpful, and I try and follow your advice. Richard has been a NURSERY WORLD baby from birth."

I am sure you are right in feeling that your little boy has got through the very frequent changes of environment which have been his lot with so little trouble just because you have been willing each time to stay with him and help him over his anxiety. I am quite certain that if you had acted on the theory of refusing to stay with a crying child, all these unsettlings in his environment would have had a very bad effect. It is on the whole undesirable for a child so young to have such very frequent changes of dwelling place. I daresay it does help to make the child more adaptable, if things are satisfactorily managed in other ways. You have certainly made these changes as little hard for the child as possible by helping him over his fright on the ship, or in the new home, or staying with relations. Perhaps your experience will help to support other mothers and nurses in what would be their natural impulse to comfort the child when he wakens crying at night, if there were not this fashion for a rigid theory which is certainly based on a false psychological view. Your little boy was fortunate that you yourself had retained so very vivid a memory of your own miseries as a child. It is a pity we so readily forget the intense feelings that we may have as tiny children. Otherwise we should not be so inclined to treat our own little children as machines.

I think sympathy towards the child's natural interest would be the best help towards his mental life during the next year or two. He will ask questions and want to understand and want to play out his interest in all the things he sees, and if he feels that you will answer questions as well as you can, and are interested in these things too, that will be the best help you can give him. He does not need formal lessons yet, but he does need to feel that you are sympathetic to his curiosity and desire to gain skill. I would not try to show him individual letters, but I would print whole words of simple objects under coloured pictures, and make books for him of stories which he tells you and you tell to him. It would be better not to introduce any figures just yet in number work, but later on to play counting games, counting with actual things; letting him help you, for example, in arranging shoes and socks or the spoons on the table and getting the number right for the people present. Paint and chalks and large sheets of brown paper are very desirable at three and four years. So is plasticine. The best kind of paint is poster paint with a large brush. You can put a little of the poster paint out at a time in a saucer. Many children in the infant schools are doing most delightful work with large materials of this kind. He will not be ready for paint, however, for another year or year and a half. He could use chalks earlier than paints. A good plan is to hang a number of sheets of kitchen paper up on a couple of tacks on the wall, so that he can draw with much bolder movements of the hand and arm. It would be a good thing to take simple carpentry tools with you as well, since most boys like hammer and nails, and a small saw and a pair of pincers, and as he is mechanically minded he is sure to be attracted to these things. Old catalogues of the big stores are often attractive to children of this age, with their great variety of objects pictured. Catalogues of motor firms, picture books of engines and aeroplanes, exercise books in which he can draw these things for himself would be all good things to take.

THEY WAKE UP SO EARLY

This week's first letter is from a mother whose children are very early birds with a difficulty that must worry many single-handed mothers

17 JUNE 1931

"A.E.G." writes: "*There are two problems I have never seen touched upon in your most interesting weekly articles. First arising out of my* two kiddies waking so terribly early in the morning. In spite of dark-ened windows (wide open of course) they wake even now as early as 5 or 5.30 a.m. on very many mornings. Last summer it was even earlier. How good and quiet is it reasonable to expect them to be? My husband and I both work hard and go to bed tired, and we find 7.15 more than early enough to get up – the children get dressed thus about 7.30. The procedure at present is to 'sit them down' when they wake and expect them to lie and talk quietly until about 6.45, when we have tea and they have orange juice and a biscuit and are allowed to sit up and play. If they sit up earlier than this, after about an hour they get to shouting and getting into mischief, tearing books, wall-paper – anything they happen to think of. Even as it is, there seem to be constant troubles, for example, they often keep on fetching me out of bed on some silly pretext or other until I get cross and the day begins in tears. I feel awfully sorry for them, as I should hate being kept in bed wide awake two or three hours myself, but what can I do? I am not over strong, and find the day's work quite long enough as it is. Their ages are four and three this month, and they are fright-fully active children, full of high spirits. They lead the normal day prescribed in THE NURSERY WORLD, one and a half hour's rest or sleep before dinner and in bed by 6.30, otherwise they are active all day. The second problem is as regards smacking. Having always followed your theories as much as possible, I have only on one or two occasions resorted to smacking, and for a definite reason. My kiddies, as I have said, are very high spirited, and they are both, but particularly the boy (three years) very excitable. They both at times get into real 'paddies', usually over some trivial matter. (The boy, like many others described in your pages, gets these crying fits of self-will very frequently.) Normally, using your methods of quietly getting my own way and yet being tactful with it, the trouble blows over in just a few seconds or perhaps a minute or two. There is, however, the other time when for no reason that I can see a most trivial trouble will lead to a real frenzy of screaming, getting more and more hys-terical. I have tried the normal method of treatment, ignoring the screaming, and it goes on and on until I have to take notice, pick the child up, kiss and coax him good, which seems to me wrong. I have also once or twice resorted to a couple of hard smacks, which has acted like a cold sponge to a hysterical person. The child had seemed quite relieved and the little girl has told me after 'she wanted to stop

*and couldn't'. Do you think smacking is occasionally justified in cases
like this? The little girl who is much easier to manage generally than
the boy, seems, if anything, to get these hysterical fits more than the
little boy, and I have seen her struggling to stop and yet unable to.
Putting them in their cots alone does not seem to have much effect.
They go on screaming until someone goes up and helps them, either
by coaxing or smacking, to calm down. The boy has more than once
cried and screamed when put in his cot until he has made himself
sick, when that has sobered him, and he calls and tells me what has
happened. These fits only occur perhaps once or maybe twice in a
month, perhaps less often. Do tell me how I should deal with them?"*

This problem of the very early waking of children is of course a very
common one, and I am surprised myself how seldom it has been
mentioned in the letters I receive. I don't mind confessing that this
is the thing I have found the most difficult problem of all whenever
I have lived with little children myself, and I am often surprised that
other people seem to bear with it more easily than I can! That last
hour or two of sleep is so very precious when one is living a very
busy life, and to be wakened up at 5 or 5.30 morning after morning
by little children who don't sleep any more, and who want to play
and talk and perhaps squabble, is to my mind more trying than anything that can happen during the day!

But that, of course, is a matter of personal irritation, not one of
anxiety on behalf of the children. In itself, it is an everyday piece of
behaviour belonging to their very ordinary physiological rhythm, and
one that cannot be prevented. I should say that your method of expecting them to stay quiet is a reasonable one. But if you could find some
quiet occupation for them I should have thought that would be a help.
When they are a little older, reading books of course will be the solution, but would they not like picture books now? I should think you
might try that, or one or two of their favourite toys to cuddle. As they
get older, however, they will find independent ways of amusing themselves in these early morning hours that will be less disturbing to you.

Then as regards the screaming, I would not go so far as to
say smacking was *never* justified, but I confess that I think that the
occasions when it is so rare that they almost amount to nothing. I
should be more inclined to try the cold sponge itself. Such fits of
screaming really *are* hysterical, and I am sure the children are right

when they say they want to stop but can't. To pick them up with firm hands, speak to them in a firm or even sharp tone, or sponge their faces with a cold sponge, does bring relief, and I should certainly try this sort of method. You can tell from the sound and manner of the screaming when it is of this hysterical type and the child should not be left to manage it alone as he can be with ordinary crying.

PROBLEMS AT BEDTIME

A little girl who will not go to sleep is the subject of one of this week's letters

7 FEBRUARY 1934

"M.R.M." writes: "*My little girl of seventeen months is being trou-blesome at the moment through refusing to go to bed at nights. She never has been very easy to get to sleep and on occasion when she has refused to lie down in her cot I have wrapped her in a blanket and brought her downstairs to the fire. In a short time, she was usu-ally asleep or too drowsy to offer any resistance when laid down. Now, however, Helen expects to be lifted every night and stands up and screams when put to bed. It is no use my merely staying with her in the room. She sobs until I lift her. The difficulty is that as soon as she is lifted she is anxious to play or look at a book and I cannot get her to sleep before 9 o'clock. Last night I sat in the dark holding her for fully an hour, making several unsuccessful attempts to lay her down during that hour. She was quite good and seemed to doze in my arms, but as soon as I put her in her cot she started up and cried. Then I tried leaving her alone, but she screamed for half an hour and I was forced to lift her again. After that I gave up trying to get her to sleep and let her sit in a chair and look at a book, which she did quite happily until 10.30. I thought by that time she must be sleepy and put her into a warm cot, but still she refused to lie down and cried until I took her into my bed at 11 o'clock. She finally fell off asleep at 12.30 and woke quite fresh at 6.30 this morning. To-day she has been most vigorous, slept for only half an hour before lunch and I have only just got her to sleep now at 8.30 p.m. Can you sug-gest any means of dealing with this problem? Is it very dreadful to bring Helen downstairs after putting her to bed, and, if so, what should I do instead?*

She leads a normal life, has a normal appetite, is out of doors as much as possible and is a very happy little soul. Her mind is intensely active, she has a fairly large vocabulary (some fifty words, most of which she has picked up without any teaching). Often before going to sleep she will lie and say over all the words she knows as if practising them. From one year old she has been extremely fond of books and pictures, picking out all familiar objects, and can now recognise her mamma or daddy or our dog in a photograph from among a group of persons. She is also very independent and fairly skilful, puts on her gloves and hat and sometimes takes off her nightdress by herself. She also climbs on chairs and tables and sofa backs with the greatest of ease, opens drawers and cupboard doors and almost manages to turn the knob of the room doors. All these things and many more she has learnt without any prompting. Helen has never been a thumb sucker, but when fourteen months old she started to bite her nails and still does do in bed or when tired. She shows no other trace of nervousness. I have done nothing about this up to now. She has slept in a room by herself since she was six months old and does not seem afraid of the dark. I went away for New Year week-end, leaving her with her daddy, auntie and devoted maid. This sleepless phase has developed since then. But she was very good during that week-end and I cannot think she is afraid of my going away again, as she is quite contented to be with her daddy if I go out of an evening.

I have never been very successful in training Helen to cleanliness although she was held out regularly. A month or two ago she became greatly improved but at present she is going through a stage of asking for the pot and then struggling and screaming if I try to seat her on it. We bought her a chair commode, but have never persuaded her to use it. Some weeks ago I slightly burned her legs through having the chamber rim too hot, but she used it for a week afterwards without protest and then started to refuse it. From birth Helen has shown signs of a strong will and now if she does not get what she wants immediately she grows very upset and even stamps her feet. I know this is common to all children, but I did not expect to see such strong evidence of a temper until she was a little older. Perhaps I am wrong. Usually her attention can be diverted fairly easily, but if I merely refuse a thing and ignore her she will go almost into hysterics. She also holds her breath. I am afraid this is very long and rambling, but I thought it better to tell you all her little ways in case you might think of something to account for her sleeplessness. To me it seems as if her brain is so active that it will not let her sleep."

The picture you draw of your little girl shows a very intelligent child. Her vocabulary is unusually large, and her other activities show that this is not merely a verbal gift but one of general intelligence. Now it seems to me that in your general method of training her you tend to underestimate her intelligence and the extent to which she will record experience and base her reactions upon it; for example, the slight burn on the leg. This will have contributed a good deal to her present fear of the pot. She is obviously afraid of being burnt again. Moreover, the sleeplessness which has occurred since you were away for the week-end, will have undoubtedly been stimulated by that loss of you, and her fear that you may go way and leave her again if she does not have you with her in the room. Then again, she knows quite well that in the past when she has been restless she has had the comfortable experience of being brought downstairs and cuddled by the fire. She now feels that she cannot do without that form of comfort. It is not only her feelings that have entered into this, but her intelligence too, remembering previous experience and building her responses upon it. It's a pity you began that practice if you did not want to continue with it. It is always unwise to bring a child down out of his room when he awakens in anxiety, because this method is so difficult to leave off. The child feels such a deprivation if we try not to give it him later. It seems to me, thus, that there are a number of different factors in your present difficulty with Helen, and that it is bound to take some time before you will be able to get her easy and contented again, and ready to accept the regular routine. The first thing to do is to make up your mind to the fact that it *will* take some time – perhaps even months – to help her through these difficulties. It is no good to think you will be able to break her off the screaming and the demand to be carried downstairs in a night or two.

WAKEFULNESS

A child cannot be forced to sleep and will probably take as much as he needs

21 MARCH 1934

"Sleep" writes: *"I am writing about my youngest charge, a boy of just two years. Until a month ago he slept with his parents and*

*on waking at about 6 a.m., went into his Mummy's bed for about
ten minutes before sitting up to play with his toys. The first few
nights I had him he screamed for his Mummy on waking, but
soon settled down and went back in his cot very nicely until 6.15.
My problem is that he is gradually waking earlier and earlier,
until lately it is 5.30 a.m. He doesn't always seem to have had his
sleep, but never goes to sleep again, and we both find the three-
quarters of an hour a long time before he sits up to play. He does
nothing but whine 'nanny', and I jump up two or three times,
tuck him up, give him a favourite animal to hold and gently tell
him to go to sleep. I have always tried to be firm but kind to him,
and he does seem to be trying to do what I ask. This morning I
put my alarm clock to go off at 6.15, and told him he could sit
up when he heard it. I thought perhaps that when he understood
this it would help him to lie more content. By 10.30 am he is very
tired, and is asleep the moment I put him in his pram at 11 a.m.
He sleeps soundly until 12.15, when I always wake him. He never
has required the average sleep for his age, and about a year ago
was having less day sleep than he is having now, either playing
about in his pram first, or going down later, say 11.30 a.m. I feel
somehow as if he is getting his sleep at the wrong time, but don't
know how to make the change. He seems young to give up the day
sleep altogether.*

*My second charge (at present in hospital) sleeps with him in the
night nursery too. He is a boy who needs a lot of sleep, and is perfectly content to lie quiet until 6.45. I think something ought to be
done with baby's early waking before T. comes back to us again. He
has his bath and then goes to bed about 6.15 p.m., and goes straight
to sleep. He is a little good thing. I have been here since before he
was born and don't have much trouble with him. One other thing,
he is a very poor talker. He has about eighteen words altogether, of
which 'Daddy', Mummy', 'nanny' are very clear, but some of the
others are absolutely hopeless; for instance, for water he says, 'gurgle, gurgle', Alfred is 'Baboo', 'sweeper' is 'forfar'. Is this anything
to worry about? I have read THE NURSERY WORLD for years and
always find help from your pages. It is through your advice that I
have got S. so well trained in clean habits, never scolding but just
keeping patiently on. At eighteen months we stopped nappies both
day and night."*

It was a good plan to use your alarm clock to try to get your little charge to rest until that went off. But otherwise it is really not any help to try to compel the child to sleep if he wakens up. Doubtless the earlier waking is due to the loss of his customary comfort of going into his mother's bed. Not having this must have been a very considerable change for the chid, and a very real loss. It is bound to take him some time to get over this, and until that happens, he is sure to go on wakening as early as he now does. When the elder boy comes back and you have to consider his sleep as well as the baby's, it would be wiser to allow the baby to sit up with his dressing gown on, and play with whatever toys will keep him content rather than letting him go on whining for you and disturbing the other boy's sleep. I don't think the early waking matters so long as he does get the good sleep in the day-time. One cannot control these processes according to the exact rules and regulations. The latter are a useful guide, but cannot be applied in a mechanical way to every child. So long as the child is well and happy and growing satisfactorily, there is nothing to worry about, and it is better to ease the situation for him by letting him play happily than try to force him to go to sleep again. With regard to the talking, quite a number of intelligent boys of his age are as indistinct in speech as he is, but become quite normal later on. There is nothing for you to worry about, except by way of always speaking clearly to him, and letting him talk as freely as he will, playing little finger games with him, and letting him join in the ordinary nursery rhymes which children of his age love.

"Two Kay" writes: *"I wonder if you can give me any help with a problem of sleep. My son, aged five and a half, is, I consider, sleeping far too short a time and, so far, the doctor has been unable to help me, though he has prescribed powder which I have given for over a month. A. falls asleep by seven every night and sleeps excellently – a deep quiet sleep – until any hour between 4 and 5.30 a.m. During the day he has a rest after dinner for half an hour, but he never sleeps then. Admittedly, A. shows little sign of needing more sleep; by that I mean he is not cross or sleepy at bedtime, but full of mischief and he goes to sleep happily every night. On the other hand, he is a sensitive and rather highly strung child and he has always*

suffered from a stammer, which sometimes disappears but at times of excitement or stress becomes very pronounced. I waited until he was five and then took him to a specialist, who put him under an experienced teacher for speech defects and both she and the doctor say rest and sleep are most important for him, as the stammer is caused largely by 'tenseness' of mind and body. Physically he is strong and healthy, and leads an open-air life with much play with his brother and other children. He was a very highly strung baby – I wrote to you on the subject of his terror of noise, etc. – and never slept as long as he should. At ten months night terrors began and continued intermittently until he was two and a half. When he was a baby he slept very well but very lightly. He slept alone from nine weeks old but the quietness of his room made him more sensitive to noise, and at times it was almost impossible to tiptoe into his room without wakening him. He seemed to 'sense' my presence even when I was noiseless. For the last year and a half he has slept with his little brother and though we knew he woke first, he was always quiet and good until the younger boy woke about seven. About three months ago I began to suspect that he woke earlier than we knew and after Christmas – when he had a chill and I slept in his room – I continued sleeping there so that I could keep an exact record of his hours of sleep. Since he was about two years old he has, every few months, had the habit of waking during the night for several nights running, and lying awake for about an hour and a half. As far as I know he has not done this for about five months. I do hope you can give me some possible reason for this. Is it allied with such problems as 'head bumping' or talking and laughing during the night, and is there any anxiety at the back of it? It seems to me unnatural in a healthy child, and given his nature, long deep rest is most necessary for him."

There cannot be any doubt that there is some anxiety behind both the general tenseness of mind and body which your boy shows, and his light sleep. The stammer is another symptom of the same inner stress as was shown in the early night terrors. But I don't think that there is any ground for anxiety on your own part about this. Since the boy has his long quiet sleep in the early morning hours and shows no other signs of lack of sleep, one has to take it that this is his individual rhythm. Although it is possible to say in the general way that children of a certain age need a good amount of sleep, yet you will always find that individual children differ, just as adults do. Some need more, others not only need less, but are unable to take more. If you keep the general conditions of your boy's life satisfactory, as you obviously do, with plenty of play in the open air with other children, correct diet, and plenty of opportunity for quiet rest, then you can feel sure that he will take as much sleep as he is able to do. We have no way of making a given child conform to the general standard, except by keeping the major conditions of his life as satisfactory as possible. I think it would be as well if you did not worry about this question of the boy's sleep, since that itself may increase the tension in his mind. Children are so sensitive to undue anxiety on their behalf in the minds of their parents. You do not need to feel that this early waking is "unnatural". As a matter of fact, it is not at all uncommon in children of his age. My own impression is that *more* children waken as early as 5.30 or 6 than sleep on to 7 or more. I should not worry about it, but let him content himself in some way that interests him, books, pictures or toys, when he wakens before the rest of the household.

"Worried Parent" writes: "I have two boys, aged five and three-quarters and four and a half years. The older is perfectly ordinary in every way, big for his age and not at all temperamental or highly strung, though quite mischievous and normally naughty and tiresome. He has been to the Froebel school for a year and loves it. The younger boy, Tony, is the exact opposite – quite tall but rather fragile looking – temperamental and does not sleep well and never has done so. I sent him to school also in the mornings this term, as I thought mixing with other little children might help. He has a habit ever since he was sixteen months old of rocking his whole body and head on the pillow at night whenever he wakes up and singing in unison; we thought it was probably due to teething at first, but he has never grown out of it, though the doctor doesn't think it matters in the least. We had a nurse who was always slapping him for standing up in his cot and for this waggling habit, and though he is rather better since I got rid of her, he still wakes up several times

*and sings and rocks backwards and forwards over the pillow. When
I go in and tell him to stop he does so and goes off to sleep, but usually wakes up later and does the same thing. Perhaps it is connected
with the fact that the nurse used to slap him so much for a wet bed
at eighteen months, though she never lifted him at stated intervals.
I kept her for nearly three years but realise how bad she was for a
temperamental, highly strung little child. He used to be very pale,
but is looking much better without such deep shadows under his
eyes since she left. Is there anything I can do about it, as the two
boys have to sleep together in the same room and it is disturbing
for the elder. Tony used to stammer at one time, but we ignored it
and he has grown out of it. He loves the school but I know that the
'waggling' has increased slightly since he started. He is a very gay,
independent, wicked little monkey at home, and seems quite healthy
otherwise except for sleeping badly, but is rather irritable. Can you
suggest anything that would help, as he doesn't seem to be growing
out of it?"*

You must be right in attributing the special difficulties of your boy
to his having been slapped by his nurse for wetting his bed and for
this rocking. It was a very bad thing to do. It is always most unwise
to whip a child for wetting the bed, since this invariably increases
his anxiety and difficulty in gaining control; and to punish a child
for such a habit as this rocking is very wrong indeed. As your doctor
says, it does not matter at all. It does no harm to anybody else, and
if it brings the boy some comfort, why should one worry about it?
The only difficulty is if it disturbs the other boy. But as the latter
is a strong and stable child, there is nothing much to worry about
there either. Tony is sure to grow out of this habit before very long,
perhaps within the next couple of years. A great many children have
habits of that type, which they leave behind in the middle years of
childhood. Commonly they pass away before the age that Tony has
reached, and this has remained with him so much more firmly fixed
just because the nurse dealt with it by slapping him. But as he gets
older, more settled at school, more secure in his real skills and social
achievements his need for this way of comforting himself will disappear. The fact that it has become rather worse since you sent him to
school this term is an indication that it is bound up with his general

emotional problems. But it is also an assurance that as he gets over the first crisis of his school life and settles in to normal relations with other children and a feeling of greater confidence, this habit will grow less dominant. I should, therefore, not give it any more thought for the time being.

WAKEFULNESS AND FEARS

19 NOVEMBER 1930

"C.P.D." writes: "I wonder if you or any of your readers can suggest any way of preventing my children waking so early. My boy is five and the girl two and a half, and they have always been early wakers. The girl is not so bad, as she very often cuddles down again in bed and sucks her thumb and, anyway, is resting. But the boy, the moment he wakes, is sitting up and getting something to play with, a book to look at, or chalks, etc. He now has just started school, and every morning he is writing figures or letters. During the summer it used to be 6 a.m. or 6.30, but since the time has changed back it is usually 5.45 when he wakes. I have tried not allowing him any toys or pencils, etc., by his bed, but it is almost worse, as he is so restless that I feel he gets

more tired than if he had something to occupy him and keep him happy. I always leave a biscuit by his bed, as I feel it is so long to wait until 8.30 breakfast, but find that by breakfast he invariably looks tired and white, but looks better later on in the morning. He goes to sleep as a rule as soon as he is in bed, and is usually asleep by 7.15. I have tried later to bed, but it seems to make no difference. I have also tried more for supper, and no supper, and that again seems to make no difference. He is a very excitable, nervy child, with very little self-control, and I have had trouble with him at night, crying etc., but that was traced eventually to hyper-acidity, which we have cured him of, more or less. He certainly sleeps much better now, though occasionally has bad dreams and wakes frightened."

I think the first and most important thing is to make sure that the boy's hyper-acidity is cured or kept down to a minimum. I suppose you have had the best possible advice on this, and arrange his diet with this in mind. Apart from this very important physiological question, all you can do is to keep the general conditions of his life as healthy as possible. I should most certainly let him have toys and writing materials beside him to keep him happily occupied when he does wake up. They will not be in the least likely to *cause* or encourage him to waken early, but they will keep him happy and contented, and therefore lessen the fatigue. Children differ very much in their sleeping habits, and it has been found that the habit of waking very early, or of lying awake at night very late, often sets in when the child has managed to overcome actual night terrors. But waking early in the morning is less disturbing than lying awake long at night, and if you can let him occupy himself contentedly there is no reason why it should be disturbing to other people.

It might be well for you to write to Sister Morrison about the physiological difficulty, as she is better able to advise you on that than I am.

UNTITLED

11 NOVEMBER 1933

This week I want to deal with two letters raising the same problem – that of whether or not a child should be left to scream.

"A.B." writes: "I shall be very glad if you can help me with two 'problems' in connection with my tiny boy (almost sixteen months old). He is the highly strung, nervy type of child. My first difficulty is over his morning sleep. He has always been a light sleeper, and we have had a certain amount of trouble over his morning sleep before. But for some months he has been sleeping well, both at night and from 10.15 to 12. Recently, he has taken to sleeping on later in the mornings, until about 7.20, so I have realised that he will not want to sleep again quite as soon as 10.15. I have therefore delayed putting him out in his pram until later – about 10.45 or 11. At first all went well. Suddenly, for the last four or five days, he has started to yell and struggle the moment I've put him into his pram – and he has gone on yelling and yelling! Each day I have left him to cry himself to sleep – making sure first that he was warm and comfortable and talking to him gently before leaving him. The first day or two he cried for about forty-five minutes and then went to sleep for his usual time.

This morning, after crying for a little while, he climbed up and tried to get out of his pram – so then I strapped him down and he screamed! He did go to sleep at the end of an hour, but only slept for about forty-five minutes, and has, of course, looked very exhausted and washed-out ever since. He needs the sleep and is always very sleepy by the time I have put on his pram woollies, etc. Am I following the right treatment in continuing to put him out each day and leaving him to cry himself to sleep? Supposing he does not improve soon, ought I to try some other plan? And if so how long ought I to keep on with the present method – a week, a fortnight, three weeks? He has a comfy little pram, and I always put him where he can see trees and birds, etc. If I do go to him to tuck him up he stops crying and smiles and holds my hand! It's terribly hard to leave him to scream.

The second problem is very similar. During the last ten days he has taken a sudden dislike to his bath. He goes in to the bathroom quite happily, but the moment I put him into the bath he clings to me, cries, and refuses to sit down. I am sure he is frightened, though I have no idea what has frightened him. Should I force him into it for several nights in the hope of getting him back to his old ways? I am finding it a great strain to hold him in the bath. I wonder whether he feels the strain and has lost confidence. He has things to play with in the bath, and used to be very happy – but now he won't look at them."

"*D.C.*" writes: "*I wonder if you would help me with my problem?
I should think it is a fairly common one, but I should like to know
how you would deal with it. My little girl (aged one year and four
months) has been brought up according to Truby King methods, kept
to a regular routine where the thing was done cheerfully. She was
a good little thing, although by no means a placid child. She went
to bed happily and was left alone to fall off to sleep, and she would
peep around the cot and see one go out of the room. Suddenly at
thirteen months she took to screaming when left in her cot. I had
heard it said that if allowed to scream children soon learned better.
So for three nights we left her to scream, and she worked herself up
to an almost hysterical condition. After this the very sight of her cot
caused her to scream, and it was most distressing.*

*Then we decided we must prevent the screaming at all costs, so
we sat with her until she went to sleep, which sometimes took over
an hour, for often when nearly asleep she would open her eyes
suspiciously to see if one was there. Next she started waking and
screaming in the night, and I have often sat with her for two hours,
while she watched to see that I did not leave her. She seemed to be
afraid of falling asleep. This has gone on for three months, during
which time she has improved, in that she does not scream so violently. Tonight for the first time, having told her 'to sing', I walked
boldly out of the room and left her. She has now fallen asleep. She
has been cutting her back teeth during this period, but they cannot
have been giving her much pain as she has been so good in the day-
time. I want you to criticise what I have done, so that were I faced
with this problem with another child I should do the right thing. And
what am I to do if she continues to wake up in the night?*"

The only criticism I would want to make of "D.C.'s" treatment of her
little girl's screaming would be leaving her in the first instance. It is a
very good thing she saw the unwisdom of this, and had the patience
to sit with the little girl and help her over her fears. It is often said
that children should be allowed to scream and so "learn better", but
I am quite sure that it is most unwise to do so. I don't mean that one
should rush to the child the moment she wakes and begins to cry.
One should obviously leave her quiet for a time and give her the
chance to fall asleep again, but once the child really begins to scream
it is very unwise to leave her to scream indefinitely. It must be a

really terrible experience to be left to scream oneself to the point of exhaustion. One must feel absolutely lost and deserted by those on whom one depends. These screaming fits and waking in the night with anxiety are very common in the second and third years. They rise from all sorts of psychological sources, and it is seldom the child can master the anxiety herself without the help and comfort of the mother's presence. If, however, she has that, the difficulty gradually passes away with normal development. It does not in the least follow that because one comforts the child in the period of the worst anxiety that one will always have to go on sitting with her. Indeed, the reverse is nearer the truth. But "D.C." found for herself how the child is gradually improving, and is probably over the worst difficulty now. The pain of teething may have had something to do with it. It is in the loneliness of the night that one would mind this pain most. In the day there are so many interesting things to occupy one, and the pain would not be so frightening, just because they cannot get away from it or do anything about it. As long as she wakens in the night and shows her desperate need for her mother's presence I would certainly go on giving it her. I would just quietly comfort her, without fussing too much, and gradually, with this quiet encouragement, she will grow over her worst fears and become more independent. The plan of telling her to sing is quite a good one I think, and could be a help.

With regard to "A.B.'s" problems, in neither case should I force the child or leave him to scream. It would be a great mistake to force him into the bath. Something must have frightened him, and I should not try to make him sit or lie down in it, but treat him quite gently and let him stand up and sponge him down. It is not essential for cleanliness that he should sit down in the bath. He can be sponged clean outside it. What the cause of the fear is I have, of course, no idea, but such fears are very real to young children. If they are met with understanding and patience they pass away in due time. If, however, we try to force the child to do what we want in spite of such fears, we put him under a very great nervous strain, and we make him fear us as tyrants and not helpers.

With regard to the day-time sleep, I think it is a very great mistake to leave the child to scream for forty-five minutes or an hour. There is reason to think that such long fits of screaming, ending in exhaustion, have a very bad effect on the mental life of the child. Sometimes they cannot be avoided, but I think they can in "A.B.'s" circumstances. It may be that the child really does not does not need as much sleep as she is wanting him to have. Even young children differ a good deal in the amount of sleep that they need or can take, and we have to respect their idiosyncrasies. It seems to me likely that "A.B." is still putting him down too early and that if she left him until a good deal nearer lunch time, say 11.30 or 11.45, he might then be ready to fall off and take half an hour or an hour's good sleep. At present I am sure it comes too soon after his good night and late morning wakening. I should try this method at once, and if it did not answer, if he refused to lie down and went on crying I should give up even this after two or three days. The loss of sleep would do the child much less harm, both physically and mentally than these enforced screaming fits which are terribly exhausting and terribly frightening to the child. I would go on for some time putting him down to rest and giving him one of his favourite toys to play with, but if, after ten minutes or so, he shows no sign of going off to sleep or of staying quietly in a resting position I should give up the attempt and let him play about happily. I have known other children of about his age who have given up their day-time sleep, although, of course, it is not very common.

HOW MUCH SLEEP?

Children, as well as adults, vary in the amount of sleep they need to keep them in good health

22 MARCH 1933

"C.M.C." writes: "I have read with interest your advice regarding 'D.R.'s' child on the subject of sleep. I agree with you that children differ. Some children seem to need more sleep than others, though 'D.R.'s' child seems a little too young to give up morning sleep. Supposing she tried putting baby to sleep, and then if she did not sleep over the half hour or hour she obviously does not need a sleep. My charge always slept for an hour and a half every day till he was just on six (after that we didn't bother). But he was always put to sleep, otherwise he would not have gone, though he must have needed it, as he always slept the hour and a half, and woke up nice and fresh. Apart from this he slept from 6 p.m. til 6 a.m. He never

slept later than 6 a.m. whether he had a mid-day sleep or not the day before. He used to make a scene and scream when I would mention sleep. But I never took any notice, only laid him on his bed and sat and sang him to sleep. He took from ten to fifteen minutes at the most to go off. He always had his mid-day sleep out of doors (winter and summer). He is a big, active and healthy child. He will be seven years next week, but most people take him to be eight or nine. I hope my letter will be of some help to 'D.R.'"

The little boy mentioned in this letter is obviously one of those children who need a considerable amount of sleep. I think it is quite possible that that is because he is a big child. It is very probable that a child with a large frame to keep up does need more sleep than a child of smaller, slighter build. "C.M.C.'s" suggestion that one should always give the child the opportunity of a day-time sleep is, of course, a good one. It is the attitude of treating the child's unwillingness to sleep as a moral offence that is so bad in its effects.

"M.M.S." writes: "I wonder if you can give me a little advice about my small daughter aged seventeen months. My nurse and I have great difficulty in putting her to bed at night and leaving her to go to sleep. This trouble only started about a month ago, when she had flu rather badly and was cutting double teeth at the same time. During her illness she could not rest, and was hushed to sleep in her nurse's arms every night, as the poor baby was suffering a good deal of pain. Previously to this, before her illness, she had her bath at 5.30 and a drink of milk and was tucked into bed at 6 o'clock as good as gold. Then the door was shut and she was left. Often we would hear her talking to herself for about ten minutes quite happily before dropping off to sleep. We very rarely had trouble with her unless she was teething or over-tired, when she might cry a little, but was usually quickly hushed with a song or two. Now since her illness she will not be left, but cries immediately the light goes out and nurse leaves the room. We have tried everything – leaving the light on, propping her up in bed with her toys hoping she will drop off, nurse coming in and out two or three times, and then not coming back eventually, playing the gramophone outside the door and gradually stopping it,

*leaving her altogether and taking no notice in the hope that she will
cry herself to sleep. Everything is hopeless. She will cry on and on
monotonously for an hour or more, until eventually we have to go
up and hush her to sleep.*

*Though not what I should call a really highly strung child, she
is by no means phlegmatic, and I feel is definitely not the type
to cry herself to sleep. The only way we can quiet her at present
is to rock her to sleep after her bath, singing softly all the while.
She drops off then quite peacefully, and in about ten minutes can
be put into her cot. We have done this because I am dreading her
getting into the habit of regarding 'bed' as a horrible place connected with misery. All the same I am afraid of getting her into
the bad habit of crying for her own way, particularly as, when my
nurse is out, and my cook, who is very fond of her, puts her to bed,
she has practically no trouble with her, simply putting her to bed
with her woolly toy and leaving her. She is a healthy, intelligent,
and extremely energetic child. Quick-tempered and determined,
but very sweet-natured, and a favourite with everyone. She is not
what I would call a heavy sleeper at any time, and when teething
or over-tired, sleep has always been our problem. She is supposed
to sleep at least a good hour in the morning, but does not always do
this. She wakes 6.30–7 and is full of energy all day, but is inclined
to get over-tired at night. She eats well, and is out both morning
and afternoon."*

I should be inclined to stay with your little daughter until she falls
asleep for the present without having recourse to all those other
devices. I am sure you are entirely right in not wanting her to regard
bed as a horrible place, connected with tears and misery. There is no
doubt that these screaming fits have a bad effect upon the emotional
development of the child. It is very likely that if you did straightfor-
wardly stay with her until she fell asleep, for the present, she would
in the course of a few months get over the difficulty quite well. After
all, through her experience in being nursed in the illness, she has
learnt to associate being hushed to sleep in her nurse's arms with
real comfort and mental peace, and one cannot expect a child of this
age to give up this comfort immediately on demand. It is bound to
mean a process of slow re-education, and we really do save ourselves
both time and trouble and exasperation if we recognise this from the

beginning. After she had got fully over the memory of the illness, and all the feelings of association with it, she would be able to give up this special comfort, but it seems clear to me that you have started too early trying to return to the previous regime, and I should certainly quieten her to sleep in the way you have been doing latterly, without feeling that this was wrong or unwise. It does not in the least follow that she will get a general habit of crying for her own way because you can be perfectly firm with her in day-time situations, which feel very different to the child from this bed-time crisis.

TROUBLE AT BEDTIME

Some night-time problems answered by Ursula Wise

3 JANUARY 1934

"E.W." writes: "I would be very glad to have your advice on the following problem. My elder boy, aged six and a half years, has, for the last two years, been very nervous at being left alone when in bed at night. It started when we were away at the sea, when he had a room further away from the rest of us than usual, and he began to call then scream for us, and said flies were buzzing near him. It was quite true, there were some, flying round as they do in summer. We tried to reason with him, and though it was terribly inconvenient we managed that someone was near or actually with him. He seems to be worse lately. As a rule nurse sits in his room, which is really a day nursery, or she is in the next room, which keeps him quite happy. But it is terribly inconvenient on nurse's night out for me, as I have to do the same, as he cries and scream with real fright if I go back to the sitting room, which is on the floor above. I tried putting him in a nearer room with his brother, aged three, but he was just as bad. No reasoning makes any difference. I'm afraid I have also been very cross sometimes as my husband thinks I have made him like he is, by giving in to him. But I know it is not all put on and he really is very frightened. He is really rather nervous in other ways, but very well and happy at morning school, and though he bullies his brother rather, and has to be scolded sometimes, he is, as a rule, very happy and is perfectly normal in every way. Will he grow out of this fear of being alone when in bed? (We always leave the light on and door open.) Do you advise me to go upstairs and leave him? My

husband thinks I am making a molly-coddle of him. The boy tells me
he thinks we will go away and leave him, that is why he doesn't like
it. But, of course, we have never done such a thing, nor has he had any
fright of any kind that I know of."

It sounds to me quite likely that when the trouble began and the
phobia of flies first developed, there had been some real happening at the seaside that had stirred up anxiety in your boy. I cannot
surmise what that might be, but it does seem very likely to me that
there was something which started off this fear. It is always impossible to control such fears by mere reason, since they arise from the
deep emotions of the child, not from the rational part of his mind.
Nevertheless, I should be inclined, since he is six and a half years
old, not to stay with him in the room. Since he is healthy and otherwise a happy child, I think it is quite possible, that real firmness
and common-sense treatment with regard to his anxieties at night
might be a help to him. I should let him have a night light and go
on leaving the door open. I should tell him that you do understand
his feelings and appreciate that he fears you will go away and leave
him, but that you certainly are not going to do so, and believe that
if he tried very hard he could control is fear by his knowledge that
you will not actually desert him. I should begin by doing this quite
firmly on the evenings when nurse is out, not reproaching him for
the fear or scolding him if he cries out, but taking an attitude of real
friendliness and co-operation with him against his fear. I should
say that while you appreciate the reality of the fear, you also think
that he can use his sense to get over it. Then I should get his nurse
to begin leaving him in the same way every other night, and keep
quite firmly to it, not sitting in the room with him – at most, only
in the next room. I think if you go on in this way quite steadily
and undisturbedly, you will find after a time that he will be able to
control the expression of his fears. When a child is very neurotic,
he cannot do this even at this age, but an ordinary child can usually learn to do so, provided the attitude of the other people is a
real support to his powers of control. Your own unconcernedness,
provided that is gentle and friendly, will be the biggest support to
his sense of reality.

"B.B.K." writes: *"Your articles have so interested and helped me that I feel I must write and ask for your advice on my special problem. My baby Peter, now sixteen and a half months, never woke in the night from the age of seven weeks to eleven months. At that age we took him to Devon and had one or two disturbed nights. At thirteen months we took him away two separate weeks, when he had to sleep in our room (he usually sleeps alone) and had very bad nights. But he was teething during this period. From about nine and a half months he would not let me leave him after I put him to bed, but I found if I shook his crib he would usually go to sleep in about five minutes, and so I started doing it. The last few months he has not slept at all well – about every fortnight he would have a very bad night. He would wake and refused to go to sleep for about two and a half hours, and I had to stop lifting him at 10 p.m. as he could not get to sleep again. Now he is getting worse. A bad night occurs once a week and last week he had two running. He wakes crying and I go in to him and shake his cot. If I don't do this he just screams. He then lies, wide awake, for about two and a half hours, and if I attempt to leave him he screams. Also he is often a great nuisance after I put him to bed, and cries and will not go to sleep for about an hour, and then sometimes wakes during the evening. I am finding the disturbed night very trying, especially sitting in his room this cold weather. I feel if I put an electric radiator on the light will aid in keeping him awake. He has cut sixteen teeth in eight months which I felt were perhaps disturbing him, but I do not think he can possibly be cutting anymore now. Do you think a night light would help him, or bringing him into our room? I could then at least stop in bed. I hesitate to do this as I am expecting another baby in April, and Peter would have to go out of my room again then, and it might upset him. I have to cook my husband's dinner at about 7 p.m. which is often very difficult if Peter wants me. Last evening I sat him up with his books till we had finished supper. I also did this in the middle of one night. He sits and looks at his pictures and is quite good for about an hour. Do you think this is bad? He is very well and jolly all day, and is very good, sitting in his pram or playing alone in the nursery before his morning sleep. He sometimes sleeps for two hours or longer in the morning. Do you think it would be a good thing to wake him after one hour? He seldom cries in the day, but cries very pitifully in the evening or at night. He is usually sitting*

up in the dark when I go to him, and I very often have to take him
in my arms to pacify him. Would you kindly let me know the best
toys to give a child of this age to last him over the next six months.
What kind of bricks do you advise? He is not very fond of woolly
animals, but do you think a Teddy bear would attract him, which he
could take to bed with him? Peter is to be in the house again a few
days after the new baby arrives, therefore I am particularly anxious
that he should get over these wakeful nights by then, because my
husband will have to look after him."

It seems clear that it was the unusual experience of sharing your
room which started off these attacks of anxiety in your little boy.
It was a pity that you started the method of shaking the crib, since
that stereotyped sort of comfort is very much harder to leave off
than merely standing by quietly and talking to the child. It is very
probable that your pregnancy has a good deal to do with his anxiety
in the last few months. It is therefore quite likely that after your
new baby is born, provided you can handle Peter's introduction to
the new member of the family quite satisfactorily, his anxiety will
get less. I would like to suggest your reading the two or three excellent letters I have published from other mothers within the last few
weeks dealing with this question of the first contact of the older child
with his little rival, the new baby.[2] If you can ensure that Peter does
not feel shut out of your love, if you can let him feel that the new
baby in some way belongs to him too, that will be a very great help
to him. I would certainly not bring him into your room for sleeping at present, since that does naturally build up an expectation that
cannot be fulfilled. It would be very much harder for him to have to
be turned out again when the new baby came. A night light is likely
to be a help to him and the plan of letting him sit up and look at his
pictures while you get the dinner cooked is quite a good one as an
emergency measure. In such complicated situations as yours is at
present, one often has to make a compromise between what would be
ideal for the child and what is desirable from your own point of view.
It is obviously not good for you to sit in a cold room without any

2 Some of the letters on this theme are reproduced in Chapter 6: Jealousy and sibling
  rivalry.

fire on, nor is it helpful to be continually exasperated by the attempt to leave the child when you have the supper to get ready. Since you have this job to do, and since your own attitude to the child is much more likely to be calm and friendly if you are not continually exasperated, I think it would be sensible not to try to get him to go to sleep until you have got through the cooking of the supper and had your own. If you can keep him warm and contented with a cuddly Teddy Bear, or picture books, he is more likely then to settle down to sleep when you can give your mind to that problem than if you and he have each exasperated the other in a fruitless attempt to force him to sleep with your mind really on the task of supper. I would not try to shorten his day-time sleep since he obviously requires this. This other method of letting him sit up until you have finished with supper would be better. If after this you have to sit with him, I should certainly put the electric radiator on, and keep comfortable, because, again, if you are in a more contented frame of mind yourself you will be more likely to help the child go to sleep. An impatient, irritated grown-up can never make a child go to sleep by mere command. The exasperation communicates itself to the child quite inevitably. But a calm, pleasant, contented chat with the child will put him in a frame of mind in which he will fall asleep without knowing it. If you find he will not go to sleep without the shaking of the crib, I should go on doing that just for the present, since it is so important for both you and the child that he should get plenty of sleep and be free from anxiety. After the new baby is born and you have got your older boy over this crisis by real understanding and consideration, you might then later on stop the shaking of the crib, being quite firm about this, but staying with the boy and talking quietly to him about the events of the day until he falls asleep.

With regard to toys, I would suggest the "fitting" toys such as the wooden train or the nest of boxes, or the peg board, supplied by Paul and Marjorie Abbatt, Ltd., 29, Tavistock Square, W.C.1. He would probably very much enjoy the "Posting Box" which they make, too. As to bricks, rather largish light wooden bricks of different shapes would appeal to him, though he is rather young for these yet in any case. He would be more likely to enjoy them in about a year's time. He might like some of the wooden animals which the Abbatts make too, and some of the toys for trundling about after himself round the nursery floor.

CHAPTER FIVE

Eating

INTRODUCTION

Eating is a most pressing issue for those looking after young children. Wise is acutely aware of the emotive quality of food and eating, where both the child and the adult are complicit. There is, on the one hand, the giving of food along with its implicit expectations on the part of the carer, and the response to this on the part of the child. Food can, undeniably, be something of a psychological battle and a pawn in power relations.

More often than not, mothers and nurses consider the difficulties around eating as to do with some form of *not eating*: not eating the right amount, not eating the right things, not eating in the right way, not eating at the right times, and so on. Wise's response, invariably, is that the adults are unnecessarily anxious and demanding about it – this is the main challenge to be confronted. Being able to have some distance on the situation and giving the child both enough space and time to eat is key. She suggests ideas about how to implement this, as well as reassuring her readers that her advice is backed up by research. Her tips, which are practical and direct, generally seem to have withstood the test of time – many could be found in parenting handbooks today.

Wise uses one of her columns to describe some observational mealtime research done in three well-known (though not named) nursery schools. This makes for an interesting read and one that is not only relevant for those who work in nursery settings, but for anyone involved with young children's mealtimes.

Wise, in keeping with the tenor of her column, does not ruminate on the psychological or psychoanalytical aspect of eating in any detail, but she does point towards this in her elucidation of the biting impulse – what it means for the child and the distinction between it and its associated behaviour and "mere wilfulness". Again, pursuing the main thread of her column, Wise urges her readers to understand the child and get to know something of their unseemly or unacceptable responses.

Given even a fleeting familiarity with Ursula Wise it would be possible to predict her views on a small child being made to eat food they disliked. As is often the case, she says this in such a straightforward and uncomplicated way that it would seem obscene to even consider the option a possibility.

Wise sees the advantages of sharing mealtimes with other children – such sociability can reduce the intensity of the meal and children can provide very good distractions and examples for each other. Though more commonplace now, at the time of her writing, when children did not go to groups or nurseries nearly so much, it might have been quite novel advice!

BEHAVIOUR AT MEAL-TIMES

The convention of sitting still does not come very easily to young children, says Ursula Wise

16 AUGUST 1933

"J.D.B." writes: "I would be very glad of your kind help on one or two matters concerning my little son aged 2 years 2 months. Until he was two years old he sat in his high chair for all his meals and was strapped in with a safety strap. Since his birthday he has had his meals at the table with Daddy and Mummy, in an ordinary chair without a strap. At first he sat quietly and ate his meal, and when he had finished he had beads to thread for about five minutes, because

I find that if I let him get down immediately after a meal, he has hiccoughs. For about a month he was quite content to do this, probably because he had not realised he was free to move about. This last fortnight he has been getting down during the meal and standing up, and we have had milk spilt, etc. I am trying to train him with love and firmness, and if I just look at him (rather reproachfully) he will say – 'I'm sorry Mummy dear, I won't get up again' – and will come back immediately; about a few minutes later he is standing up, or down again. I do not expect him to sit still without a little variation, such as kicking the table (if he starts kicking I suggest a little more, and he soon stops then); helping to pour his milk, putting the lid on his honey, etc., because I realise he is a very active child and must be 'doing' all the time, but am writing to ask you if he should remain at the table the whole of the meal time and a little after.

He has plenty of scope for using up energy in the forms of a climbing frame (I had one made very cheaply), sand pit, boards to climb up raised a little off the floor at one end, and a bucket with a little brush and cloth to scrub boards and the floors. This latter is the greatest pleasure of all. He has copied my woman help since he was a tiny mite, even to a kneeler and apron. Am I giving him too much freedom in allowing this last occupation? It is considered 'awful' by the other occupants of our flat.

My other question is – how can I put his little mind at ease about bicycles? Three weeks ago, a little girl from upstairs was cycling round the lawn, and although I was there, David suddenly ran out of a shed, with a big ball, on to the lawn and was knocked down and hurt quite badly; having a cut and bruises on his face and a bruise on the back of his head. He was very upset at the time and now seems frightened if he sees a bicycle, shouting – 'A bicycle, Mummy', several times. I tell him it will not hurt him again, but do not think I am quite right in saying this, because he is very sensible and knows it may hurt him again if he gets near one. We hope they will stop cycling round the lawn, but cannot be sure. Do you think David will gradually forget the incident, or will it cause any nervous disorder later on? At present he is a happy little being, and I am anxious to keep him so."

First of all, it is an excellent plan to let your little boy enjoy himself scrubbing the floors or doing other things which interest him in the activities of the grown-ups. It would be "awful" to refuse him this pleasure when he wants it, and there is no reasonable ground for denying it to him. He is gaining a real skill, and living himself imaginatively into what grown-ups do for his comfort, in a way that will help his later social development. It is always a good sign of developing social sympathy with people and interest in the world generally, when little children want to imitate the activities of grown-ups in this way.

As regards mealtimes, it is quite general for children of his age to want to stand up and walk about during meals. The convention of sitting does not come very easily to young children, and if we demand it we have to realise it will take time for the child to achieve. Two years is indeed rather young to expect a child to sit through a meal with grown-ups, and follow grown-up notions of manners and politeness. It would be better to postpone this a little longer – or at any rate, to make a transition, by not expecting the child to sit for more than a few minutes at table after he has finished his own meal. Another year's growth would make a great difference in the child's capacity to control his impulses, and I should be inclined to let him eat by himself for a little longer – perhaps having him at table with you as an occasional treat, or for part of the meal only. In any case, patience and skill are required in training the child to meal-time customs.

It is sure to take him time to get over his nasty jar with the bicycle, is it not? We, too, should feel shaky and nervous with any comparable experience – and a little child has so much less to go on in getting such an experience into perspective. He is bound to be nervous of all bicycles for a time. I should not tell him baldly that it *will* not hurt, but rather if he is careful not to go too near it, or to run about without looking what is there, it is not likely to hurt him again. I do not see any reason why it should cause a permanent upset, if you take the incident, and his own fears, quite calmly and sensibly, and help him to see just what happened.

UNTITLED[1]

3 APRIL 1935

"Thirty-three" writes: *"For some time now I have been very much troubled about my small son's appetite. Daniel is four years and five*

1 The title was irrelevant as it referred to the first letter of that week (not printed here).

months old, height 3 ft. 7 ½ inches (both sides of my family have been very tall), weight 2 st. 12 lbs. He is an only child, as I was very ill after he was born, and he is, I think, a fairly normal boy for his age, except in eating, both in behaviour and his attitude towards food in general. He never seems hungry or thirsty. When we call him to a meal he seems quite uninterested and frequently does not bother to come until he is fetched. He then wriggles on his chair (it is seemingly impossible for him ever to be still except when asleep!) and may or may not attempt to eat the first mouthful – the rest of the time he just jigs about, wants to get down or else he plays with the food, making volcanoes, cakes, etc., etc. Very occasionally he eats a normal meal, and I hope that our meal times may be peaceful at last, but always he slips back to the old ways. I have tried ignoring the matter, persuasion, and reasoning, also quietly taking the food away. The only times he eats are when we happen to talk of something which interests him very much; he will then – if someone puts it in his mouth – eat quite absent-mindedly. He is an imaginative and excitable child, but not at all fearful. I have other children to tea with him sometimes, and if he is not too excited – which is frequently the case – he will eat better then, but if he has one good meal (one slice of bread and butter and one small slice of home-made cake is a large meal for him) he almost invariably wants nothing at the next meal! He has three meals a day, with a cup of Ovaltine before bed at 6.30 p.m., and as much fresh air as possible, but even after a morning 'working' in the garden or a run on the Downs when we come home feeling ravenous, he'll sit and play with his food! Another thing, his behaviour at table is that of a child of two years (that too, I have corrected, and ignored, hoping it was a phase which would pass). He seems very clumsy and backward in using his hands and, unless reminded, even eats with his fingers. He has chalks, plasticine, etc., and loves 'carpentooling' – he has the use of his father's tools and can hammer nails into a piece of wood as well as I can, yet handles a spoon or fork so badly! I have noticed that he does not hold his hands, particularly the right hand, in the ordinary relaxed manner when not using them, but keeps his fingers pressed close together and nearly out straight – also he is left-handed, though he can use his right hand when gently reminded, though I have not pressed the point. No one else is left-handed in the family, and strangely enough his father and I are both artists, and his father especially is a clever *craftsman and can simply make his hands do anything! I am telling you this as I wondered if there was some connection between eating and managing the spoon, etc., with hands. Daniel also does not seem in the least interested in dressing himself and cannot do a thing beyond putting on his socks, yet is most anxious 'to be a big boy'. He knows a lot about building houses, machinery, and foreign countries, etc., but time and all the little everyday practical things seem completely left out! How can I best help him to be more self-reliant and a little more practical without upsetting his individuality and imagination?"*

It is very probable that the difficulties your little boy feels about food and eating have their ultimate origin in the circumstances of his life soon after birth and your own illness. It often happens that feeding difficulties in the toddler period can be traced back to some sort of disturbance of the normal relation of the child to his mother in the suckling period. Where this is so, there is no way of getting over the difficulties but patience. He will not go on being so reluctant and difficult all his childhood, but he may continue with this moodiness about eating until he goes to school and eats among other children. You would find that that would be the most effective help towards normal feeding, namely, if he could have his midday meal amongst a group of little children in a nursery school. It happens so often that a child forgets all about his reluctance and difficulties about eating as soon as he shares a meal with other children of his own age. I am sure you are right in thinking that the curious posture of your boy's fingers and his clumsiness in handling spoons and forks etc., are connected with the difficulty about eating. I should be inclined not to worry him about table manners for the present. A child who has emotional difficulties about eating feels these things much more acutely when he is bothered about table manners as well. He will get these all right a little later on, especially if he can be with other children. I wonder whether you could not find a nursery school or group of children with whom he could have at any rate his mid-day meal. You have yourself noticed that he eats better when other children are with him at tea, and this surely gives a strong hint as regards the best way of getting over his difficulty. All the more general aspects of his development

would be helped by companionship in play and handicrafts. Self-reliance and practical common sense will grow later on. They are never conspicuous in a boy of four, especially one who has this sort of emotional difficulty about food. I should therefore not worry about his general development.

MEALTIME DIFFICULTIES

Pressure and force and over-persuasion make these difficulties persist whereas gentler, more tactful methods will cause them to practically disappear

25 AUGUST 1934

"Jill" writes: *"I should be so grateful for any hints you can give me with regards to my little son of two and a quarter years. The vexed question is solid food. He seems thoroughly to dislike any meal that means his sitting up to the table. His Daddy (for whom he will do almost anything) has spent as much as an hour giving him his dinner, and then he may be sick of it all in the end (due, I am sure to*

emotional disturbance at the time). He will just keep a spoonful in his mouth and won't swallow it. Bovril, milk, biscuits, orange, or 'sweets' present no difficulty. I know the usual procedure is to take the food away and take no notice of him, but you cannot very well produce a full dinner at tea-time just before bed, and then he eats a little tea and can go till breakfast (only a cereal and perhaps a piece of toast and half an orange), continually missing his lunch without question. I am sure it is not a pose or want of notice, but he is extremely active and bright, and I think he is genuinely bored at having to waste time! His table manners are not good – at least he is always restless, but both his nursemaid and myself have had to allow him to take anything in any possible way, such as running round a room. My doctor suggested force, but how can you force a child of that age, besides being very bad for his nerves and digestion. He is still fairly wet, and although he can ask for his 'chay', won't always do so. He has never been unduly bothered about it by us, and quite cheerfully wipes up after himself. He is cutting his last four back teeth at present, so things may improve afterwards, but he has always been a most difficult feeder, and I really feel he is undernourished.

You might be interested to hear how I successfully treated him for terror at bedtime on the lines you consistently recommend, as there have been several queries lately. I had to send Peter to a nursing home for a few weeks in the summer (he was one and a half then), and I think my leaving him and the fact that they tried to force him to take full (rather over-full, I am afraid) meals, gave rise to a terror of being left in his cot at 6 o'clock. However, I stayed with him and talked a little and put him on my bed (lying beside him) for a few nights, and gradually shortened the time till he was normal again. He now quietly goes to bed, with no trouble, in his own room in the dark. I think it is just confidence they need to overcome the fear you are going away for ever."

You are certainly very wise in feeling that it would be useless to attempt to force your little boy to take food that he objects to. The fact that he is sick with the food that he has taken even under the pressure of persuasion shows very clearly that he could not possibly digest food that had actually been forced upon him. These difficulties in feeding demand the utmost tact and restraint on the part of the grown-ups who are dealing with the child. Every bit of evidence I have been able to gather, both from my own experience and that of other people, goes to show that the more we fuss over the child's dislikes, scold or reproach him for them, or attempt to persuade or force him to get over them, the more they persist and the worse the difficulty becomes. Whether or not the method of ignoring helps, depends on the attitude with which it is adopted. If it is done in a cold stern way, it is little better than reproaching openly; but if it is done in a cheerful, unconcerned way, a manner that emphasises to the child the willingness of the adult to help and understand without fuss, then it does really aid the child. I would not suggest that you should produce a full dinner at tea-time or give the child a heavy meal just before going to bed. I should try to follow the plan of giving him a very small amount of solid food on his plate at the mid-day meal, not even trying to make it more for the first few days; and then beginning to increase it only by a very little at a time. This reluctance to take solid food is not mere wilfulness on the part of the child, but comes from very deep feelings connected with his fear of his own biting impulses in rage against persons. That is one reason why the companionship of other children at mealtimes helps him to get over his anxiety about solid food. I should not worry about table manners at present, as the feeding itself is more important than that, and mere restlessness does no harm. You have proved for yourself how sense and consideration will help your boy over such an acute difficulty as the fear of being left, and the same thing applies to the feeding difficulty.

During the last few months I have been able to have some careful observations made with regard to the frequency of feeding difficulties in relation to the methods of dealing with them in several well-known nursery schools. These observations have demonstrated even more clearly than I anticipated would be the case, that pressure and force and over-persuasion make these difficulties persist, and cause a nervous excitement that is very bad for the child as a whole. Whereas gentler, more tactful methods, based upon some understanding of the reality of the child's feelings will cause them practically to disappear. I am sure that many mothers and nurses will be very interested in these facts about the results of different sorts of methods in dealing with feeding difficulties. I will quote from three different nursery schools. The detailed description about the two-year-old child in the third nursery school mentioned is very interesting in showing the way in which these skilful teachers enabled the boy to get over the tremendous change of food and of circumstances that the nursery school meal meant for a child who until then had not been weaned.

Nursery School 1 – Some persistent feeding difficulties with a few children occurring every day; with others, only when certain articles of diet appear.

Compulsion frequently used: the adult constantly urging and encouraging – "Hurry up and finish your dinner", "You *must* eat it up", "Bite it up quickly". Children who are slow, or who are playing with their spoons and forks instead of eating, are fed by an adult. If a child screams and kicks in temper, spoonfuls are pushed in when its mouth is open. Any intimations on the part of the child that it doesn't want any more, such as by shakes of the head, firmly closed mouth, appealing looks or entreaty, are completely ignored by the adult, and the child has to finish even to the last spoonful.

Two children, who have learnt that this is inevitable, make valiant attempts to finish their dinner; but they eat so slowly that it soon becomes cold and unpleasant, and each mouthful is taken with a shudder, and sometimes held in the mouth for some time before swallowing. They resort to all kinds of devices when trying to swallow these mouthfuls – playing with spoons and forks, digging their forks into the bulb pots, pulling the flowers to pieces, rocking movements and wriggling. On one occasion, a child was given no pudding because she had refused to finish the first course. Quite often the children are very excited during and after the meal, and frequently at the end of the meal they throw their water about, or tip it out on the floor.

Nursery School 2 – No feeding difficulties or only occasional ones if a child is poorly. One case of a little girl who said she did not like meat. Miss X. gave her a very small portion and said she would "help her to like it". The child asked for a second helping, and had no further difficulty over feeding. No compulsion is used: the children seem to be quite ready for their meals and eat what is put before them. The fact that those that finish first sometimes help themselves from another child's plate, is an incentive to the slow ones to eat more quickly; also, the fact that someone else wants their dinner, seems to make them want it all the more. Sometimes, however, a child, who for some reason doesn't want his dinner, will give away spoonfuls to other children or pass his plate along for them. The adult in charge makes no comment on the amount eaten by the child: the plate is removed if the child says he does not want his dinner. The adult's attitude in such a case is one of sympathy and understanding. It is a rare occurrence for any food to be left on a plate.

Nursery School 3 – Many children have feeding difficulties on first coming to school, but lose them during the term. Very small portions are given at first. One little girl sat before an empty plate for several days because she refused her dinner. When at last she asked for some, only a very tiny portion was given, the adult taking the attitude that she considered it too much for the child, and when asked for a second helping, querying whether there would be enough for the other children. A child of two years, who had not been weaned when he started school, had no dinner for several days. A mug of milk was placed on the table behind the piano, and one day the boy found it and drank it up. This happened every day, and one day he came to ask for more. He was persuaded to sit with the others to drink his milk, then the milk was put in a shallow basin and he was given a spoon: he began to eat milk puddings, and finally after two months, he was eating the same diet as the others.

THE CHILD WHO WILL NOT EAT

27 JULY 1932

"Worried" writes: "I should be so glad if you could help me with the problem of feeding my little boy, who is two this month. Food as food alone does not interest him at all, but if he is allowed to look at picture books, spin his top – in fact, do anything which interests him – he will eat it. We have no nanny, and my sister-in-law and I look after him between us. Up till quite recently I have been making him eat his dinner by means of a threatened smack if he did not, which was constantly carried out with good results. However, we decided this was not the right method, so I stopped feeding him and handed mealtimes over to my sister-in-law, as she is very patient and just and yet does not spoil him. Some days dinner goes down well, with lots of conversation about birds and outdoor things he has seen, but to-day nothing was any use as he wanted to play with a tin, which she wold

not allow him to have, with the result that nothing would induce him to eat. What do you advise me to do? We are so afraid of starting bad habits of playing at meal times, and yet he cannot afford to go without his food or have these mental struggles, as he is very advanced mentally and understands everything we say to him."

I do not know if you have read any of my replies to other letters dealing with the problem of difficult feeders. I have from time to time dealt with quite a number of these cases, and I very often receive confirmation of the general lines of advice which I have offered. Other people working with children in, for example, nursery schools and places where careful observations can be made, all fully agree with me in holding that the biggest and most frequent source of difficulty with little children who will not eat is the too great anxiety on the part of the grown-ups. When we start urging a child to eat what we consider he ought to have, we turn the question of eating or not into a sort of contest between the child and ourselves, and the child's natural appetite often has no chance at all against his pleasure of being fussed over, or the sense of contrariness which the fuss arouses, or the actual feeling of power that he gets from being able to make the parents so worried.

It has been found by experienced nurses and nursery school teachers over and over again that a child who will not eat when the grown-ups show their anxiety that she should, will begin to do so when the food is simply put before her and she is left free to eat or not. It is the rarest thing in the world to have a child who will really let more than one meal pass by if the food is put in front of him and he is left with it without any urging or comment. It is, of course, important that the food should be of the right kind and attractively cooked and served; that goes without saying, but once that is done it is far better to leave the child alone even if he does not seem to us to be eating as much as we imagine he should. There is, of course, a fairly settled average amount that children of particular ages do normally eat under healthy circumstances, but nevertheless they differ amongst themselves quite a good deal, and not only so, they differ from time to time even while they are healthy and growing. Very often the whole difficulty starts when the child is off his food for a day or two without any apparent reason, and mother or nurse starts pressing or urging him. He feels contrary, and the whole tiresome circle of refusing and being persuaded and refusing again and needing more persuading goes on and on. Once this attitude is set up it is far from easy to break. It can usually be most easily altered if the child shares his meal with two or three other children of the same age who are eating normally, as when he goes to a nursery school. I have myself seen many children whose mothers said, "He won't eat", and were really extremely worried because they ate so little, begin to eat normally and readily when they found themselves in a group of other children all enjoying their meals and with the grown-ups saying nothing at all about it.

Now I do not know, of course, how your difficulty with your little boy began, but it does sound to me as if you had been urging him for a long time and never really left him alone about the question of eating. There are occasionally cases of children who are difficult in this way from their weaning, but when they are it still holds true that it pays far better to leave them to get over it by natural development and healthy surroundings than by persuading, urging and punishment. When these latter methods are followed, the mealtime becomes associated in the child's mind with reproaches and punishment, and he is therefore bound to come to it with the very opposite attitude from the one that would bring a good appetite. In your circumstances, I should be inclined to put the child down to a pretty, pleasantly arranged small table of his own, with the right size of chair, and leave him alone with the meal, giving him a reasonable time to eat it in, and telling him without reproach or fuss that you would be soon clearing up the meal if he had done eating it. I should then carry this out. And I should try this method for a little time. But it would be a great help if you could arrange for him to share at any rate an occasional meal with another child, using the same general methods. I do not think that you will get over the difficulty at all along the present lines, but will simply go on worrying and persuading and scolding without any improvement.

THE CHILD WHO WILL NOT EAT[2]

24 JANUARY 1934

"Gee" writes: *"I read your columns of THE NURSERY WORLD with much interest and am venturing to ask your advice about my*

---

2 The same titles were repeated over time.

small boy aged four years next month. The main problem at present is that he will not eat, but will sit and dream or play with his food during meal-times. He has his meals with us, as we have not room for a day nursery, and it is inconvenient for him to have his meals alone. I have tried playing with him, forcing him to eat (i.e., feeding him myself, which he usually objects to very much), taking no notice of him and making him go without his food. But none of these remedies seem very effective. He is very fond of sweets, but I try to limit him to one during the morning and two after lunch or tea. He is tall for his age and although not fat, is far from skinny, with the exception of his legs, which are extremely thin and very double-jointed, which means he is constantly falling down. He is very healthy indeed, and never sits still for a moment, except when in bed. He sleeps well and has an hour's rest before lunch every day. His father has a very small appetite, and I am not really a great eater, so do you think it is just natural for him to eat very, very little? Even as an infant he was always rather 'difficult' with bottles. He has never been 'spoilt' nor allowed much of his own way, but if he really doesn't want the food, shall I just let him leave it? I hate people to be 'faddy' over food, and am so afraid he may grow up to be one of those people who 'don't like this' and 'can't eat that'.

As regards his legs, is there any other way – apart from sending him to a dancing class, which I have already done – in which I can help to develop them? He is never free from bruises caused by his falls, and although he never cries, I don't think it can do him any good. Could I massage them in any way?"

It sounds to me as if you had fussed too much about your boy's not eating. So often this situation is created at the first sign of any reluctance to eat what he is supposed to eat – perhaps soon after he first gets on solid food. If one does then start pressing and urging, the child may go on expecting this and being unable to eat unless he gets it. I cannot tell from your letter whether this has been the history. It does happen that there are children who are very difficult from the beginning, and you do say that he was difficult even in the bottle stage. And yet it seems to me likely that you have had too much anxiety about the whole thing, as you say you "*hate* people to be faddy over food". Children readily sense the emotions of adults about these things, and this very often increases rather than lessens the difficulty. I should certainly be inclined to try the policy of consistently leaving him alone, making sure, of course, that the food is attractively prepared and offered. After all, if his father has a very small appetite and you not much more, and the child eats with you, it is hardly expected that he will develop a large appetite, since this would be bound to feel greedy to him. One of the best helps would be if you could arrange for him to have a meal, even if only an occasional one, with other children of about his age, who do eat well. Somehow children seem to get so much reassurance from the sight of others their age doing things they are reluctant to do. It acts more effectively than any amount of urging or persuading on the part of adults. But if he is so healthy and well developed, I don't think you need to worry as much as you have done, providing you are sure that the food you offer is well balanced, varied and attractive.

I have no doubt that there are ways in which you could help to strengthen the boy's leg muscles, but I am not competent to give you detailed advice. You would need to be shown how to deal with it. I would suggest your writing for information about the question to Miss Vulliamy, of the Hampstead School of Physical Culture, 1, Broadhurst Gardens, N.W.3. She would be able to tell you where to go for the detailed information you need.

UNTITLED[3]

16 DECEMBER 1931

"D.W." writes: *"Would you very kindly give me some advice as regards my little boy aged sixteen months? He will hold his food in his mouth having had a few spoonfuls. Nothing will make him swallow it. I try forcing him to drink in order to try to make him swallow the food, but he usually nearly chokes, and consequently brings back what he has already eaten. He takes his gravy and vegetables fairly well at midday, but immediately holds milk puddings in his mouth – perhaps for an hour. Sometimes I have to force his mouth open in order to take the food out just before his afternoon outing. He will*

---

3 As with the previous untitled letter, the title referred to the first letter printed and was irrelevant to this letter.

eat a little bread and butter at teatime, and perhaps a sponge finger, but after his bath, about six o'clock, he has rusks and milk with a little cream and sugar, and it is at this meal especially that he holds his food in his mouth. It has been suggested that I should starve him for a while in order to make him really hungry, but as he is not a fat baby and not over bonny, I am not anxious to do this. My other trouble is that he continually wakes up in the night and sits up and cries, and if I do not tuck him down again he falls forwards and sleeps on his face. At least a dozen times in the evening and during the night he sits up and falls asleep on his face. He does not always wake up. Perhaps he will do this twice in a quarter of an hour. I have tried to tie him down, but he still manages to wriggle up. He is quite a happy baby."

This is a very difficult problem, yet not an uncommon one. I should be inclined to find some way round it, since it is obviously useless to make the child choke and vomit by trying to make him swallow food he doesn't want. Such experiences are bound to increase the difficulty, not to lessen it. These strong dislikes that little children get to certain sorts of food are far more important than grown-ups often realise. I can myself remember experiences like this and the real horror a child may feel of being made to swallow food that he dislikes. And, after all, milk puddings are not *absolutely* necessary to a child's health, even at sixteen months. If the boy would drink the milk, he can get what is necessary in that way; and many people consider that starchy puddings are definitely not an ideal diet. The rusks and bread and butter might be preferable. Would it not be better to drop out the supper meal all together and make the tea meal a little later and rather more solid? If he will eat then you might avoid the difficulty of the meal after his bath. I agree that it would not be wise really to starve a boy of this age in order to make him hungry, but I would certainly not try so hard to force him to swallow food, and I would definitely try to avoid the foods that he objects to so strongly. The other trouble is certainly not so easy to deal with except by constant observation. I should not try to tie him down. The annoyance of this is likely to make him want to sit up more than ever. I should rely simply on him growing out of the habit as he gets through this second year of life, and not worry about it more than is just necessary at the time to see that he doesn't smother.

TROUBLE AT MEAL-TIMES

22 OCTOBER 1930

"L.H." writes: *"My charge, aged six years and five months, has developed a strange attitude, and this has been going on for some time. He will come to his meals quite all right, and then commence a series of nonsense instead of getting on with his food, and when told he must stop and start to eat, he throws down his table napkin and says, 'Very well, I won't have any', and folds his arms, pouting his lips, and sulks for quite a time. When out with his father alone he is quite happy, but as soon as he arrives home is very rude to him, and gives one the impression he doesn't like his daddy. It has always been the same with him, and as his father has to be six months away from him during the year he naturally feels it, for no child could have a more affectionate father. The child loves to go out 'exploring' with his daddy, but why this sudden change directly he returns? There are also times when he is rude to both his mother and myself. When spoken seriously to he says he never knew and didn't mean to be rude, and cries about it. If you could help me in this matter I shall be very grateful. Naturally, I ask myself, 'Am I at fault in his upbringing?' or is it that he is a most extraordinary child?"*

It is not easy to understand the causes of this sort of behaviour without a good deal more knowledge of the child than your letter gives me and of the ways in which he is dealt with. I would suggest that you try to deal with the difficulties on much the same general lines as I have pointed out to other readers with similar troubles. For instance, with regard to the meal time problem, I think you would find it better not to tell him to "stop his nonsense and start eating", but to leave him alone, going quietly on with your own meals and clearing away the food in the ordinary course when everyone has finished. If you explain this to him, quietly and pleasantly, beforehand, and then keep to it quite firmly, showing no concern at all whether he eats or not, you will probably find that he will stop the "nonsense" and eat his food. When he says, "Very well, I won't have any", and folds his arms and sulks, he really wants you to persuade and scold and battle with him. He does not really mean not to eat his dinner, but only to enjoy this fuss beforehand. You did not tell me what the "nonsense" was, and so I can hardly judge how much attention should be given to it, but I think that you would find that this method of just letting the meal take its natural course, and letting the boy find that he lost the opportunity of his dinner if he did not take it when it was there, would soon bring both the nonsense and the sulks within bounds.

The boy's behaviour to his father is of a trying and puzzling kind, but it is by no means unusual. There are children who can be most affectionate and friendly when they are with either parent alone, but who cannot seem to manage the situation when both are there. He must, of course, be a very jealous child underneath, but it would be a mistake to tell him so or to scold him about it. The only way to deal with this kind of behaviour is for both parents to be consistently firm and gentle, so that the child has no opportunity to play one parent off against the other. To say this is not, of course, a great deal of help to you as the child's nurse, except in so far as a little more understanding of the child's problem may help you to be more sympathetic and more firm. With regard to his rudeness to his mother and to you, I wonder if you have tried to observe what sort of occasions call out for this rudeness? It is often a help in knowing how to treat the child if one can see something of what is going on in his mind. E.g., one of the occasions of rudeness may be the one you described in the first part of your letter, the meal-time problem. Now, I think you will find that the rudeness there will tend to disappear if you change your methods in the way I have suggested. It won't do so all at once, of course, but this different way will give less occasion for a direct tussle of wills. If you could take each situation in which the boy tends to be rude, and consider it on these lines, you might find ways of getting the child to co-operate more willingly and to feel less blindly defiant.

WHEN THEY WANT THEIR OWN WAY

A little girl who is very difficult at mealtimes

1 OCTOBER 1930

"M. McK." writes: "*I should be glad of your advice about my daughter, aged twenty months. She is a very lively, intelligent child, with a strong will. She is usually very obedient, but we are now having*

struggles at meal times. She always fills her mouth really cram full,
and gobbles her food tremendously. I find the only way to stop this is
to keep her toast on the table and hand her a very small bit at a time.
This means that she sobs all the time, which I'm sure is bad for her
digestion. I also have difficulty over feeding her with a spoon, as she
will hold the spoon herself, and cannot manage to pick up the food
with it; but she will not let me guide her hand, as she gets furiously
impatient. So, there is little prospect of her being able to feed herself
soon! She is very obedient in every other way. My chief reason for
bothering over this is that her digestion is a very weak point with
her, and I am sure this bother over meals is not good for it."

I am sure you are right in thinking that these struggles and the sobbing are very bad for a child with a weak digestion – probably quite
as bad as the gobbling you are trying to prevent. I think it is often
forgotten by mothers and nurses who want to keep the discipline of
the meal-table very strict that the unhappy frame of mind which this
leads to in the child may be the worst possible thing for health and
digestion, often much worse than the small faults that it is aimed at.

Somehow or other the little child's co-operation has to be won in
seeking to establish good habits of eating. We can never establish
them if we start out by making the child fretted and miserable. We
must make her feel that it is not only more comfortable, but more
fun to eat more slowly and chew things up. And the very first thing
towards success in this aim is our own attitude of mind. If we are
cross or stern, if we treat the child's quick eating as mere naughtiness, she is sure to be either defiant or frightened, as well as puzzled.
We must be good-humoured and patient in the training, and find
some way of making a game of it.

In your little girl's case, it seems that she should be allowed to
do her best to feed herself. She can only learn to get the food into
the spoon by trying. The fact that she takes a long time to get each
spoonful up, and gets only a little at a time, is surely a useful safeguard against gobbling! With her impatient temperament, she will
learn more quickly by her own effort than by having her hand held.
To have one's hand held brings a sense of helplessness that many
children dislike very much indeed. And at twenty months she should
not have any difficulty in feeding herself, if the spoon is of the right
size and a deep enough bowl to scoop up a mouthful easily; and if the

food is broken up small and put, not on a flat plate, where it would slip away from the spoon, but in a deep saucer, which gives the child more chance to get it up. As regards the toast, that, too, should be cut up small, and two or three bits at a time put on the child's plate for her to feed herself. And only a smallish portion of food should be put in the dish at one time. When the child has finished one portion, I shouldn't forcibly keep her waiting for another; the mere interval whilst the next lot is being put into her dish will help to slow down the rate at which the food goes into the stomach. And smiles and pleasant talk will ease things and make the child more amenable.

You will remember, won't you, that eighteen months is the average age for children to learn to feed themselves with a spoon? If your little girl is normally forward, then she is bound to feel irritated at having her hand held and being spoon-fed as if you tied her to a chair in straps when she was running about!

If you can get her frame of mind easy and happy, and let her feel the sense of power and pride that comes from being able to handle her spoon by herself, then it should be quite easy to win her to eating more slowly and putting less in her mouth by pleasant suggestion, saying, for example, "Will you try to go more slowly?" or "Look; try that little bit first. Now, that's gone – another weeny piece", and so on, rather than "Don't eat so quickly".

A FEEDING PROBLEM

A letter from a mother whose little boy will not eat is the first of those answered this week

8 JANUARY 1936

"E.G." writes: "I have read with much interest your advice to mothers and nurses on childhood problems, and would be grateful if you could advise me regarding my son, aged two years. Until a few months ago he enjoyed all his meals, with no fuss or fads whatever, now it is the most difficult job to get him to eat after breakfast. I am afraid, perhaps, that I am to blame, for when he first began to be difficult I pleaded with him instead of ignoring him, in fact in desperation I even gave him things to play with to keep his mind occupied while I fed him. After reading your advice to other

mothers regarding fussy feeders, I decided to adopt your methods and ignore him. Should he not take his first course, I remove it without comment and let him have his sweet. If he chooses not to eat that I treat it in like manner. This has been going on for weeks now and apparently he shows no sign of improvement. I have tried nearly every cereal for his breakfast, but all I can get him to eat is the yolk of a new laid egg with crisp toast and milk to drink. This is usually all he has all day unless I can distract him while I feed him, which I am convinced is quite wrong. David, I might add, has never been given scraps between meals. Perhaps it may help you to know how he spends his day. He is brought down to breakfast at eight o'clock. I tried the raw apple at seven o'clock but he just threw it away. After breakfast he uses his 'pot' and is placed in his cot by the open window, and is very happy there until 10.30, when he is bathed and cold sponged. The cold sponge he has had since six months old. After bath he has his orange juice and is put in the garden to play. I must say he is a quite happy little boy and amuses himself until 12.30 when he is offered dinner, which often consists of steamed fish with two vegetables, chicken another day and brains another, followed by milk pudding and fruit. After dinner he is put into his cot and sleeps for an hour or more; then he is taken in his pram for a walk for half an hour and then returns to play in the garden until 4.10 teatime. I spend the whole afternoon with him. 6.00 to 6.30 he is put to bed and usually sleeps till 7.00 a.m. On the whole David looks wonderfully fit, has rosy cheeks, real hard limbs and is full of energy, but I am wondering how long he will be so fit if he doesn't eat. Do you think this may be all due to his teeth? He has yet to cut his four molars. At present his weight is 29½ pounds. I should be so grateful for your advice as I am expecting another baby in four months' time and should so like to get David back to normal. I might add I have the entire housework, etc. to manage so have to fit David's routine in accordingly."

It is possible that you are worrying unnecessarily about your little boy's lack of appetite, since he appears so perfectly healthy and energetic: and there is no doubt that in the beginning it would have been better not to plead with him. It is understandable that you should be so anxious, and if there are any signs of his losing weight, or being in ill health because of the lack of appetite, you would be justified in coaxing him. But I wonder if you will not find it helpful to get some first-hand advice from the doctors who are engaged in the work of the Child Guidance Clinic in your part of the world? You could go to one of them, and perhaps take your little boy with you to see him as a private patient. I suggest them, however, because they do understand the psychological factors in the problem of feeding, just as in the difficulties of behaviour. It might be a real help to you, because they might be able to suggest ways in which you could change your handling of the boy in a way that would increase his appetite. Doubtless his teething has something to do with the difficulty, and it may be that you do not need to worry about it at all. I should not hurry to do anything at present until his teething is through. His routine sounds good and he seems happy and jolly with you. There is nothing much to worry about, but if you have any special difficulties at the time of the birth of the new baby, or if the appetite does not improve, it would be sensible to get some first-hand advice from someone who can inquire into all the details of the way you handle him, both in general and in the feeding difficulty.

The address of the clinic is: The Child Guidance Clinic, Sheep St, Birmingham.

A FEEDING PROBLEM

3 FEBRUARY 1937

"Irish Brian" writes: *"I would like your advice regarding my son aged nine and a half. I rather think, although cannot be sure, that the trouble arises from diet, and would be ever so grateful of you could give me some dinner menus. He dislikes potatoes so much that they make him heave very often. He likes them chipped or roasted in fat, but do you think that he should have them in that form every day? He will not eat any form of stew – even without vegetables – just shin and kidney and a very little water. He won't touch milk in any shape or form, except a milk jelly or Nestle's milk on Rice Krispies for breakfast. This, by the way, is the only cereal he will eat. Porridge, milk, milk puddings, suet puddings, etc., actually make him sick. He likes a mashed banana and greens of most kinds except cabbage. I am wondering how I on earth I can contrive dinners for a week on such a slender list, and am wondering also if bread would*

take the place of potatoes for dinner. He likes pancakes, a fried (not boiled) egg, sausages, roast meat or cold boiled meat, ham, tongue, beef, etc. He suffers from indigestion, but, of course, this is to be expected. He loathes fish, and you may think a lot of this is my fault, but from a baby of one year he would not eat certain things and would rather go without. He has been operated on for umbilical hernia when four, rupture when seven, and adenoids. He is now on the list for having his tonsils removed. All this, of course, has made it difficult to make him eat certain things which I know to be good for him. Despite all this, he is an extremely healthy, bonny child and most sturdy, his weight being most satisfactory. He is an expert dawdler! He will take from half an hour to an hour to dress or undress or preparing to practise his violin, all things he dislikes doing, but has abundant energy for anything he likes doing. This dawdling causes more unpleasantness than anything in the house, as, of course, it results ultimately in a mad rush, no time for things he should do."

Your boy seems to be getting enough of the different kinds of food to keep him healthy, and I would not worry over his difficulties of not eating. It is, of course, a practical problem for you, but I do not think you ought to be too concerned about it from the point of view of the boy's health. You say he has had feeding difficulties from the age of one year, and some emotional disturbance is probably being expressed in this way. The operations the boy has undergone will also have been an emotional shock to him, and may be a contributing cause in this present difficulty. These feeding difficulties are, however, quite common in children, and experience has shown over and over again that it is best not to force the child to eat food which he does not like. You say that certain foods actually make your boy sick, and the child really cannot digest food which is distasteful to him. With regard to the actual diet, let him take any particular food in the form in which he likes it. For instance, with milk, since he likes milk jelly or Nestle's milk or milk with Rice Krispies, let him have it in these ways. Does he like cream? If so, you could let him have a little cream with his mashed banana or, if he won't eat the cream, Nestle's milk. Or you could introduce the milk in a disguised form in savouries – soups and gravies and sauces. He might take it, for instance, in onion, celery, artichoke or tomato soup; but if he does not like these, it is possible to put a certain amount of milk into a gravy soup. Have you tried cocoa made with milk or part-milk? (When introducing a new form of food to the child, it is best to allow time to get used to the flavour. Give only a very small quantity at first and do not force the child to eat it, but say in a matter-of-fact way, "Perhaps you will like it when you get more used to the taste", and try it again on another occasion.) Since the boy likes chipped or roasted potatoes, I don't think they will do him any harm provided they are well cooked and tender. But he could have a slice of bread, preferably brown, with or without butter, with his meat for a change sometimes; or you could try him with Vita-Wheat or some kind of unsweetened (but not dull) biscuit. If he likes fried eggs, sausages, roast meat, cold boiled meat, greens and banana, milk in certain forms (and he may like it in some of the other forms I have suggested), I think he is getting enough nourishment. Have you tried a little liver? Let him have plenty of fruit; he would probably like fruit juice if not the fruit itself. The main thing, however, with regard to your own attitude in the matter is not to make a fuss, but to treat it in as matter-of-fact way as you can. I would not let the boy think that he is putting you to a great deal of trouble, or he may really tyrannise you in this respect. But I think you can introduce some changes and disguise the food without too much trouble. Could you have some of the boy's friends to meals with him sometimes? It is often found that children will eat things when they are with other children who enjoy their food, which they will refuse when alone in their own homes. But your boy is likely to outgrow some of his present dislikes; and he will do it all the more readily if you do not force him now to eat things which are distasteful.

With regard to the dawdling, it is best not to nag or keep on urging the boy to hurry, but to let him suffer the consequences of his delay – for example, if he were late for school. I notice you include his practising of the violin as among the things which he dislikes doing. It seems a pity that a thing like music, which can bring so much pleasure, should be regarded as a task. Would it not be possible to let him enjoy any music he can make, without regarding it as practising?

CHAPTER SIX

Jealousy and sibling rivalry

INTRODUCTION

Jealousy, for Wise, is part of the human condition and cannot be entirely avoided. It can be helped by being handled well. However, that way of thinking was not generally accepted in the 1930s, as can be seen in the debates about jealousy in the "Over the Teacups" column. Wise takes on the challenge of responding to this at length in "Prevention is better than cure".

As might be expected, the main area of concern for Wise's correspondents is that of jealousy associated with the arrival a new baby. While making plentiful suggestions as to how a young child might be prepared for a new baby, including referring to readers' suggestions, Wise also points out that young children cannot be made immune to jealousy. She considers just *how* much to say to a child in terms of preparation – knowledge will not safeguard against all jealousy.

At that time, too, as well as the arrival of the new baby there was also the issue of the extensive absence of the mother. It was not uncommon for middle-class women to spend several weeks in a nursing home when having a baby. A young child might go from spending the majority of the day with their mother to then being parted from her for three weeks, maybe more. Many of Wise's readers ask for advice about dealing with these lengthy separations.

Wise advises candidly about the needs of the child at such a difficult time of change, suggesting that "to ask adults to accommodate themselves to the emotional crises of little children is surely not difficult or unreasonable". Jealousy, however it might be expressed, is not something that a child should be blamed for or accused of but supported through, however inconvenient that might be for the adults. Allowing the child to feel and express what is "natural" about the baby is key, and important in enabling it to pass over time.

Wise, too, points out that hostility towards a new baby can be converted into hostility towards others – aggression towards a sibling can be transferred onto something or someone else. Similarly, feelings of jealousy can be experienced in a different form, such as guilt or showing an over-keen interest in the baby. Such manifestations are not so easily recognised as having their root cause in sibling rivalry. Jealousy can be diverse in its unconscious expression.

Wise offers some particularly intriguing advice to a family where there is a large degree of jealousy – advice, indeed, that is of its time and not likely to be given today!

In this selection of letters, there are passages where Ursula Wise speaks particularly beautifully about the relationship and love between carer and child – for instance, she refers to a 'mutual concern' between mother and child – one of many gracious turns of phrase that are moving to read.

DISPLACED

The emotional crisis faced by first children with the arrival of a new baby

2 JULY 1930

"Petal" writes: "I would much appreciate your advice about my little daughter, now aged twenty-two months. I have just returned home after three weeks' absence in a nursing home and where my baby son was born. Since my return, Audrey seems to whine and cry – real sobs and tears – if things are not quite to her liking, and if I bring her into the drawing room to see visitors we have quite an outburst. She has always been very shy, and would not go to strangers even when quite a baby, but I thought she was getting a little better.

She is very conservative, and does not like any new experiences, new toys or new faces, and she took some days before she would come near the new baby, but she is now very interested in him and not the least bit jealous. I had not been with her a great deal for some months, so she has not felt my absence.

Ordinarily, she is a cheerful, happy little person, and sits in her pen quite contentedly chatting to her toys, so she has not been spoilt or been the centre of attention. In fact, I wonder whether I have kept her too quiet. We live in a very quiet country village and do not have many visitors, but the grannies and the aunts think I ought not to pander to her idiosyncrasies, but I cannot make her if she does not want to. She is quite all right with people she knows, and not so bad with young people, but elderly people – usually large and dressed in dark garments – seem to inspire her with dread. I may say that my husband and I are very reserved people and do not shine in company, while I also was a very shy little girl, so do you think the trouble is hereditary? It used not be so bad when Audrey just sat speechless on my lap, as she usually brightened up sooner or later, but now she clutches me tightly and sobs, and I usually have to send her out of the room.

I shall be most grateful for your advice, as it seems such a problem. She is perfectly healthy and most independent in other ways."

I don't think there can be any doubt that the new baby is the immediate cause of the whining. Even though the child does not show jealousy in any open way, her querulousness is but a sign of the great effort she is making to deal with the situation. However careful and tender mother is, the little newcomer is bound to cause fears in the older child, and the fact that your little girl would not come near the baby for some time suggests how strong this was. It will take her a little time to accept the baby brother wholeheartedly, but as her direct interest in him develops, and as she finds that your own affection for her is as sure and warm as always, things will become a little easier for her.

But just for the present I should certainly not force her to see visitors who distress her. She is sure to be rather more sensitive all round just now, and fear every sort of change even more than she normally does. You want her to grow out of such excessive shyness, of course, and she probably will do in time; but she is more likely to do so if she is not forced to meet people who have no intrinsic appeal to her, or those who seem frightening to her – even if her fear does seem silly and unreasonable to the people themselves. I should choose rather carefully the grown-up friends who I did bring her in to see, and should arrange to send her out for a walk when someone was coming to the house of whom I thought she probably would be frightened. If she can make one or two really good friends among grown-ups, and her circle is gradually increased, she will gradually lose her fears and shyness and become much more at ease. If, however, you insist on her seeing anybody and everybody, including those who frighten her, the outbursts of fear and crying must tend to make her worse rather than better, as she is bound to feel ashamed and unhappy about it afterwards. And as the nervous ones among us grown-ups know, it isn't easy to feel happy and at home when we meet again people with whom we have already been social failures! Failure makes for failure, and nothing succeeds like success! So I should go slowly, and let her have a few really happy and agreeable friends, among the grown-ups. After all, she is no more than a baby herself yet!

And if a situation arises where you can hardly avoid her being brought in to see someone whom you know she does not feel at home with, I should let it be no more than a greeting, and send her back to play again after the briefest possible time.

JEALOUSY IS OFTEN THE CAUSE OF TEMPERS AND TANTRUMS

*The interesting problem of hostility and aggressiveness in children of varying ages from eighteen months to four years raised this week shows the type of difficulty with which **Ursula Wise** is so well qualified to deal. She is always pleased to hear from mothers and nurses*

8 JULY 1931

Three of the letters I am replying to this week all raise the same essential problem, although, of course, there are differences in detail. The problem is that of aggressiveness of one kind or other. In the little girl "Petro" writes about, the aggressiveness seems to be unusually open and marked, showing itself whenever the child is thwarted. With "R.D.A.'s" boy and "H.T.C.'s" little girl it seems to be definitely connected with jealousy, but the little girl, although so young, has somehow managed to deal with her hostility to her little brother, turning it on strangers and other children.

"H.T.C." writes as follows: "*I have so often read your advice to others in THE NURSERY WORLD, and now I am asking you to help me. My little girl, aged one year and ten months, has become very difficult to manage, owing, I expect, to jealousy, as she has a little brother of five months. At first she would hit him and start whining whenever I picked him up. I have not taken any notice of these fits, and never asked her to do anything for him, as I realised it only made her more angry. I am pleased to say this has been very effective, as she now asks to tuck him in and mind him for me. She also offers him her toys, although she does not like parting with them. The real problem now is that she absolutely refuses to have anything to do with strangers. If anyone says 'Good morning', or speaks to her at all, her reply is nearly always a very definite 'No, don't', or 'No, won't'. She screams if they touch her or try to pick her up.*

This has been going on for some months now; it started before baby was born. If I refer to it and tell her it is rude she is much worse. I have tried ignoring it for some time now, but she still carries on. It makes it rather difficult for me as she is rather attractive and has a lovely complexion, as she is always out in the open. We have a large garden with plenty to amuse her. She has a bunny and baby chickens, and is passionately fond of animals. She can point out any fruit tree in the garden and name it, as she is not at all backward.

I have tried having other children to play with her, but find she screams as soon as they go near her or touch her. She is quite all right as long as they don't speak to her. If strangers ignore her she will immediately start talking to them, but very few do ignore her; and it always means a scene, besides making people think she is spoilt. Her daddy makes a great fuss of her and is really very patient, and very rarely gets angry. She worships him, and is really very upset if he is cross, but often whines and carries on when he is there. Hazel knows that she is being naughty, as she often comes in from a walk and tells me 'a doggie said "No, don't", and he is rude'. It is very difficult to explain everything, but perhaps I have made it clear that she is continually having scenes when other people are near, and is quite capable of being exceedingly sweet and lovable."

It is clear that the little girl's first reaction to her brother was of open jealousy and direct hostility. These feelings, however, would be naturally frightening to the little girl herself, because she would at the same time have impulses of love and tenderness to him, and because she would be afraid of losing her mother's love if she showed her jealousy so openly. What, then, happened was that she turned her jealousy on to strangers, other grown-ups and children, and so freed her relation to her baby brother from this distressing emotion, and became wholly maternal towards him, tucking him up and taking care of him like a little mother.

Now, the problem is, what should be done about her attitude of fear and hostility towards strangers? Well, what I should do in such a situation is to leave her largely alone about it, trusting to her natural affection and her proved abilities to get over her less desirable impulses to carry her out of this difficulty too. I would leave *her* alone, but I would very definitely ask the grown-ups not to touch her or take any marked notice of her, telling them that if they would be just quiet and responsive she would be sure to talk to them and be friendly. She is quite certain to grow out of this in a year or two if her experiences with grown-ups are happy.

To ask adults to accommodate themselves to the emotional crises of little children is surely not difficult or unreasonable. What is the use of *our* superior self-control and politeness and reasonableness if we cannot exercise them to help little children over a stile? If we were talking to a friend who was in a temporary emotional difficulty of some sort – the loss of a loved one or some other trying circumstance – we should surely give them special consideration. We should not expect them to do and say exactly what we wanted them to. It is only with little children that we let ourselves be offended so readily when they cannot immediately respond to our advances. And, after all, what right have we to demand, any of us, that a child who doesn't know us should immediately like us and be friendly? If we want the friendship of a child we surely have to earn it, and we don't deserve it if we insist upon picking him up and talking to him the very moment we meet him. If, however, we can be just quiet and friendly in his presence he will very soon come and make the first advance, as "H.T.C." finds that her little girl does.

Whenever Hazel is going to meet quite new people it would be worthwhile just telling the strangers beforehand that if they leave her alone for a time she will be sure to make friends. She will then grow out of this particular difficulty as she becomes assured that grown-ups are friendly and understanding people. With other children, of course, it is not so easy, as one cannot very well explain to them as one could to grown-ups. But one could very often say, "Hazel will soon come and play with you if you leave her quiet for a time".

The way Hazel puts her naughtiness on to the doggie, saying it was the doggie who "was rude and said, 'No, don't'", shows how hard she is struggling with these impulses of fear and hostility. It is not an uncommon way of dealing with a feeling of naughtiness – quite ordinary in small children. I am sure you are right in feeling that she becomes worse if you tell her that she is rude not to be friendly with people, and I think you can rest quite secure that she will grow out of the difficulty with the sort of help I have suggested.

"Petro" writes: *"Thank you so much for the help you gave me with my small son. I am again venturing to ask your advice, this time about my baby girl. She is so different in nature to her baby brother; it hardly seems possible they are from the same family. What really worries me is her wilful temper. Almost her first little definite action was to throw out her hands and scratch and tear at anyone nearest her. Now, at the age of twelve and a half months, she is worse than ever. If anyone happens to touch a toy in her possession she immediately flings out to claw at them, and, if she cannot reach, she will scratch at her own face. Scolding does no good, but produces a scene of screaming and kicking. This is not only done when her temper is aroused. Sometimes while happily loving someone and stroking their face she will suddenly pinch and claw them in a most spiteful way. I am always afraid of holding her too close to another child for fear of him being hurt.*

We are so afraid, if given in to a nature so difficult, she will grow up a bad-tempered and self-willed child, and be disliked by friends as are all spoiled children. Once or twice I have tried tapping her hand, or rather more gently clawing back, other times ignoring it, all with no good results. She is healthy, generally happy, loves her toys, sleeps well, and is average weight, but is put into a wildest temper at the slightest provocation. If you could help me once again, I would be more than grateful."

Such clawing and scratching is by no means uncommon in infants, although it is more marked than usual in your little girl. Such a very fierce temper is, of course, difficult to deal with. I don't think it helps at all to hit the child's hand or claw back. But a firm protest against her hurting anyone else is another matter – not scolding, but simply saying quite firmly, "Please don't scratch". I don't think you ought to give her any more indulgence than normal because she feels denials so keenly, but I should, of course, make sure that any denials and thwartings that she did experience were soundly based on real necessity. Teasing, or really unkind handling, or severe reproaches and scolding would be no good whatever to such a child; they would only confirm her in her aggressiveness. She needs the constant sense of love in those around her, and firm, consistent handling. I think she may well become less aggressive and temperful as she gets a little older, with this sort of general care. If, however, she did not show more affection and amenableness by the time she was, say, two and a half or three, I think I would then suggest getting more direct advice on the basis of first-hand observation. If you will write to me again later on I shall, of course, be pleased to suggest someone who could give you this sort of help.

"R.D.A." writes: "I have read with very much interest your articles in THE NURSERY WORLD, which I am sure must have helped numerous people with the management of their children. I should be so grateful for your advice on how to manage my small son, who is going through a phase of throwing things at us, either when he is told he cannot do something he wants to do or when we are trying to make him do something he refuses to do. John was four years old at the end of March. He is a highly strung and very intelligent child. About two years ago he was very ill with intestinal poisoning,[1] which went on for six months. When I say 'very ill' I do not mean he was in bed. He lived his ordinary routine, but was dieted and never had normal motions. I took him, in the end, to a

---

1 Whorton (2000, pp. 83–85) argues in his book *Inner Hygiene: Constipation and the Pursuit of Health in Modern Society* that fears of the ill-effects of "intestinal stasis" (constipation) resulting in "autointoxication" were rife throughout the 1920s, abetted by patent medicine advertisements for powerful laxatives in print and on the radio.

specialist in London, who advised me to let him go to St Mary's home. They cured him there, and he has steadily improved in health ever since, and really looks awfully well. He is of the tall, thin kind. This doctor in London told me to keep him from getting over-excited as much as we possibly could and not to allow him to go to children's parties. We have done this; but I wish there were more children of his own age around here he could meet when he is out, and have to tea. The few there are, are much younger, but he is very interested in them. I have a young Norland nurse[2] of whom John is very fond, and who understands and manages him very well now. While he was ill I had a nurse who was terribly 'nervy' and who could not manage him at all. This, I am sure, reacted on John, and affected him badly. John is the only child, but I am going to have another baby this month, which I told him some time ago, and he seems awfully pleased about it, and talks about the toys he is going to give 'baby sister'.

This throwing business started quite recently. This morning when my nurse told John it was time to get up and go to his bath (warm water first then a cold sponge) he wouldn't, and then threw a little dispatch case he was playing with, full of toys, at her. They went all over the floor, and of course, she made him pick them up, and, as it was late, she said he must go without his bath. (He has a warm bath at night as well, of course.) If he is thwarted he will throw whatever he has in his hand, a stick, or a shoe, and one day he hit a nurse with a pramstrap across the shins, and hurt her, as the buckle caught her. He is very sorry afterwards if he hurts anyone, and is very kind and fond of animals – in fact, he hates to see anyone or anything hurt. He throws things, I think, only at nurse and myself. I do not think he has thrown anything at my husband, who, by the way, can manage him very well, and when nurse is out and John is being very obstreperous, my husband can usually make him do as he tells him, and John knows this.

My husband, however, thinks that when he throws things at one he ought to be given a good spank immediately he has done it (by

2 Norland nannies were trained at Norland College, founded in 1892 by Emily Ward. Originally the college provided day care and boarding facilities for infants, and was a training college for nannies. The college is now based in Bath and is solely a provider of child-care education and training.

him), and then say and do nothing more about it. Do you agree with this or not? Have you known this phase to pass, or does it continue usually and become worse as he gets older? I am so afraid he might throw dangerous missiles at other children later on in life if he isn't checked now. It is the same idea as when he smacks us when thwarted, and he is then nearly crying, but tries hard not to. I suppose it is his defence against us. He is such a darling really and very friendly, and awfully sweet to me about my not running about as usual, and lifting heavy things. We are not living in our own house at present, but with mother, and other grown-ups do make him excited and more difficult to manage. In many things he is so sensible and independent. The throwing started when we were not here, but by ourselves. The last few weeks he has had a pimply rash on his face, not bad. We have given him something for this; also my dentist tells me that his first back permanent teeth are already beginning to swell up in the gums, which, of course, is very early. I know all this must make him feel irritable. John adores playing football, cricket and bat and ball, at which, for his age, I think he is really quite good."

Here we have quite a complicated picture. The intestinal poisoning must, of course, contribute to the irritability both directly and indirectly, and the other physical troubles at present will certainly act on John's temper too. In spite of John seeming so pleased about the baby sister, there is probably some fear and potential rivalry, and, as you realise yourself, the situation is always more difficult for children when there are so many grown-ups around. Bearing all these things in mind, I should not be too distressed about the present phase of throwing things. I don't think I would spank the child for it, but I would firmly express my straightforward displeasure and ask him not to do it. With a child who is otherwise loving and genuinely sorry if he has hurt, and who lives in a happy environment where he is loved and understood, there is really no risk of him going on doing these things in a dangerous way when he is older.

It is quite a common and a natural reaction for children to pick something up and throw it when they are angry. If he were entirely neglected, or if he were severely treated, then it might be dangerous later. But it doesn't sound to me in the least likely that this will be so with John. On the other hand, I would not put too much strain on

him by demanding consideration for yourself beyond what is reasonable to expect from a little boy of four, or by expecting him to
express loving sentiments towards the baby that is to come. Let him
be natural about it and feel that he can show his rivalry in words
if he feels it very strongly. And, above all, let him have lots of big
boys' games, like the cricket and football, which I think are excellent outlets for his emotions and a very promising tendency in his
development. In other words, I should in general treat him as much
as possible as a big boy, being firm when he is unreasonable, but giving him courtesy and respect in general, and letting him have lots of
fun and companionship with other boys away from the atmosphere
of the nursery.

THE EX-BABY

*The arrival of a new baby always causes conflict in the mind of
the child he has displaced, and unless the situation is handled
understandingly, contrariness and bad temper often result*

16 MAY 1934

I have two letters this week that raise much the same problem, and
may be answered together.

*"B.E." writes: "My little girl of four simply will not behave herself at
the table. Before her baby sister came a year ago she was perfect, sat
nicely and needed no correction. If I have visitors she is much worse,
talks the whole time and throws her arms about and is thoroughly
naughty and will not do as she is told. How can I get her to eat and
behave well at meal times? She has always been so good until the
last year, and so sweet tempered and so happy, but now she seems
quite the reverse, and is always whining and crying. At one time, she
would play for hours and be contented all day. She is kept to a certain time on everything, but now she seems not to know what to do
with herself. I know she is older and perhaps needs something different to do, as before she would amuse herself with almost anything.
What toys, etc., should she need? She is really still a very lovable
child, as when she is tiresome and naughty, she always says, 'I never
mean to be naughty', and 'I'll never do it again'. But she seems to*

forget. She is nervous and highly strung and gets easily tired. She has always been difficult to feed, never wanting anything much, and I have never fussed about it, but just taken the food away. Also, how do you advise me to act in the case of a baby of one year who gets in a temper?"

"E.M.A." writes: "Will you kindly give me your help with my four-year-old daughter, who, up to the age of three years, was a perfect child and such a good baby, no trouble, was most contented, cheerful and very obedient and was always happy. At three years she had a baby sister and was not at the time at all jealous; she was told about the baby before its birth and was most happy at her arrival. But now she has completely changed, will not do a thing she is told without a lot of fuss, and is continually naughty, and I seem to be always correcting her. She had always gone to bed splendidly at 6 p.m. without a light up to the age of three and a half years, but now she is frightened of the dark and always calling me, and wakes once or twice during the night. She is rather a nervous child and highly strung. I do hope you will be able to help me, as we should so love to see her again the obedient and happy-natured child she was. Could you also tell me the sort of toys a child of this age requires? She has always played happily by herself up to now, but at present seems to need other things to amuse her."

It is clear that each of these little girls is suffering from very acute conflict about the birth of the baby sister, and is quite unable to deal with her feelings of rivalry and inferiority. Neither of these mothers tell me just how the elder child was prepared for the birth of the baby and dealt with at the time. "E.M.A." says her little girl was told about the baby before its birth, but as so much of my correspondence on this problem has shown, it is not so much the mere telling that helps the child, as the way in which the whole situation is handled. The knowledge that a baby is coming will not help her very much if, when it arrives, she has plenty of reason for feeling shut out of things and lost and neglected.

I do not say that either "B.E." or "E.M.A." have done this with the child, but both letters do strongly suggest that the natural and inevitable jealousy of the older child has not been sufficiently allowed for, and ways of getting her to feel she has a part in the new baby have not been found. It would be a great help to both children if the mother could give a definite period of each day entirely to the child for play and talk and mutual concern. And it would be very helpful if ways could be found of letting the child feel that she can share in the baby sister, help with the bathing and dressing and feeding and be allowed to ask questions. The right sort of toys and play material would also help her, but what would be the most valuable for her can only be found out by experiment. It is possible, for example, that a baby doll of her own of a good size, with clothes that would take on and off, and a pram to take her out in, would be a great help. Others are more helped by having a puppy or kitten of their own. Others, again, by being shown how to make something that a baby sister could use; for example, to sew some beads on a coloured coverlet, or to wash one or two of the baby's garments in a bowl with soap-suds on a low stool, where splashing would do no harm. All the ordinary child's toys, dolls and dolls' house and pram, etc., are a help in a crisis of this kind, but especially so if, for one period of each day, the mother will share in the child's play with her doll baby, and allow the little girl to play the part of the mother and the hostess.

The difficulty about the child's naughtiness when visitors come could be helped if, occasionally, the child were allowed to give a tea-party all of her own, and receive visitors and act as the hostess; sometimes a real one with little girl friends, or even pleasant-mannered grown-ups, who would for the occasion adapt themselves to the little girl's needs and allow themselves to be *her* guests; sometimes with a toy tea-set, a mother and an aunt or two or three dolls to be her guests. There are endless ways in which we can meet the need of the child to get rid of the feeling that she is unimportant and shut out – neither a baby nor a mother. Entering into the child's play and letting her not merely assume important parts in play, but have occasional real responsibility, for example, as a hostess, would help to adjust the balance that has been upset. These little girls are rather young for sewing material, but they could use large darning needles, threaded with bright wool, to sew soft material and make dolls' garments or real aprons and coverlets, etc. They love threading coloured beads, and washing real things in soap-suds and water, ironing with a play iron and doing all the things that help them to identify themselves with mother and nurse.

With regard to the fit of temper of a baby of one year, there is only one thing to do – to remain quiet and calm until the temper has passed. All healthy babies of this age get into occasional tempers. One needs to find out what has caused it, whether the situation can be avoided, but, above all to realise it itself is a normal thing, part of the child's normal growth. There is no need to do anything but remain quiet and pleasant until the fit passes and then just go on with whatever has to be done, never letting the child feel that she has committed a serious crime by showing temper.

THE NEW BABY

Jealousies and the behaviour problems consequent upon them are bound to arise when a second child is born. The wise Mother prepares the elder child for the event

30 OCTOBER 1935

This week I am dealing with two letters which raise the question of how to prepare a child for the advent of another baby. In addition to those which I quote, I have letters from "Nannie of One" and "Anxious" on the same subject, but have no room to quote this week.

"O.D." writes: "I would be glad of some advice in dealing with the problem of the 'new baby'. My little boy will be three and a half when the second child arrives in the autumn. I'm afraid he may feel the change in the family life rather acutely as he has been so much alone with me. His father is away all day, and it is only recently that we have even had a maid with us, except in the mornings, so that he is rather a 'mummie's boy'. However, he thinks babies are dear little things, and is pleased that we are going to have one of our own. He says he is going to help bath it and dress it. He asked me a great many questions about where it was coming from, so I have explained a good deal of this. What is really worrying me is that I have to go to a nursing home for the event and I am afraid that W. will be very upset at my leaving him. He is used to being left with Granny for an afternoon occasionally; but if he knew I was not coming back at bedtime he would be very distressed. Would it be best to say nothing about not coming back that day, and leave him to get used to it gradually? I thought of leaving a parcel with a new toy in it to distract his attention when he first begins to worry about my absence.

What would be the best attitude for Granny and his father to adopt if he keeps on asking for me? I thought of telling him that I have to go to a nursing home for the baby to be born because it will be so little at first and will need a doctor and nurse to look after it, but that very soon it will be strong enough for us to look after ourselves. Would it be a good idea for him to have a photo of me in the nursery while I am away and for me to write him little post-cards from time to time, or would it be better for him not to be reminded of me? I intend to come home as soon as I can get up – after a fortnight, I hope, and have a nurse in the house for a week or two. I imagine that a child must not be allowed to think that the baby has made his mother ill? But as I am bound to spend the mornings in bed at first, would it be all right to explain that mothers are a little tired after growing a baby? I must apologise for all these questions, but I shall be very grateful for any advice you can give me as I am very anxious for W. not to feel more jealousy than can be helped."

"H.E.D." writes: *"Perhaps you would be good enough to tell me what general steps to take to prevent what appears to be the inevitable awkwardness of a three-year-old when her baby brother or sister is born. D is already (about a month before) going through a nervy phase, which I partly blame to an attack of measles which, though very light, was a bad experience for her as she had been lucky enough never to have to stay in bed for even one day before. She is quarrelsome with other children, wanting her own way all the time, and has become afraid of noisy motorbikes, trains and large animals, such as horses, cattle and large dogs. We have discussed the new arrival in the hopes of sparing her the disappointment that the new baby will be rather useless as a playmate for some while. She is most interested in learning that she was very new once, and is always asking to be told about what happened when nurse was here to bath her, etc. I have wondered if she is already subconsciously jealous of the new arrival. Are all first children awkward when a second arrives, or can this trouble be avoided?"*

There is no method by which we can *altogether* prevent the first child's feeling of jealousy. Jealousy is too deeply rooted in human nature for such a typical and essential situation as the arrival of a new baby not to evoke it. But we can certainly make it very much harder for the child to bear, or help him to master his jealousy, by the way we prepare him beforehand and deal with him afterwards. It is always worth telling the child that a new baby is coming, because he then feels that he is not shut out of the magic circle of the love between his parents. It lessens the frightening sense of mysterious events in which he can have no part, as well as increasing his sense of love and confidence in his parents. It is worthwhile answering any of the questions that he may put as to where the baby is coming from and how it begins to grow, for the same reasons. It is doubtful whether we can give the young child much real understanding of what happens, however, even if we should wish to. Very often we find that children of ten or twelve years who were told quite fully about the birth of babies when they were small are just as ignorant of the matter as children who have been brought up on stories of gooseberry bushes and storks. But it is equally true that children who were told about things have benefited, not through *knowledge*, but through the sense of sharing with their parents and trust in them. They do not get so strongly a feeling of secrecy and evasion on the part of the parents. The idea of telling the children the truth about babies, however, will not work as a panacea for all ills; it will not solve all the child's problems. A sense of proportion has to be kept about this, as about everything else to do with the education of children. If the child prefers not to ask questions or shows reluctance to talk about the matter, it is best not to force explanations upon him. But this is very seldom the attitude of the quite small child. It is shown more often by the child of over six or seven. The small child who has an affectionate relation with his mother does not feel privileged and pleased to be told by her about the event, since he will in any case have surmises and wonderings about the changes he sees in his mother and in her activities and plans. With regard to the best way of dealing with the actual arrangements for the birth, e.g., the mother's leaving for the nursing home and having to be careful of her health when she returns, "O.D.'s" suggestions are all excellent. "O.D." has evidently realised how lost a little child may feel when the mother leaves home in this way, and how much it will help him to have constant and solid proofs of her continued love and interest in him. The plan of leaving the parcel with a letter and a new toy in it, and of letting him have a photograph and sending him postcards are all excellent. It will certainly be far better to do this than to leave him without any reminder. There is certainly no reason why children should not be told that that mothers want a little extra rest after growing a baby, and need the help of doctors and nurses to achieve so important an event. As regards the actual day of leaving, it probably would be best with so young a child not to tell him beforehand, but leave a little note behind and a picture or toy for him.

The same steps would be very helpful for "H.E.D.'s" little girl. I have no doubt that the child is already aware of some impending change, although her feelings and ideas about it will hardly be conscious. She will, however, get over the difficulty if she is sure of the mother's continued affection and interest, by consideration along the lines suggested.

THE PROBLEM OF JEALOUSY

... between the ex-baby and the baby who displaces him is a common cause of trouble in the nursery

7 MARCH 1934

"G.B." writes: "Last week I wrote to a daily paper regarding my two little boys, and they advised me to write to you. They are aged six years and two months and three years and ten months, and were quarrelling rather a lot. That, however, has improved a little, as the elder recommenced school last Monday (mornings) and my maid tells me that they have agreed very well while out in the afternoons. I would still like advice, as the elder teases the younger, who does not seem able to stand it. Do you think I should interfere? I do so now, and am wondering does the little one make a fuss to draw my attention? They are rather rough, and I am always correcting them. Do you think this is necessary? I have often smacked them, but have decided not to do so anymore, and already they seem to be better for it. Do you agree with me in this? I think the elder boy is sometimes jealous of the younger, as he is rather peevish and irritable with him. I do not make any distinction between them, so am wondering could you suggest something to make him less peevish? Also, he is very rarely asleep before 8.30, although he is nearly always in bed before 7.15. I warm the spot where his feet will be, as he very often said his feet were cold. I have also tried giving him something to eat; now he

*has only a warm drink, but still, whatever I do he remains the same,
and always has been. The elder always awakens first between 7 and
7.30. He is very quick at school, his teacher says unusually so, and I
wonder is his brain too active to allow him to go to sleep? Then, too, I
leave the bedroom door open, and I have to keep a light on the landing which shines into their room, so wonder has that anything to do
with it? Between tea and bath time they play with bricks, trains, and
all that type of toy, as Daddy is at home just then and he won't allow
them to be noisy while he is in as he really comes across for a rest; so
they don't get over-excited before bedtime. Whatever the cause, it is
something that doesn't affect the younger. But he is the stolid type
and the elder is excitable. I feel sure that ten and a half hours' sleep
is not enough for a six-year-old."*

It seems as if you were worrying unduly about the question of your
boy's sleep. Children do differ in the amount of sleep that they need
or can take, and whilst I should certainly do everything to help him
to sleep, I don't think you need worry so much about it. If his feet
tend to be cold, why not give him a hot water bottle? Nobody can
sleep with cold feet whatever the coldness is due to. Doubtless your
elder boy is jealous of the younger one, and has been so from the
time of the latter's arrival. You are certainly wise in not smacking the
boys, since that is not a helpful way of dealing with their difficulties.
How does your elder boy spend his afternoon? Does he get out for
open-air exercise? If they have an enforced quiet time between tea
and bed, he certainly needs to spend every moment of the afternoon
interval in outdoor exercise. Also this should be of the free kind, not
just soberly walking, but running and jumping and ball games, or
digging and playing on the beach. If his school has outdoor sports
in the afternoon, as some schools do, it might be a very good thing
to let him join in with these. But I am sure it is very important that
that afternoon time should be one of free outdoor activity, so that he
is thoroughly satisfied and healthily fatigued when bedtime comes.
The quarrelling of the two brothers, as you have seen from your
experience, is most easily helped by giving the elder one a life of his
own with the boys of his own age. He will be more easily able to be
friendly to the younger brother when he is with him if he has plenty
of opportunities for games and exercise and friendship away from
him. The two problems you put to me seem to be interconnected, and

whatever you do to help the child's relation with his brother is also likely to relieve the sleeplessness.

JEALOUSY

29 MARCH 1933

"S.I.C." writes: "*May I ask your kind advice on a problem of jealousy? I have three children, two girls of eight and a half and five and a half, M. and E., and a boy of two and a half, F. I have always had trouble with M. over jealousy of E. from when the latter was a baby. Owing to the help I got from a psychologist, we quite cured this for a time by never making a fuss of E. in front of M., and by showing M. plenty of affection and never scolding her for teasing. As E. is a very attractive golden curly-haired little person, we have constantly had to be on guard against this, and two new nurses who came had trouble with M. at first with her teasing, until I explained matters to them. M. is very fond of a few people who she knows really love her, but she does not show affection as readily as E., whom everyone seems to love at once.*

Recently I have had to leave them with an aunt, and the same situation has arisen, as she adores E., and their nurse writes to me that this is again causing jealousy and teasing. The particular occasion was when their aunt took E. to sleep with her, owing to a cold. When she returned again to the nursery the teasing stopped. M. also said to her nurse, 'Why does aunty love E. so much more than me?' Now, throughout life, these two are not always going to have a mother or nurse who understands this problem. M. is a very sensible, intelligent child. When I am with her again, do you think I could now discuss the matter openly with her, explain the misery that a jealous nature is to anyone, tell her that she must try to control it? She and her sister play very happily together when there is none of this feeling, but you would not call them devoted. M.'s father is devoted to her, and she is a constant companion to him, and I do my very utmost to show her all the affection I can, and yet I have the feeling that I must never show affection to E. in front of M., which is so unnatural. Also, what should I reply when M. says to me, 'Which do you love best, E. or me?' I generally reply, 'I don't love one of you more than the other, but as you are the eldest I've loved you longer'.

Do you think it would be wise when school age comes to send them to separate schools? Although here the advantage would be on M.'s side as she is much more intelligent than her younger sister, allowing for the difference in age. But this might give E. too much of a sense of inferiority."

It is always a difficult situation when there is a child who suffers such uncontrollable jealousy, and another who is naturally so attractive that she gains everybody's natural affection and interest without any trouble. These situations are always so cumulative. The attractive child whom people naturally love has no motive for jealousy or peevishness. She has only to be her own sunny self and she gets all the care and attention she wants. The other child suffers the sense that people do in fact prefer the other child, and are aware of her jealous attitude and less attractive personality, even if she does succeed in controlling open shows of jealousy. Undoubtedly one helpful solution to this problem is that of separating the children, wherever occasion allows. After all, they are not likely in adult life to be in situations which would arouse these feelings in quite the same way, and this can be off-set against the other fact that you mention, namely, that she will not always have considerate nurses and mothers who will avoid stimulating the child's jealousy. I should certainly send them to separate schools. It would be very unwise to perpetuate the rivalry between them in school as well as in the home. If M. can develop her own friendships and her own circle of activities she will have least provocation towards the jealousy. I think I should go on trying to avoid open demonstrations of affection to the younger child in front of the elder. It is quite true that in a sense that is unnatural, but M.'s jealousy is *natural* enough. If we are expecting her to control her feelings of jealousy, surely we can expect ourselves to control our natural impulses towards open affection with a younger child. I think your reply to her question about whom you love best is quite a good one. But of course it is not easy to satisfy jealous enquiries of this kind, since the child is perfectly well aware that she is not so lovable as the other. I would again emphasise the wisdom of sending them to separate schools, so as to lessen the acuteness of the rivalry and give each child the chance to develop her own life independently.

JEALOUSY IN THE NURSERY

2 MARCH 1932

She appears to adore her brother but is secretly eaten up with jealousy

"*Jealous*" writes: "*I have read many of your interesting articles, and hope you may able to help me with the problem of how to treat my little girl's temper and jealousy. The girl is now six and a half years old and her brother one year, so there is a big difference in age. Her trouble is two-fold – terrible tempers and jealousy of the baby. She has always been rather hard to manage, and being an only child with few companions, living in the country, I sent her to school from the age of four and a half.*

She is very happy and gets on well. She is a quick and most amusing child and was, of course, made much of before the baby's arrival. She appears to adore her brother and keeps saying how lovely it is to have such a nice baby, but she is secretly eaten up with jealousy. She has no reason for this as, except for occasional walks with nurse,

it is I who looks after her entirely, and have done ever since she was four. In the drawing room in the evening she can never leave the baby to play alone, but must always be interfering and so keep in the limelight. If her daddy is there, which is not often, and wants to play with the baby, it is most trying to see her fling herself on him in a way she would not do otherwise. We have tried, in vain, explaining that the baby has his 'play time' with us, and when he has gone hers will come, but she continues to interfere. To get her own back we have found her hitting the child, so had to forbid her the nursery for a week unless Nurse or I were there. A few weeks after this she again hit him. Then her tempers, I feel, are subconsciously forced so as to have more notice taken of her. They have been terrible lately and are thoroughly getting on my nerves. She is not in good health at the moment, which makes it worse, as I feel sure she will be less cross when her physical being is better, but I feel that too much spoiling is making her worse. She had a bad cold and septic spots in December, and no sooner was she better than she had a bronchial cold, from which she has not quite recovered. She fusses over all her food and has no appetite, despite a tonic. She argues incessantly and will take no answer or reason for any refusal, and gets into a terrible rage, kicking the door and yelling. I usually put her in a room by herself to scream, telling her when she is quiet she can come back. She frequently comes back and continues the argument, which seems amazing to me for a child of her age. She is very rude to me, too. I sometimes take no notice of her nagging at me, and then, too, she flies into a rage. Some months ago, when in a bad temper, her Daddy gave her a beating, which usually did her good for a long time, but as she is not well we have refrained. I was at the end of my tether yesterday and did give her a smack, and the result was terrible. As soon as I can I will send her back to school, for I am sure she will be better then. She suffers from boredom, having no resources of her own. She is very independent and good at doing jobs around the house, but I cannot keep her busy with them all the time. Perhaps my attitude is wrong as I never refer to her naughtiness and try to be quite pleasant after the tempests. She is rather a hard-hearted little thing and never comes to say she is sorry. On days when she has been good she frequently asks if she has been good! I am sure the shrieking is often forced as my neighbour came yesterday in the midst of a storm, and when the child heard her she stopped quite abruptly!"

From what you say, I rather get the impression that your little girl would do better with distinctly firmer handling. I don't, of course, mean whipping, but I do mean firm control, and I do even mean showing displeasure when she is either unkind to the baby or tempestuous. After all, she is six and a half, so it is not like handling a child of two or three. One can really demand a good deal more self-control for a child of six and a half, and, moreover, a child of this age often thrives better if she is more firmly handled. It is, of course, quite certain that these tempers and uncontrollable jealousy spring from very deep anxieties in her own mind which would repay psychological treatment. But, nevertheless, it is also true that a child who is suffering such anxieties is often helped more by having rather high standards of behaviour demanded of her and being controlled rather firmly than if she lives in an easy-going environment. If, for instance, she will not let the baby have his play time with you and her Daddy, on the understanding that she has a full measure of you both when he has gone to bed, then I think I would say that she could not be there with him. I wonder whether perhaps she feels that you demand that she should say, "How lovely it is to have such a nice baby". It may be that her saying this is partly to cover up her jealousy, but also partly to make herself *feel* nice by *saying* nice things. I assume that you won't demand that she should say these things. All you can demand is that she should control her hostility so as not to hit the child or to interfere with his play. Let her feel that while you don't condemn her for the jealousy, you nevertheless expect her to control its worst expressions. I wonder whether you ever give her opportunity to help with the baby herself – to take him out or help bath him, or get his things ready for a meal. It is quite possible that this might be a very good thing, as it will give her a chance to make up for her jealousy and show her that you believe in her power of making good. Of course, you do make allowances for her physical illness. Her irritability and lack of control are bound to be worse when she is unwell. I don't think I would ignore her nagging at you, but should respond to that quite firmly. Of course, I would make sure that my demands upon her were reasonable, and that I did not nag her in turn. I think it is quite likely that she is trying to provoke you into being angry, and the more definite expression of your displeasure at an earlier stage might really be a greater help to her than letting her go on until you do lose your temper. But I am sure you are right in wanting to get her back to school. It may very well be that she really cannot manage her jealousy at home.

PREVENTION IS BETTER THAN CURE

The "jealousy" question is discussed this week by Ursula Wise

25 DECEMBER 1935

"P.C.E." writes: "Acting on the theory that prevention is better than cure, I am writing to you for advice. I have one small boy of just two years two months, and am expecting a second child at the end of February, when he will be two and a half years. He has always been such a good tempered and easy child to manage and exceptionally good at night, that I am anxious to do all I can to prevent upsets at the second child's arrival. Perhaps you may be interested in his life up to date. He was breast-fed until eight and a half months and took the usual five weeks over weaning. I have always looked after him myself with the exception of an odd three weeks or more when I have had a temporary nurse for holidays (always the same one). Last month we left him in her charge while we were away for ten days. She came a week before we went, and he was perfectly happy with her and very good. Now I am hoping to get a nice girl as nurse-housemaid to help with him, so that he may have got quite used to her by February. He is not a great eater and I do not force him. He is very small weighing only twenty-three and a-half pounds, but as my husband's family are all very slight, I do not worry, especially as he is so fit and full of energy. He did not walk till twenty months and has not a very big vocabulary, but understands all that is said to him. He rather resented weaning and showed it by refusing to allow anyone but myself to give him milk to drink – not even my maid, of whom he is very fond, although he will let her bath him, etc. Now we are over the difficulty as he holds his own cup – also he has fed himself since twenty-one months. We have not had any bad 'pot' troubles, he is dry in the day mainly by being held out at regular intervals as he will not ask for it. I suppose he will in time: also, he will not use it if it is placed on the floor – only if he has it on my lap. He is a very contented child and plays by himself – he has the run of our small garden for about an hour each morning. He has a sand *pit, but the novelty has rather worn off; also, I hope to get a climbing frame for him later. He is very fond of children of all sizes and has several small friends (all boys by coincidence) and meets them quite often for tea, etc. I shall be at home for confinement and am having the same nurse as before. He knows her, as she visits us quite often. My chief problem seems to be later when I shall be more occupied with the baby's feeds, etc. I want to do as much as I can for him so that he will not feel slighted. Bath time seems to be difficult – at present he is bathed at 5.45 and goes to sleep immediately after or at any rate lies quietly without crying or having to be sat with. If he is still put to bed at that time, when I would be able to bath him and the nurse-maid the baby, it will mean that he will be disturbed later by the baby who would not be ready till about 6.20 or later. I am so anxious not to spoil his excellent habit of settling down so well. Would it be better not to put him to bed till 6 p.m. so that he could help with the baby's bath, although it would mean that I would not be able to bath him for some months? The nursemaid would have to bath him at that time. Would this make him jealous unnecessarily? I would be so grateful for any advice you can give me to prevent the upsets I so often read of in THE NURSERY WORLD, following the arrival of a brother or sister."*

I have chosen this letter to reply to this week because I have been very interested in the letters in "Over the Teacups" protesting against the notion that one should assume that the child will be jealous when a new baby comes. It is not clear what correspondents who write about this imagine the harm in such an assumption to be. It seems to be vaguely suggested that if it is taken for granted that a child will be jealous, that will make him so, or perhaps that some sort of moral injustice is being done him by expecting him to be. And, of course, I agree that if we make this assumption in a clumsy way and show the child that we are expecting him to behave in a bad or disagreeable way, we certainly shall not help him. Moreover, I do agree that there are plenty of children who do not show their jealousy in any direct or obvious way. Sometimes they show it by an exaggerated, fussy affection, one that is likely to break down into teasing or tormenting at any time. Sometimes they show it by being off colour themselves, unwilling to eat or to play, or by being more fractious and liable to tantrums. There are children of so sunny a temperament and who are so well handled that the natural jealousy is mastered very quickly, without any strain. Such children are very fortunate, and it is fairly safe to say that where this happens, mothers and nurses are wise and understanding people. It may not always be easy to say precisely what method of handling has helped a child. More important than anything else is the attitude of the mother or nurse; the even justice and calm unbroken consideration for all the children equally, the ready sympathy and constant love. If a child has a mother or nurse who shows all these qualities by nature, without having to turn to any theorists or, anybody else's advice, then the child is likely to get over the rivalry with another child with the least possible friction. But many letters I have published in these columns show that this does not always happen. It is an advantage to be prepared for the possibility of open or indirect signs of jealousy on the part of the child, because then one is not so likely to over-emphasise the naughtiness of such feelings and to make it harder for her. One is not likely to treat the child's behaviour as abnormal. It is much better to recognise that such feelings do occur with very great frequency, and are perfectly natural but that we can help the child to get over them by consideration and unswerving love and care. The element of justice must be given due weight. It does not really help a child to neglect the baby for her. She is often made guilty and unhappy by this just as much as by the fear that the mother loves the baby best. All-round consideration and steadiness of affection is what the child really needs. It does help her if the mother can convey her understanding of the child's feelings, as well as her conviction that the child will learn to love the baby and to overcome her hostility.

In the case of "P.C.E.'s" little boy of just over two, the fact that he is very fond of other children already is a very good sign. Even if he does have a little difficulty at first, he is very likely to be able presently to find pleasure in the companionship of the new baby. I have no doubt, too, that it will be a help rather than a hindrance that the confinement is taking place at home. I do not know what the general evidence is, and wish people would take notes about it from their own experience and that of their friends, but I think it is quite likely that the child is more disturbed when the mother goes away from home for her confinement. It seems to me a greater loss, and he is, in fact, much more cut off from her. When the confinement is at home, he can see his mother and the baby within a few hours, and at more frequent intervals. It is also a great help that the maternity nurse is already a friend of the little boy. There seem to be many helpful points in the circumstances of this child.

With regard to his bath-time, it would probably be better on the whole to let him help with the baby's bath and see the baby put to bed first, since that will give him a sense of privilege and being the older boy. On the other hand, the fact that the nursemaid will have to bath him may be a disadvantage. If he does show distress at not being bathed by his mother, there is no reason why she should not try the other plan. There is no reason, indeed, why she should not make occasional change in one direction the another; but as he does let the maid bath him, it may work out all right. I do not know whether "P.C.E." saw the wise suggestion made in these columns by one mother a year or two ago, who pointed out that it was very hard if the older child made the first acquaintance of the baby, and had the first sight of the baby after the confinement, with the baby in the mother's arms, or at any rate if the mother looked down at the baby, instead of at the older child perceptibly; when he came into the room. On the whole, it would probably be better to let the nursemaid hold the baby and introduce it to the other child, leaving the mother free to give him a few minutes of affection and caresses. A child is bound to know that something has been going on that is painful for the mother, and will be anxious about her. A few minutes quite direct communion with the older child will be a great help to him, and he can then be introduced to the rival baby, and even allowed to hold it for a moment. After this, throughout the next few weeks, he should be allowed to share in everything that concerns the baby as far as possible, and to talk about his feelings freely.

WHEN CHILDREN ARE JEALOUS

20 MAY 1931

"Lynette" writes: *"I am writing to ask if you can give me any help-ful suggestions regarding my eldest son, Peter, aged nearly seven. He is becoming more and more 'difficult', and I am really at a loss as to the best way to manage him. He seems to have a particularly aggravating quality which upsets and irritates everyone with whom he comes into contact! It is very difficult to explain briefly, but I will*

try to do so. For instance, he takes not the slightest notice of any reproof or suggestion to do anything unless spoken to with a distinct air of command. He teases his brother, aged four, unmercifully, and delights in getting him into a temper. (I suppose this is fairly normal in itself, but it is very trying, as it invariably leads to 'scenes' and when the younger boy retaliates with angry words and blows – also very difficult to deal with justly!) Peter always wants the toy Roy is playing with, and is not satisfied until he has taken it from his little brother – if two identical engines, for instance, were given the two of them, I think he would still covet Roy's. I believe he is really very jealous at heart, much more of Roy than the third child, a baby of sixteen months. Of course, Roy is taken a considerable amount of notice of, as he is rather an attractive person and seems to have 'a way with him'. But Peter never gets left out of any treats that are planned, in fact he gets outings Roy is too young to share – such as a day at his grandparents', or going out to tea perhaps. Last week we took him to the cinema for the first time, and Roy had to stay at home.

Another difficulty with Peter is that he really does not seem to mind being punished. I have tried all kinds of punishments, sending him to his bed, depriving him of sweets, etc. Whipping, I am sure, merely hardens him. He will listen with a heart-rending expression of 'penitence' to a 'good talking to', whether delivered with anger or merely in sorrowful exhortation and disappointment! But the moment it is over, his tears and distress vanish miraculously, as if they had never been, and he is down again playing with his train upon the floor. If brought to book for obvious disobedience, he will glibly recite what he has done, and what he was told not to do, showing that he did not just forget, but deliberately disobeyed, knowing he was doing wrong. But he will rarely tell a lie to save himself, and looks one fearlessly in the eyes even when in a serious 'row' (he is always in some kind of 'hot water'). I am wondering if in about a year's time boarding school might be the solution to the 'problem of Peter'. I do not think he would mind, as he welcomes any change, such as a new nurse, any and every visitor, and seems to enjoy his kindergarten school. He is very fond of me, I think, and does not like me to go away – but is quite happy after I have gone! He is affectionate, quite good-tempered, full of energy, and is a regular chatterbox. He is, however, very excitable and highly strung – as a toddler one could never romp with him as he became over-excited

*at once. I might add that he is infinitely better behaved when alone
with one than when several are present – in the latter case, he gets
very silly, often showing off and doing senseless little things. For
instance, one afternoon, I took him out with me, and he behaved
quite nicely until we were back again in the house, when the sight of
the maid in the hall seemed to have a bad effect upon him; he rushed
at her, pulled away a rug she was folding, and disarranged it, and
then threw his hat and gloves about, and generally behaved in an
unnecessarily babyish manner.*

*I am afraid I have not explained very well, but it is most difficult
to do so, as it is all so intangible. But I hear of this irritating quality
in Peter from everyone (beside feeling it myself!), from his school,
his father, the nurse, the maid, and even his very affectionate grannie! But perhaps it is just a matter of time, and he will grow out of it!
I do hope so, for his sake as well as other people's, as he antagonises
so many, and really he can be very nice and lovable. Perhaps I have
not laid enough emphasis on the difficulty in controlling Peter without severity and many 'Don'ts'. He is so strong-willed, and leads
Roy into all kinds of scrapes. He seems to love 'baiting' us all, and I
feel sure gets satisfaction from doing so."*

I don't find it easy to make any helpful suggestion to your problem,
although I sympathise very much with the difficulty. It is not, however, easy to see from your letter just what is wrong, if anything, in
your general treatment of Peter. It may be that you have perhaps
not been firm enough with him throughout, and not quite consistent
in your demands and reproofs, but I don't feel sure that this is true,
and don't want to imply any reproach of this kind. I think, however,
it is possible (reading between the lines as far as I am able) that less
exhortation and fewer "appeals", with rather more matter-of-fact
firmness, even to the point of a mild strictness, might be helpful.
"Mild strictness" perhaps sounds a contradiction in terms, but it
expresses what I mean – as few demands, and those as reasonable as
possible, with mild punishments, but these strictly and consistently
enforced. But I know how difficult it can be to handle a boy who has
got into this attitude of mind. It is the whole situation which somehow needs to be changed. There is no good in niggling away at this,
that and the other in turn; one has to try to get a broad general policy
of treatment which can be steadily followed under all circumstances.

One thing that does seem to me probable is that the boy needs to be treated with a good deal of respect and given as much responsibility as possible. As you yourself suggest, his rivalry with Roy is the main key to the whole situation. The fact that Roy is such an attractive person by nature must be very trying for the older boy, once he has got into these more difficult and less attractive ways. I think it is quite probable that a boarding school will be the solution for Peter's problem just because his main difficulty is the rivalry with Roy. People have sometimes been shocked when I have suggested that it may be a good thing to send a difficult boy away to school. They feel that it is just shifting the responsibility onto the schoolmaster, and that parents ought to be able to face it. In a general way, of course, I agree with this, but nevertheless it is certain that there are some children who never can solve their difficulties at home, and who do develop more happily when they are away at school. This is often true where the difficulty springs from an acute rivalry, but there is sometimes another reason too, one that I think is probably operating with your Peter. At nearly seven years of age he wants to be treated as a big boy, but home and mother and nurse and the younger boy all make up a situation in which he cannot act like a big boy. They are all reminders of his nursery difficulties and too closely linked with these. But if he gets away into an entirely new world, where there are bigger boys and new friends and he is treated like a man, he may be able to break away completely from his petulance and contrariness. I hope very much this will prove to be true with Peter.

CHAPTER SEVEN

When expert advice is needed

INTRODUCTION

For Wise, the majority of cases of childhood outbursts and eccen-
tricities are par for the course and just a passing phase, but there
are those cases that she considers need specialist attention. The well-
established phobias, the extraordinarily strong will or temper, the
shyness that has gone beyond regular inhibition, the wakefulness
that is more than the usual sleep disturbance. For these she recommends a consultation with a psychological expert usually found at a
Child Guidance Clinic. In "The real problem child", Wise gives her
readers some general information about these relatively new clinics
and the thinking behind them.

Wise highlights throughout her column the difficulty of separating
out the physiological and the psychological. Does the child's trouble
originate from a physiological difficulty or is it a sign of a psychological
disturbance? Far from pathologising a symptom, Wise delivers a strong
message on the importance of checking out the physiological side of
things first – babies and young children can suffer from many minor
ailments that cause a lot of discomfort and unsettledness. She by no
means overlooks this in favour of suggesting a psychological or emotional interpretation. The physiological should not be underestimated.

Having said that, as focused on in Chapter 3, one of Wise's main
messages is to bring to the attention of the reader those disturbances

in a child that are not necessarily due to real events. As she explains, these can be very common in small children and not inevitably a matter for concern. However, as well as recognising the significance and place of these manifestations, it is important not to overlook the fact that in the 1930s there was very little awareness of the sexual abuse of children compared to today. Many of the symptoms that Wise is told about, such as bed wetting, extreme anxiety, or excessive fears might nowadays be understood as raising the possibility that a child is being sexually abused. That is not to deny, of course, that there is an equal danger if every symptom is taken as an indicator of a real event.

Similarly, at the time Isaacs was writing there was less awareness of learning difficulties than there is today. "Sister" writing in "The real problem child", for instance, lists a whole series of symptoms that would nowadays make a psychologist vigilant to the possibility of an autistic spectrum disorder.

There are the more technical complications, such as a stammer, that Isaacs is most cautionary about. Such a difficulty requires expert handling and should never be meddled with. Isaacs offers pointers to her correspondents as to how they might contact a suitable practitioner, at times recommending specific clinicians. On several occasions, she invites her correspondents to get back in touch with her to let her know how they get on.

Isaacs is unconditionally insistent that a child should never be scolded or punished regarding a problem. Often the behaviour results from a deep disturbance not necessarily or obviously connected with a *real* event as such. Not only is there no reason for punishment, but it would only cause further turmoil and exacerbate the problem.

In this chapter is a particular piece of advice that may cause us to balk today – Wise's recommendation of a residential nursery school. Though residential nurseries were commonplace at the time of this advice, it seems so out of kilter with her sympathies and her understanding of the child's emotional wellbeing. It is a difficult matter to understand, especially given that she contributed some insightful and influential work about the problems of residential care in 1941 with *The Cambridge Evacuation Survey.*[1] It is, perhaps, reassuring to know that even Ursula Wise had her inconsistencies!

1 *A Wartime Study in Social Welfare and Education* – edited by Susan Isaacs.

THE REAL PROBLEM CHILD

25 JUNE 1930

I have had a number of letters lately from mothers and nurses who have wanted help in dealing with difficult behaviour in their children which seems to be of the kind that psychologists term neurotic. When we say it is neurotic we mean that it is not just ordinary childish self-will, or temper, or fear, that can be dealt with by ordinary methods of education, but something much more irrational and uncontrollable, seeming to have little or no ordinary cause. When a child is actually threatened by another child or by a large animal, we understand his being afraid; and in the ordinary way we know that he will stop being afraid when the cause is removed. We have no difficulty in understanding a young child's feeling a little cross if an absorbing game has to be interrupted, or if he is denied some pleasure that he keenly desires. We are not surprised if he is sometimes a little disobedient and defiant, or occasionally shy with strangers. All those things are part of the normal behaviour of little children. We know they will grow out of it, and we try to help them to do so. But when a child is persistently angry and defiant and perverse, without any cause that we can ascertain, we feel there must be some deep trouble behind this behaviour. When he is so terrified of strangers that he cannot bear to leave his mother at all, when he is excessively frightened of ordinary animals, of being in the dark, of other people's laughter, of the rain or a waterfall, when he stammers or will not try to talk, when he bites his nails or wets his bed – in all such cases we have come to understand that the causes lie far below the surface of the child's mind, and have little to do with real events. Sometimes these troubles may perhaps have been made greater by unskilful ways of handling the child, and a change of method will help him a good deal. But sometimes they occur even in children who have had excellent mothers and nurses, where there is little to alter in ways of training. And in any case the roots of the difficulty really lie in the deepest level of the infant's mind. To understand them in any particular child calls for considerable knowledge and experience, and it is little wonder that mothers and nurses feel themselves at a loss in trying to deal with these problems.

Neurotic fears and defiances do, of course, shade off into ordinary childish wilfulness and anxiety. Whether or not actual treatment is required, or whether some change in method of handling the child and in his general environment will bring a real improvement can, as a rule, only be judged by a psychologist who sees the child himself and talks to the mother or nurse.

It is just for this kind of problem that Child Guidance Clinics are being developed. Their work is based on the co-operation of physicians and psychologists, who give definite treatment to the child or practical advice to the parents, after a close first-hand study of the whole problem.

The five letters I quote this week are all about just such difficulties as really call for this first-hand observation. They differ very much in detail, but they are all of the kind about which fruitful suggestions can only be made by someone who sees the child and makes a proper diagnosis of his trouble.

I very much want to urge each of these parents to take the child in question for a proper consultation at a Child Guidance Clinic. There they would receive help and advice far more reliable and detailed than any that I can offer myself on the basis of a letter, no matter how full and accurate. I would suggest, that for those who can get to London, the Child Guidance Clinic at 1, Canonbury Place, Highbury. N.5, of which Dr. W. Moodie is the director. I haven't any doubt that a consultation there would lead to suggestions that would relieve the trouble very greatly and bring most valuable and permanent help to these little children and their parents.

Letter one: *"Robin"* writes: *"I should be very grateful if you could advise me re my little boy, who is an only child and will be five in September. He sleeps well, is very energetic, and is thoroughly healthy in every way.*

Lately he has developed the habit of blinking and screwing up his eyes every few minutes, and also, when we are out walking, I notice he keeps lifting up his shoulders and twitching his arms. It is not shyness, because he makes friends quickly and has a word for everybody. He talks nicely, and has no signs of stammering. I shall welcome any suggestions."

Letter two: *"E.T."* says: *"I should be so grateful if you could advise me in the matter of my little girl. She is now two years and eight months, and is a perfectly robust and healthy child, but apparently* *suffers from nightmares – which must be intensely vivid, as spasms recur during the day. She frequently wakes in the night, frantic and screaming, because she fancies there are animals about the room and in her bed. All my efforts to reassure and pacify her are useless for a time, and when finally she ceases screaming, she keeps clutching at me and will not go back in her bed. She has always been very fond of cats and dogs, and cannot pass one without wanting to love it; in fact, she shows great interest in all animals. I took her to the Zoo last week, which I now fear was quite wrong, for since we have had trouble every night and day spasms. The latter we did not have previously.*

She has her tea, from 4.30 to 5 p.m.: milk, wholemeal bread and butter, honey and perhaps a biscuit or sponge cake, and goes to bed soon after 6 p.m. The trouble commenced about last August. She was sleeping in a cot in my bedroom. When I ran up to see what was wrong she was trying to climb out and seemed terror-stricken. Nothing would induce her to go back in the cot. She said, 'An animal bite her feet'. I put her in a spare bed, and she gradually forgot it until a few weeks back.

If there is any treatment for cases of this kind, I should be much relieved to know of it."

Letter three: *"H.R." writes: "I should be much obliged for advice about my little girl, C., aged two years seven months. She is a large, apparently perfectly healthy person, nearly as big as her sister, aged four years, but not soft and fat. From a baby (with weight 9 lbs) she has been a very bad sleeper, waking from 2 to 4 a.m. and about 5.30 in the morning. She is better than she was but still wakes and talks almost every night for from one and a half to two hours, and usually is awake between 5.30 and 6 a.m. The last three months she has dropped her midday sleep entirely. I should think she was able to do without sleep, except that she is so peevish. When in a good temper she is sunny, full of sense of humour, and often leads her sister in inventing games, etc. This is usually so after good nights. But at the least thing going wrong there are howls and yells, and, if not tears, an irritating insistence on getting attention. She is extremely ingenious in going from one thing to another till you are driven to a refusal, and then there is a row. These rows occur with the grown-ups or other children equally. They want to play something, and*

C. settles down to arranging her doll 'first'. Nothing will hurry her, and if they go without her she sits down and screams. With grown-ups even, if she is going somewhere for a treat, she will go on with her own jobs at her own time, and scream if interfered with, even if the treat will be missed. She is left as much liberty as possible, and given warning before anything is to happen – bed, or rest, or meals. I think she has a healthy life. Out at 9 or 9.30 into a garden, where she plays with her sister and the gardener's children, of the same age. There they have a sand-heap, dolls and dolls' pram, wheelbarrows, horse-reins, etc., and seem perfectly happy. Rest from 11.30 to 1, pram walk 2 to 4, tea 4.30, and play with a grown-up till 6, bed-time. No supper. Midday rest is a serious problem. The older girl likes kindergarten games and reading, the younger rackets the whole time; won't listen to reading or allow the other to, and if playing demands attention ceaselessly, and cries if she doesn't get it. If put by herself she calls nurse on some excuse or another the whole time. She drives her sister, who is a very highly strung child, nearly to tears by her perpetual teasing.

I think the trouble is that she is too advanced for her age. She tries, and mostly succeeds in doing everything her sister does – 'Me a big girl'. We give her all we can to do – dresses herself, washes herself, has a baby doll to look after, and feeds the hens, eats with a fork, sits on a 'big chair' at meals, has a 'grown-up' plate instead of her own platter; but I think she is living too fast for her age. If kept away from the older children she is more unhappy and more peevish. She has worried for months to go to her sister's dancing class. I let her go last week. She danced like one of the older children who told me, 'I watched and she knew what to do' – but for the next two days she was quite impossible.

I have tried various foods to see if it is digestive, and have tried more and less exercise: but she will be fairly good sometimes for as much as a month or so, and sleep fairly, and then we suddenly go back unaccountably to a period of being impossible. It is particularly important now, as I have a new baby, and some of the children will have to sleep together. Would a tendency to tonsils affect her like this? She had enlarged tonsils in the autumn, but they seem to have gone. I don't think she is spoilt. We try to give her as few orders as possible, but she is not allowed to disobey if an order is given. I have tried to find things she can do well, in case she is worrying at the *older girl being cleverer, but she won't do anything unless it is 'what Isabel does', and won't allow anyone to show her the difficult things – 'Me can'. Of course, she can't, and then gets cross. She won't try to do things properly – 'No, I do it this way' – unless, of course, it's her sister she can copy."*

Letter four: *"M.H.R."* says: *"It is with much interest I always read your articles in THE NURSERY WORLD, but more especially this week, as you have written about nervous children. I have a little girl of four-and-a-half years who has been very ill, and at last I took her to a specialist in London, but she screamed and kicked so much directly she was shown into his presence that he was unable to touch her. My own doctor has been treating her with all sorts of different things, and I am glad to say she is better, but still very nervous and your suggestion in THE NURSERY WORLD about having advice from a psychologist is exactly what I should like to be able to have, but I have no idea where to find such a person. I would also like to ask if the fee is very large. I have another little girl, who is nine years old, who is a born egotist. I want her to wear her hair in plaits, but nothing I can do will make her go to school with two small plaits; she says she hates the girls saying things about them, even if they liked them. That does not help matters, and were I to insist it would reduce her to tears and make her so unhappy; she would far sooner let me have her hair cut short which I am contemplating doing. She is a very loving, gentle and good child, but so terribly sensitive – to frown at her almost makes her cry – that I believe her life at school would be perfect but for her shy and sensitive nature, which causes her a lot of inward suffering. All these things could be helped tremendously, I believe, with psychological treatment, and I wonder if you could help me."*

Letter five: *"Sister"* writes: *"I should be so glad of your advice regarding my sister's small son of three years. He has been staying with my little folk – boys of four and a half and three and girls of one and a half and three months. The difference between the two three-year-olds is amazing and makes me think that there is something wrong.*

He is a well-built child, although not so sturdy as his cousin. He has a poor appetite and is very slow over the little he does eat.

He has a little sister of nine months, but has most of the character-istics of the only child, e.g. he will not play with the others, is selfish with toys, etc., and will not leave his mother. He is very backward with speech, only his mother being able to understand anything he says. He appears to keep his lips and jaws almost rigid.

He never wants to play out of doors, either alone or with his cousins, unless his mother is there. When he is indoors he is never absorbed in anything except a fairly difficult jigsaw puzzle, which he can solve almost as quickly as a grown-up. There is no picture to do it to guide him, but he did it straight away, although it is quite beyond the efforts of my own two boys.

He has the habit of picking his nails, and when he is not doing this he gives vent to a particularly irritating screech. All this makes him appear very dull mentally, and I should like to know whether you think it may be due to his difficulty with speech.

Thanking you for your most helpful articles."

BROTHER AND SISTER JEALOUSY

12 MARCH 1930

"E.G." writes: "If you can possibly solve the problem about my little daughter's extraordinary temperament I shall indeed be grateful. She is three years old, and very intelligent, but extremely nervous. If she should fall in the house, and slightly hurt her knee, she will scream to have her outdoor leggings put on to cover it, and if we remain firm about not putting them on, she will cry until she is ter-ribly sick, and her heart beats twice as quickly with fright.

The biggest problem is her behaviour when seeing me or being with me. When I am not about she is full of laughter and happiness, and quite good with Nannie and her baby brother (six months). But as soon as I come upon the scene she whimpers and whines, and will not let Nannie do anything for her. She says, 'Mummie, you do it'. You can imagine how I long to be with her at times, but have to avoid her owing to her getting upset. The extraordinary thing is, she loves very much to be with me, and I with her, but once I am there she no longer seems to be happy. Her daddy says we should give in to her, because of her nervousness and strong spirit, which I, naturally, do not wish to break."

I think you have a very difficult problem with your little girl. Her nervous anxiety is obviously very great indeed. Many children are more difficult with mother than with nurse, but not usually to so marked an extent. And many children are frightened by a trivial hurt to knee or arm, but not to such a point of terror and physical distress. I don't think even the best educational methods can alleviate anxiety as acute as this, and the help of a psychologist is definitely called for. It is usually found in such cases that there is an acute jealousy of the baby, as well as of other people – so strong that the child is quite unable to deal with it, although it may not appear on the surface. When so acute it has to be looked on as an illness, and not open to ordinary moral controls. You can, of course, help a little by your way of treating her. For the present you should try to be with her only when you can have her to yourself, not when nannie and the baby are there, too. And you should try to let her have a few special privileges in her relation with you. Do you spend a little time with her after she is in bed? If you could, and occasionally have her to tea with you alone, and sometimes take her for a walk without the others, it would help her feel the comfort of your firm affection. And when you have to deny her anything, or to insist on letting Nannie do things for her instead of you, you should be perfectly firm and unmoved, but *not* reproachful. Just keep quietly to your decision. "Giving in" and "spoiling" her won't help. But never let her have any *real* cause for the fear that you don't love her as much as the baby.

I don't, however, think these or any other educational methods will do more than touch the surface of a trouble so deep and acute, and I would strongly urge you to consult a specialist with a view to psychological treatment.

STAMMERING

Even the mother of a large family is often confronted with an unaccountable phase of behaviour in one child with which she finds it difficult to deal. The young mother is even more bewildered with certain aspects of her child's development

21 MAY 1930

"A.B.C." writes: "I should be very grateful if you could advise me how to treat a tendency to stammering in my son. He is an only child aged four, and thoroughly healthy in every way. He is highly strung, but not abnormally so. He has always been rather backward at talking, but we have not worried about this. He is naturally right-handed. He has always led a regular life and had plenty of sleep. The stammering has only developed recently, and I have thought that it might go when he had better command of language, but I feel worried to see his difficulty. It is almost always the first word of a question over which he stumbles (e.g., what, why, how), and the aspirate seems to trouble him at present – he over-emphasises it and stammers over it. Can you advise me how to treat his difficulty wisely?"

The treatment of stammering is a highly technical affair, upon which one cannot give general advice without first-hand observations of the child. So much depends on the sort of difficulty and still more upon the underlying cause. Stammering usually starts in some specific emotional disturbance, which can only be ascertained by a psychologist who understands the deeper aspects of emotional development and has also specialised in difficulties of speech. I should like to urge you to consult one of the trained workers either at the Central School for Speech Training, Albert Hall, S.W.7 (Miss Elsie Fogerty is the Director), or at the Child Guidance Clinic, 1, Canonbury Place, N.6 (Director, Dr. W. Moodie). Even if it were not possible for you to keep your boy up in London for a course of treatment, it would be worthwhile having the consultation, for at either of these places you would receive practical advice based on a real diagnosis of the particular difficulty. Until you have such first-hand advice from someone who understands something of the psychological cause of the stammering it would be best for you yourself to take no notice of it at all. If you try to correct it without special knowledge, it is quite likely that you may do the wrong thing and increase the difficulty. If you keep the general conditions of the boy's life and his relation with you, as pleasant and healthy as possible, that is all you *can* do without detailed advice from a specialist. I do hope you will be able to arrange this very soon as the sooner the trouble is attended to the easier the cure will be.

THE DESTRUCTIVE CHILD

An unusually strong and destructive little boy of three is the subject of one of this week's letters

13 JUNE 1932

"Worried" (Wallasey) writes: *"I am writing to ask you to give us some help by your advice on how to correct our little son, who had just turned three years of age. He has a terrible propensity for breaking things, not just his toys, but any kind of furniture. He is very strong and, before anybody is aware, he has smashed glass windows and mirrors, and broken furniture (except, of course, solid chairs and tables, but these he scratches). He recently made three deep scratches along the keyboard cover of a four-year-old piano that cost nearly £100. He throws articles about, and always tries for one's face, and my husband to-day had his glasses knocked off and smashed. China and table glass are also often broken by him. We married four years ago on a none too large income, and now, when one feels the need during this crisis of being careful, this sort of thing goes on. This is a small house and I only have an eighteen-year-old lady help. Kenneth likes the girl, who is quiet. My husband plays noisily with Kenneth and they both laugh a lot. I daresay, with*

household worries and some others, I am a bit preoccupied and seri-ous, but I try to play and be jolly with him now and again and when the girl is out. Kenneth is very affectionate and hugs and kisses me, when in his cot especially. He is healthy and also fairly forward, and is picking out the letters of the alphabet. He doesn't play well with children, though he likes to watch them playing. We do not seem to be able to find enough outlet for his tremendous amount of energy. We haven't a garden, either back or front. We have tried every kind of punishment."

You certainly have a specially difficult problem with a child who is so unusually destructive and strong. I know how very trying it must be to have a small son who can carry out so much destruction and do it suddenly in that unexpected way. It must give you a very great deal of anxiety, but it is quite certain that no mere punishment will effect any change. Punishment would have to be extraordinarily severe to check such a destructive impulse, and then it would, of course, sim-ply ruin the development of the child's whole character and perhaps disturb his mental life permanently. I feel sure the key lies in finding opportunity for active exercise of a kind that is free and vigorous and yet not harmful to other people and their possessions. Such a child wants extra space for running about, extra opportunities for learning to climb and throw and use tools, and of course, the companionship of other children under skilled supervision. Now, it seems to me very likely that in your circumstances you will not be able to find a sat-isfactory solution in these directions. I think the first thing I should want to do for such a boy is to find a really good nursery school for him, where he would have proper training, and ample opportunity for the active play and exercise that he needs, and the right sort of material to enable him to develop skill and emotional satisfaction. I would go to any amount of trouble to discover such a school by, for example, advertisement and personal enquiry, and I would not rest until I had either found one or fully satisfied myself that there was none available. I think I would then quite definitely arrange to let the boy go to one of the really good residential schools for children of nursery age, of which there are now quite a number in different parts of the country. If you need addresses for this I should be very pleased to do what I could to help you. The other suggestion that I should like to make in case your difficulty gets worse, or in case the nursery school solution does not seem a possible one, is that you should get first-hand advice from the Clinic for Child Guidance, at York House, University Settlement, Nile Street, Liverpool. I think that a talk with Dr Barton Hall there would be of very great help to you, since you would be able to let him have much more detailed information about the way the boy is handled, and he might then be able to discover the main causes of difficulty.

LEARNING TO TALK

Many mothers worry over a child's slowness in learning to talk. But the normal child of fifteen months only knows a few words

21 JANUARY 1931

"Mother of One" writes: *"I should so much like your opinion and advice on my baby who is now fourteen months old. Ordinarily she is a very happy, healthy baby, and has made quite normal progress with teeth, crawling, standing and walking, but is very slow to learn to talk. She says only five or six words, and these she has been saying for several months. In fact, she is slow to learn everything we actually try to teach her, like talking, or holding her cup or 'asking' to be held out. On the other hand, she seems very intelligent in finding things out for herself or in learning through watching. For instance, she calls a horse and a dog both 'bow-wow' on a large composite picture, and recently recognised her daddy on a small snapshot. The two things that worry me about her are the restlessness and excitability. She cannot settle down to play with anything for more than a minute or two at a time. She will be sitting on the floor, apparently very interested in putting bricks in a box; the next minute she will be crawling across the floor to cuddle her Teddy; then she will go back to the bricks, and half a minute later she will be looking at a book. She has always been very active and energetic, and has plenty of things to play with – I sometimes think too many. She is quite friendly with strangers if they give her time to get used to them and don't try to touch her or talk to her at once. But though she quite likes visitors, she gets terribly excited in no time, so much so that she seems hardly to know what she is doing. For instance, in the ordinary way she understands almost all we say to her, and will point*

out her dolly, her ball, the 'tick-tock', etc. But in her excited state she mixes them all up. Lately she has developed a sort of squealing cry when she is excited or angry, which is very upsetting. Also, she has begun to show signs of fear of moving objects, such as swaying branches or a swinging electric light. She is a very light sleeper, and now never sleeps more than thirteen hours out of twenty-four. She is often restless at night, and gets outside the bedclothes to sleep. Some of her restlessness may be due to teething – she has cut twelve in the last eight months; but as I had rather a worrying time before she was born, and there is something of a neurotic history on one side of the family, I am afraid she may have a tendency towards nerves. She leads a very quiet, routine existence, but now that she is over a year old I feel that she ought to see more people. I should be very grateful for your advice."

On the facts you give, your baby is if anything a little ahead of the normal in her speech. The average fifteen months child only knows four words besides "Mama" and "Dada"; so that your little girl is not by any means slow in this respect, and there is nothing for you to worry over there.

With regard to excitability, I think I should try to keep the general conditions of her life as quiet as possible, and not have too many visitors just now. It is too early to say whether the excitability is just a phase which she will pass through, perhaps within the next year, or whether it is so marked that psychological advice would be helpful. If she doesn't calm down and get a little more emotionally stable within, say, the next twelve months, then I think it would be as well to see a psychological expert. But at this stage I really don't think there is anything to be distressed about. Your description gives me the feeling of a child who is just a shade more excited by pleasure than most children, but it suggests nothing, so far, that may not be lived through if you keep her quiet and content. There is no particular reason to feel that she ought to see more people, provided she has some companionship in play and friendly interest from those she loves.

Then, again, those quick changes of interest are perfectly normal at that age. One does, of course, find children of twelve to eighteen months or two years whose interests are not quite so volatile. But they are not any more representative of the ordinary child of this age than your little girl: if anything they are less so. Your baby will obviously have a lively, energetic temperament, but we don't want everybody to be stolid do we? I sympathise with your little girl about only feeling friendly to strangers who don't try to touch her or talk to her at once. That, again, is far more often true of children as a whole, especially in the second and third year, than most grown-ups realise.

There are very few children indeed who don't need a little time to get used to strange adults. If, however, they are left quietly alone by the stranger, who is content to remain passive for a little time, responding to the children but not making advances, they will, as a rule, soon become easy and friendly.

I think it would help your little girl most if you could yourself feel a little less anxious about the possibility of neurosis. If you can keep her in a cheerful, calm atmosphere, and not show any particular distress about small difficulties that arise, she will very probably grow quite happily and satisfactorily. If, later on, you would like to have further advice and will write to me again, I shall be very pleased to suggest someone to consult.

AFRAID OF WATER

2 APRIL 1930

"April" writes: *"I should feel much obliged if you could tell me how to deal with my little girl, aged ten years. She is very frightened of rain and running water.*

When we are out for a walk, if she hears water running anywhere, she will not pass it, nor go near the spot again. We have some gardens here, with a small waterfall enclosed, and we cannot get her to go anywhere near it. I have great trouble in getting her to go to school unless I can promise her that it will not rain before she comes home. She often starts for school, and then comes back because it looks cloudy. We have taken her straight back to school, but cannot get her to go in. She is terrified at the prospect of thunder. All the time the weather is settled she goes to school regularly, and is quite pleased when it is foggy as she can't see the sky. She has been like this for two years. We have been hoping she would grow out of it, but she seems worse, if anything. She was very delicate as a young baby, and has always been of a very nervous temperament. Should she be punished for coming back after being sent to school? She has to wear glasses, and the doctor told me not to worry her, but her school teacher seems not think she ought to be punished."

It would be quite useless to punish the child for a phobia of this kind which is quite definitely a mental illness, not a piece of naughtiness, nor even of ordinary cowardice. No sort of punishment would cure the inner difficulties in the child's mind from which such an unreasonable fear springs; but it might very well increase them. Such forms of deep anxiety have nothing to do with *real* causes of fear, and are not open to the control of reason. They will yield neither to discipline nor to persuasion: but they can be cured by skilled psychological treatment, and I would ask you to seek the help of a psychologist, who will be able to find out what difficulties are hidden behind the fears. If the child goes on without such help, her general social development is bound to suffer severely. One can hardly imagine a greater handicap than a fear of rain and running water for anyone, or one that would interfere more with general activities. I very much hope that you will be able to consult a specialist and arrange for definite treatment. I shall be glad to let you have some suggestions as to possible consultants.

AFRAID TO BE ALONE

13 AUGUST 1930

"Worried" writes: *"Like so many others, I have read your letters to mothers with interest and wondered if you can help me with my*

little girl, aged two years and four months. She is a very determined, nervous and rather highly strung child, and the chief trouble is that she will not be left alone in a room. She has a little brother of fifteen and a half months to play with, but she screams whenever I go out of the room, even to fetch something and is rapidly making the little boy nearly as bad. Even when playing in the garden (which she will seldom do alone), if I move away she cries and runs after me, wanting to hold my hand. I have tried being cross and taking no notice, but you cannot ignore a crying child completely. She is very backward in talking and a bit underweight, being only twenty-six and a half pounds, although she looks exceedingly well. I have sometimes wondered if some of the trouble and fretfulness is due to indigestion, from which I suffer a lot, and did as a child. She often has a high, patchy colour, particularly after she is asleep at night. She is fed on Truby King lines, and only has three meals a day, but I feel there might be something to account for it.

I wondered if you could advise me of a good children's doctor, or even a psychologist, if you think that might help to cure the trouble. She is terribly shy with strangers, and will often cry bitterly at the sight of an aunt whom she should know fairly well. She has lately taken to picking and biting her nails, and we keep her in thin gloves. I was a very nervy and whiny child myself, and went through terrible phases which I want to avoid at all costs. She is much better with my Nanny than with me, but at present Nanny is on holiday, and I am having a terrible time, as she will not be left a minute. I should be very glad of your help, as I feel the child cannot be completely well or happy. Although looking so well, she has not gained at all the last two months, and even has lost a little. I enclose a stamped envelope for your reply, which I would be glad to have, as if I am to take her up to a doctor I should like to get it fixed up soon."

I think it would be quite advisable to take your child to see a children's physician who has specialised in cases of this type. From your description, it might seem that the child's nervousness may have a physiological origin. Sometimes it is very difficult to know whether this sort of trouble originates in a physiological disturbance, either glandular or digestive, or whether really it is the other way about, the psychological trouble being at the bottom of the physical signs of nervousness. For this reason, it is just as well to tackle the difficulty from both ends, and I should be pleased to suggest a doctor who has understanding of both aspects of the difficulty. Meanwhile, the only practical suggestion is to keep the general atmosphere in which the child lives calm and quiet, and to be both firm and gentle with her. I should avoid scolding or punishment, since it is quite clear that the difficult behaviour springs from some cause that is outside the child's ordinary control. I hope very much you will be able to arrange for a consultation as soon as possible.

"Baffled" writes: "I read your splendid articles each week in THE NURSERY WORLD with the keenest interest, and now I am writing for your kind advice on a problem of my own. My small son of just two years is the healthiest, happiest little man one could meet.

When he was eleven months old, I was bringing him back from Egypt, and on the boat he suddenly developed a very bad form of ophthalmia. He was extremely ill, and lay for the best part of a week in a kind of torpor and quite blind. The only thing that comforted him was to chew his sheet. We had to give him the most painful dressings every two hours, during which he cried and cried, then directly it was over he would seize the sheet and drop into a semiconscious state, chewing hard. Naturally, I couldn't bring myself to deprive him of it, and that started the bad habit. When we arrived the eye trouble cleared up, and he got quite fit again; but the minute he was put in bed he would start to bite his sheet. At this time he cut his first tooth, so probably this was the cause of the sheet-biting in the first place, and not his illness. He has, of course, been cutting the rest of his teeth since. Periodically I have made attempts to break him of this habit, and with no result. He has never sucked his fingers, and obviously the tough sheet is comforting to the swollen gums. Then we came out here again, when he was twenty-one months, and for a month of two we were living in hotels where the bed linen was washed by natives. The problem worried me very much, as the Arabs are filthy² people, and none too particular over their washing. So

---

2 The words of the correspondent. I have not censored the original documents of casual racism and racial prejudices in order to preserve socio-historic accuracy. While shocking to the contemporary reader it seems typical of the time in that it was not challenged by either Isaacs or the editors.

when we got into our own home, Nurse and I made a valiant stand to break him of the habit. He still has his last eight teeth to come – the four eye and the four back molars.

Well, I made a large pillow-case for his mattress, so that he couldn't gather up any bits to put in his mouth, and as it is very hot I was able to dispense with the top sheet altogether. I gave him a hard piece of apple to gnaw while settling down to byes, gave him his favourite toy, and left him. This was his mid-day sleep time, when he always sleeps solidly for two hours during the heat of the day. However, he soon missed the sheet and started to cry and cry. I steeled myself to letting him bellow the whole of the time, with the result that he didn't sleep at all. I felt sure he would be so tired at night he would fall asleep at once without a sheet – but no, he cried piteously for an hour, and then I felt it was being too cruel, so gave up and took him a sheet, which he stuffed in his mouth with a happy gurgle, and he was asleep inside five minutes! I have tried again at intervals since, with the same result. I have also removed it entirely once he was asleep, but always, about 3 a.m., he has wakened and cried hard till we gave it him again.

Of course, we always remove it from his mouth the minute he is asleep, but if he half-wakens, once his first heavy sleep is through, he will reach out for the sheet. I really feel that sleep is more important to him – especially out here – and we are making him a restless and light sleeper, where before he has always settled down without a murmur and slept the clock round. He is a child who needs a lot of sleep, and if he doesn't have enough it makes him discontented and 'grizzly' all the next day.

Also he has had two ruptures. A bad one in the groin, which developed at five weeks, and which the doctor now declares healed, but he still has a tendency to an umbilical one, and always has to wear a pad. I am afraid to let him cry too much for this reason.

He still wets his bed terribly, which all points to teething. At present we have reverted to giving him a sheet to settle down with. Nurse washes them, so we know they are clean. He has plenty of hard food through the day, including hard-baked crusts, which he loves. This may seem a silly problem, but it is a bad habit, and I should be so glad to have your wise advice. I wonder if it is more harmful to try and break him out of it than to let him go on."

I think you are perfectly right in your general feeling that it would at the present time do more harm to make a determined attempt to break the child of this habit than to let it continue. From the grown-up point of view we like to call this sort of thing a "bad habit", but I think we often greatly exaggerate its undesirableness. After all, if one remembered all the little ways in which grown-ups indulge themselves – for example, pipe and cigarette smoking – one might be rather less severe on what is really the same kind of indulgence in the young child. If *we* find it not very easy to do without this sort of irrational satisfaction, how much harder it must be for the tiny child to give it up! He has not our other resources and satisfactions, in social life, and games, and art. He has nothing but these sensory pleasures to comfort him when things are difficult and he feels fretful. There are plenty of grown-ups, efficient, wise and happy people, who retain some such childish way; and one cannot see that they are in the least the worse for it. I know one lady of forty, a splendidly useful and pleasant person in University life, who to this day never goes to sleep without rubbing a little piece of flannel between finger and thumb, and putting her little finger in her mouth!

In view of the particular difficulties in which this habit started with your little boy, and the ruptures, one must be more lenient with him than with a perfectly healthy child. Provided that you can be sure the sheet is clean, I cannot see that the habit is likely to do any harm. This particular habit of biting the sheet seems certainly less harmful than thumb sucking.

If, later on, you felt that it would be desirable to cure the habit altogether, then I think you should only do so under the detailed guidance of a psychologist; otherwise you might easily do more harm than good.

CHAPTER EIGHT

Eclectic letters

INTRODUCTION

Whether it is because the topic is interesting and relevant, or the writing is eye-catching, the selection of letters in this chapter would have been difficult to leave out. "D.Sc.'s" letter was irresistible, not only due to her effusive tone but her amusing and somewhat surprising terminology – I had no idea that a particular expression she uses was in circulation at the time.

Wise turns her hand to a range of issues including "where babies come from" and death – both preoccupations of many young children at some time or other. She also takes on the topics of leaving a very young baby whilst on a holiday; the truth about Father Christmas and friendliness versus robotic manners (for which she comes up with a delightful phrase). Early rudimentary research into left-handedness, including rather dubious ethics, and a vivid description of woman having a "permanent wave" (which we would now call a perm)[1] at the hairdresser's provide us with enlightening historical insights. Through the letters she chooses, Wise highlights the distinction between routine and rigidity: though a firm believer in

---

1 It seems from this that the perm as we know it today is not such a dramatic spectacle!

the necessity of some degree of regularity and routine for the young child, she opposes inflexibility.

Wise's foresight on the topic of *praise* is an example of her being well ahead of her time. She comments on overdoing the praising of children: while praise can be good for children some of the time, getting to the point of dependency on constant flattery is not a good idea.[2] Since the time of these columns, the issue of praising children has escalated as an area of research. Carol Dweck and Claudia Mueller[3] have been investigating the effects of different sorts of praise for well over a decade. Among their many findings is the suggestion that children who are told how clever they are become less able to learn and may even lie about their achievements, compared to those children who are commended for their efforts alone.

This chapter contains a letter showing Wise at her most forthright, even indignant. In the case of a child going through a lot of anguish and suffering due to the parents' deeds, she does not hold back with her reproach of the adults. Though her usual manner is to be sympathetic to all involved in the difficulty, Wise's priority on every occasion is to advocate for the child and here we have her at her most uncompromising.

WHERE BABIES COME FROM

14 MAY 1930

I have had a number of further very interesting letters dealing with various aspects of the problem of "where babies come from". I should like to quote from some of these, and discuss two or three further points raised by them, and by some of my earlier correspondents.

"N.G." writes: "*I am so glad you are dealing with this question of telling facts of the origin of life to children. It is a question every mother has to face, and a vital one at that. You asked for personal experiences of telling children the truth, and here are mine. 'Daddy' and I were most clear beforehand that we would tell ours*

2 A point illustrated powerfully by Stephen Grosz (2013) in *The Examined Life: How we Lose and Find Ourselves*.

3 See, for example, Carol Dweck (2007) *The Perils and Promises of Praise*.

*whenever they asked, as the only truthful and honest way. My boy
of three asked one day, seeing his baby brother in the bath, what
his 'little hole' was. 'That's his navel.' 'But what is it for?' And in
explaining how the baby got his food before birth, I naturally had
to explain where he was then. The boy was most interested and
intrigued, and said with sparkling eyes, 'Say it again! I mean that
part about his being so tiny and growing and growing!' So I said it
again. Here I will say that his reception of the telling proves what
an interest and delightful wonder the natural facts are to a child,
at least as fascinating as any fairy tale, and it seems a shame for
any mother to deprive her children of that. The 'pretty illusions' of
storks and gooseberry bushes are 'not in it' with the wonder of the
real thing. At about four, my boy asked me, when our charwoman
brought her new baby, 'Where did she get it from?' He had not
forgotten it 'grew inside her, safe and warm', but wanted to know
'how did it get inside her?' I answered his meaning in saying it
'had not got inside her as a baby, but had just grown from a little
sort of seed inside her body, just like the plants come out of the
seeds in the ground'. It has never occurred to me, so far, to tell him
'not to talk to anyone about it', as some correspondents seem to.
Why should I? There is nothing offensive about it. So far no 'awkward situation in mixed company' has arisen. Personally, I think
it much more likely that embarrassing situations would arise with
uninformed children, as so many things might provoke questions
in public. As to the informed child telling his playmates, it is really
too far-fetched to let the feelings of a few misguided other parents
stand in the way of our children receiving the truth we believe to
be so important for them. We should have to refrain from all sorts
of things at that rate! Is it any less desirable for some children
to hear, possibly, the plain simple truth from us, than for us to
risk having garbled and lying rubbish from them, or even nasti-
ness engendered by curiosity? I should have thought there was no
one left who didn't agree about telling where little babies grow
before they are born. What really is a little perplexing seems to be
when to let them know how the baby is generated, i.e. the father's
part. However, here again, honesty with one's children must be
one's great guide, and the belief that truth is clean; and personally
I am prepared to tell my children when they want to know regardless of age. My boy already knows about the male and female*

flowers, and that it is the pollen from the former that makes the latter able to start 'new baby plants'; and whilst this in itself will not necessarily lead him to the deduction 'human beings are the same', still it will prepare his mind for that knowledge and save it being a possible shock. One final word, it would be so valuable, I think, to many readers, if you could refer them to Miss Coster's article on 'Sex Education' in the Report on the Conference on Mental Hygiene held in London in 1929. Miss Coster as a headmistress had had a big experience of girls, and her article is intensely interesting and illuminating."

"Red Clover" writes: "As I have four children between the ages of nearly one year and nearly nine years, I am very interested in your articles and letters on children's questions about birth. The eldest, a boy, nearly nine, is the only one interested so far. He accepts quite naturally the fact that birds lay eggs; dogs and cats, puppies and kittens, and mummies lay eggs. Last summer, when baby was born, he noticed no difference in my figure (I am very slight), and I told him we were hoping to have a new baby soon. He asked no questions, but after she was born, he asked me how she got out – was it through a little hole? I replied, 'yes', and at that moment the conversation was interrupted, but I feel sure he was going to ask where it was. Since then he has never alluded to it, except that a few weeks ago he suggested that baby was getting rather old, and he thought it was time I laid another as he was so fond of them! I think he is just ready to ask further questions at any time when circumstances might remind him of the subject; and I should like to be ready. At what age is he likely to connect the father with birth? He will go to a boarding school at the age of 12 or 13. Is it advisable to tell him any more before he goes? At present he keeps birds in a small aviary, and knows that a mummie bird will lay her eggs and hatch them out if she has a daddy bird to help her look after the babies; but nothing more. I have the book 'Where Did I Come From?' which advocates telling a child about the parts of the body, and fertilisation, etc., but I would like your opinion."

"Friend" writes: "The other day a friend asked me if I knew of a book which would help her to tell her girl of fourteen the facts of life in a simple nice way, but as I don't know of any such book, I said I would *write and ask if you could help. I shall be so glad if you can tell me of a good book."*

1   First of all about books. I have already referred to the one by Miss Norah March, "Towards Racial Health"[4] (Routledge, 5s.), which is a very helpful and suggestive book, approaching the problem through the study of plants and animals. For parents who really want to learn more of those general facts of human biology which will help them to explain things to their children, a very good book is Dr. S. Herbert's "An Introduction to the Physiology and Psychology of Sex" (A. and C. Black, Ltd., 7s. 6d.). And for a scientific and humane account of the general biology of sex and parent-hood as a whole there is nothing better than the excellent volume "Sex", by Professors Thomson and Geddes, in the Home University Library (Williams and Norgate, 2s. 6d.).

2   With regard to the father's part in procreation, which most people feel to be the most delicate and difficult aspect of the problem; there is no particular age at which children become interested in this. Some ask about it earlier, and some later; some never ask at all, but come to their own conclusions about things. The letters of "N.G." and "Red Clover" illustrate how widely children may differ in the age when they ask questions. *If* he asks, then he must be answered about this, just as much as about the mother's part, and just as simply and truthfully. The father plants the seed which the mother shelters and nourishes, and which presently grows into the little baby. The child is intuitively prepared to receive this knowledge by his spontaneous interest in the family relationships of animals, as well as his immediate sense of the special closeness of "daddy and mummy's baby". "Daddy and mummy" co-operate in beginning the life of the infant, no less than they do in loving him and caring for his needs after he is born. Why should the essential meaning of the special relationship of fatherhood be clothed in shadow and mystery, any more than that of motherhood? Sooner or later children may have to come to know this too. Let it be learnt from wise and understanding parents rather than from hole and corner informants!

4 March's book made an early and important argument for sex education, but its title and contents are also a reminder of the widespread support for the "eugenics" movement across the political spectrum in the 1920s and 1930s.

3   It has interested me very much to find that so many correspondents seem to fear that if children know these truths about the
origin of babies they will not want to play imaginative games, nor
be interested in fairy tales. Some have even implied that those
educators who think the truth about these things is essential do
not believe in fairy tales in general. But neither of these suggestions is sound. Little children go on playing their delightful
imaginative games of "mummy and daddy and children" just as
freely and happily when they know that babies spring from the
mutual love of daddy and mummy, and are sheltered and nour-
ished in mother's body before birth, as if they have been told
about storks or gooseberry bushes. Indeed, they often seem to
play *more* freely and imaginatively – because they are less afraid
of their own thoughts and of what mummy would say if she knew
of them! The children of truthful parents will, of course, not play
at "storks", but they will invent endless games of mother and
father and babies, of nurse and doctor, of washing and feeding
the baby, putting him to sleep, taking him for walks, visiting and
going on picnics, etc. This greater freedom of the imagination in
dramatic play is one of the very boons which mother's sympathetic understanding of the child's interest in babies, and her kind
honesty in answering questions, is able to bring to the child. It is
when mother suggests that the subject is taboo that the child's
imaginative play is more likely to become inhibited.

4   Nor is the value of fairy-tales in general in the least affected by
this question of truth about real events. No one who knows little
children could wish to deprive them of the joys of the fairy-tale,
as imaginative experience and as literature, any more than one
would wish to deprive the grown-up of imaginative art in painting and poetry and drama and the novel, because of the growth
of scientific knowledge. We do not need to believe that stories
and plays are real historical truth in order to enjoy them! Nor
do they give us less delight because we also take pleasure in the
facts of biology or astronomy or actual human history. And the
little child goes on loving his fairy stories, and having as much
imaginative need of them, when he understands the true facts
about important real things. Indeed, he can let his imagination
roam all the more freely because his real life is rooted in truth
and honesty. He is not forever wondering whether what his parents say is *true*, and does not feel so perplexed about where the

The best way to help children to understand about birth is to let them keep animals and their young.

real ends and "pretending" begins. He can give himself up to "let's pretend", and to convention of the story, with the same security that we have when we yield to the magic of the theatre or the novel. To share imaginative literature with the child, and to tell him untruths about real events, are two quite different things, which it is very important to distinguish.

The article of Miss Coster's to which "N.G." refers would certainly interest readers very much. The Report contains other papers on the same subject, and on the topics of great importance to anyone concerned with the education and mental health of little children. It can be had from any bookseller. "Report of the Conference on Mental Health" (National Council for Mental Hygiene), 1929, published by Adlard and Son, Ltd., price 2s.

A CHANGE OF ROUTINE

... may be the best way of getting round temporary difficulties with tiny children, says Ursula Wise

27 APRIL 1932

I am publishing the following letter from "D.Sc.", although it puts no question to me, because I am sure it will prove both interesting and encouraging to other mothers who have the sort of difficulty mentioned. I am sure "D.Sc." is right in suggesting the value of a change of routine as a way of getting round temporary difficulties with tiny children. It is far better to do this than to look upon the question as one of "winning a battle" against the child, or "breaking the child's spirit". With regard to the older child's jealousy of the baby, readers will remember the letter from another mother some months ago who also found that the misery and jealousy got much less when the baby was put in the same room as the older child. The most reasonable explanation of this is that when the baby was there with the older child the latter did not feel that she was left out in the cold whilst the baby was getting all the mother's care and attention. I don't doubt that the older child feels, too, that the baby is in some sense "hers". A boy of seven spoke to me only yesterday of his younger sister as "my baby". When the older child can feel this it seems to take the sting out of the jealousy, and, of course, helps to develop a protective, parental attitude towards the younger child.

"D.Sc." writes: "I wonder if it will help any of your correspondents to hear of the simple way in which I have tackled one or two difficulties in the upbringing of my two baby girls? When J. was two and a quarter years old she suddenly refused to do her big job after breakfast, and when I (unwisely, now I think) insisted upon her sitting still, in spite of shrieks and tears, she retaliated by messing her bed several mornings in succession, after she had had her orange juice, but before she was dressed. We were nearly desperate, when I thought that an abrupt change of routine might break the spell. So I took her out of bed on waking and gave her her orange juice and apple in front of the dining-room fire, and let her run round in her dressing-gown while breakfast was being prepared, until I was ready to dress her. It worked like a charm! She forgot all about the unhappy complex she had developed. She asked for the chamber to do her daily job some time during the morning (I affected complete indifference as to whether she did it or not, only making her diet more relaxing when she was inclined to be constipated, and vice versa), and after some days she settled down once more to her 'after breakfast' habit. Within a week or so we returned to the usual routine without any danger of a relapse. When N., aged seven months, suddenly began a fit of screaming on being awakened for her 10 p.m. feed each night, I decided to try the same remedy – i.e. a change of routine. So, for three or four nights in succession I left her to sleep until 2 a.m., and fed her then instead of at 10 p.m. When I returned to the normal routine she had forgotten her scream-ing fits, nor have they returned during the succeeding two months. After the baby's birth J. became frightfully wet, both day and night, as a means, I suppose, of attracting attention to herself. She would scream until she was changed and I often had eight or ten pairs of knickers, four pairs of pyjama trousers and four under-blankets to wash every day. I had her water tested, but there was nothing wrong with it. A few weeks ago, however, she had a bad cold, and the baby caught it from her. To facilitate the nursing I moved baby into J's room, and, to my surprise, J. immediately improved tremen-dously, both day and night. Within a month she was dry during the day, and a good many nights also. I can only suppose that the baby's presence during the night calmed J.'s jealous fears, which had showed themselves through the wetting, though she was actu-ally very fond indeed of her little sister. In this case, of course, I have not re-established the old routine. The two kiddies still sleep in the same room."

AT THE HAIRDRESSER'S

A little boy who saw someone being permanently waved, and has been terrified of the hairdresser's ever since, is the subject of one this week's letters answered by Ursula Wise

4 SEPTEMBER 1935

"M.L." writes: "Ian is two years and four months old – very active and forward for his age. He walked at thirteen months, and is talk-ing like a child of four. Six weeks ago I took him as usual to the hairdresser who has always attended him from one year old. He has never shown the slightest fear before – always playing with small bottles whilst she cut it. This time we were five minutes late for an appointment and she had taken a permanent wave. Ian happened to see this woman strung up to the ceiling and gave one shriek and ran sobbing to his nanny. He was in such a state that I didn't force him *to stay, and since then he will not allow either of us to go near him with scissors. I manage to keep it tidy over his ears while he is asleep, but can't manage the back. Could you advise me what to do to get over this fear? I did stop outside a perfectly new hairdresser's with a small boy friend who went in. My son was so upset at Oliver going in that I had to take him home, and he went to sleep sobbing 'man won't hurt Oliver'. His hair is a disgrace and I'm quite ashamed to take him out. But what can I do?"*

I can quite understand that the sight of a woman undergoing a permanent wave would be terribly frightening to a small child, who could not understand in the least what was happening. You will have to allow time for him to grow out of his feelings about this. Have you tried to explain to him what it was that was happening? He is, of course, very young to understand, even with patient explanation, but I think you could do something. You could say, "I know it looked to you as if the woman was being hurt – perhaps having her hair pulled off – but she wasn't at all. She was simply having it made nice and wavy as she wanted, and she had gone there because she wanted to, and it doesn't hurt in the least little bit". Can you draw? If so, it might help if you could draw a picture of the straight hair and the wavy hair, and even a picture of the woman in the gadget. Meanwhile, while this is sinking in, your quiet confidence and good humour is helping him to *believe* that it had not hurt. I should leave him alone about his own hair. After all, there is no serious harm in his having long and uneven hair for a bit, is there? It surely does not matter for a little time. It is far more important to help the child to get over the fright. One does need a sense of proportion about these things. The child's feelings are far more important than uneven hair, especially as it is for only a short time. I should let him play with scissors, perhaps try to cut up paper, or cut off a doll's hair to make it neat and tidy. Gradually you will find the intensity of his feeling will get less, although it may be some time before you will be able to persuade him to go to a hairdresser to have it done. The plan of letting him see other children go and come out alive and happy is certainly a good one. Has he seen his little friend Oliver since the day when the latter went in to have his hair done? You could tell from the way he sobbed himself to sleep how urgent and intense his fear is. You could not expect such a fear to disappear all in a hurry. But it will do so, with time and patience, and far more readily if you do not worry him with the scissors in the meantime.

GOOD MANNERS

If we are consistently polite and considerate to the child it is very rarely indeed that he will not respond with equal courtesy

1 APRIL 1931

"Anxious" writes: "I shall be so grateful for your advice regarding my little daughter, who is three years eight months (four in June). She is a perfectly bonny child, happy, a lovable disposition, and I think quite intelligent for her age. There is just one thing that worries me, and that is when she is spoken to she very nearly always pretends she has not heard, and the first word that follows is 'Eh?'

I've proved repeatedly that she does know what has been said; it is just a habit she has. Also, I've corrected her and told her that if she must ask what has been said to say, 'Pardon?' or 'What did you say?' but she will not grasp it. Now I just ignore her when she says 'Eh?' and she immediately says, 'Pardon'. Do you think this is the best way of breaking her of it? I've been treating her this way for over a week, but she still continues. She also forgets to say, 'Please' very often. When this happens I either say, 'Is that the way to ask?' or 'I should say "please"' (in quite a friendly way), and she at once corrects herself. I'm sure it's not because she is dense or dull, as in other ways she is all that could be desired, and has never had to be told more than two or three times before she has grasped it. She will say, 'Excuse me', 'I'm sorry', and is quite polite in every other way without having to be told. It is so disheartening day in and day out to find she does not improve, and I shall be most grateful if you can help me in any way. I read your articles with great zest, and am usually able to overcome these little difficulties by following the advice you offer to other mothers and nurses. Finally, perhaps I ought to say that M. is an only child with no other companions."

The whole question of training in politeness is a delicate one. If one cares only for obtaining the form of politeness, the actual words "please", "thank you", "sorry", and so on, one can as a rule get these by strict demands and punishments. But obtained in that way most of us would feel they were quite worthless. The whole point about these conventional modes of speech is surely that they indicate a real wish to please others, and a real sense of considerateness and friendliness. If one can ensure that state of mind, the conventional speech can be left to take care of itself. The state of mind, if genuine, will last on through life and ensure happy social relations wherever the child goes. The form of words, unless it springs from friendliness in the mind, will only last as long as we are there to demand it.

This attitude of mind cannot be made to appear in the child on *demand*. It is a matter of growth, and it grows in response to our own friendliness and consideration. It will come naturally from the child's actual living experience of friendliness and consideration in the grown-ups around him. If *we* are consistently polite and considerate, treating the child as a *person*, with all the personal respect we should give to a grown-up, it is very rare indeed that he will not respond with equal courtesy.

From your letter it sounds to me as if your little girl had these general characteristics of lovableness and friendliness which you desire in her, but that for some reason she has developed this single habit that you find so tantalising. Now I think that your suggestion of ignoring her "Eh?" is much the best. It is much more likely to lead her away from it than any scolding or reproach. But in any case, if a little girl of three years and eight months were perfectly polite all the time one would surely suspect she was a little machine and not a human being at all! It would really be quite unnatural. I should not worry very much about her sometimes forgetting to say "please", but I should be very careful to say it to her myself. And I would not accede to any request she made in a domineering or tyrannical tone. I don't think, however, that it would do any harm to make your friendly request for her to say "please" without being distressed if she forgets, and without making too much of it. If you fuss about it, you run the risk of really spoiling her whole relation with you.

IS LEFT-HANDEDNESS A DRAWBACK?

We are never justified in trying to make a child change his preferred hand

16 DECEMBER 1931

"D.G.V." writes: "I should be most grateful if you would advise me about my small daughter, aged two years five months. She seems to be distinctly left-handed, and I do not know whether to try and rectify this or to leave it quite alone. I am afraid it may be rather a drawback to her when she goes to school and later on in life. Neither I nor my husband are left-handed, and I am wondering why it should be. My little girl is rather forward, I think, in everything but talking, and even with that she is coming on now and can string quite long sentences. She tries to paint, draws (scribbling, of course), thread beads, feeds herself, irons her dolls' clothes, and hits a ball with a minute golf club very accurately; but these are all done entirely with her left-hand, and so far, I have done nothing whatever to check it. I am told that if I try to make her right-handed it may lead to stammering in the future, and, though I can hardly believe this, I should very much like to have your opinion on the subject. Writing, it seems to me, will be the only real difficulty. I presume she must learn to write with her right hand. She is a very independent *child for her age and full of life and energy, although we live in the East, in a very hot place, and her health is very good."*

I am very glad you asked me about this, and hope very much that you have not already tried to make your little girl use her right hand whilst you have been waiting for my reply. There is some connection between the speech centres in the brain and those centres which control the movements of the hand and arm, and it has very often, if not always, been found that if we try to correct left-handedness we are liable to produce a stammer. The reasons for this are not fully understood, but the fact is one of simple observation. Only yesterday a specialist in disorders of childhood was telling me of a group of right-handed children whom someone had tried to train to be left-handed, just as an experiment, and with them also a stammer had resulted. This is the first case I have heard of where the attempt was to change right-handedness into left-handedness, and it was by a trained doctor who was sceptical of the idea that there was any connection between the centres in the brain that control the two sets of movements, those of speech and of the hand and arm. The results of this experiment bear out what had previously been concluded from the very frequent attempts to make left-handed children use their right hand. For this reason, we are never justified in trying to make a child change his preferred hand, and if the child himself doesn't mind being left-handed in a right-handed world, it is hard to see why anyone else should mind. To the observer it does, of course, look very clumsy, but the child himself does not mind it, and it is surely his own concern. There are successful left-handed tennis players, bowlers, and batsmen, and lots of left-handed people who write just as easily as any ordinary person with the right hand. I should very definitely leave your little girl to please herself which hand she used, and, even when it comes to writing, should make no attempt to change her in this point.

THE EFFECTS OF CHANGE

15 JANUARY 1936

"V.L.C." writes: *"I should be so grateful of your advice in my particular case. I have a little boy of fourteen months old whom I have looked after entirely myself, with the help of a little maid of fifteen who is very good with him. I left him last week for the first time with his grandmother (whom he adores) to look after him. He was quite happy and good during the day but gave her terrible nights, often being awake from 10 p.m. until 2 a.m. He is sleeping quite all right again now I am at home. But I wish to go abroad for a month in February. I can leave baby with perfect confidence with mother and my little maid, but mother refuses to have the responsibility of him without a proper nannie. I would like this also except that I am afraid that to put him in the charge of a perfect stranger will upset him very much. I would so much like your advice. Would it be better to have a trained nannie for a month, or to leave him to the rather uncertain mercies of my little maid, who is very fond of him and of whom he is very fond? I cannot quite make out from your various letters and answers how much a change like this is likely to upset a child. Is it only for a day or two or is it likely to have far-reaching effects?"*

I confess that I should not myself want to leave a little boy of fourteen months, who had shown himself so disturbed by parting from you at night, for a month. One cannot say how much emotional disturbance will be involved. It is certainly more likely to have a far-reaching effect than to be a purely temporary thing, lasting for a day or two. But it is perfectly true that some children would not suffer any permanent ill-effect, whereas others would. I cannot tell which would be so in the case of your little boy, and you alone can decide whether the reasons for going abroad for a month are good enough to justify putting the particular strain on a child of his age. A year later it would be a different matter, but at fourteen months to part with one's mother for a whole month is a very big experience, which I myself and a good many other people would not feel justified in imposing on a child, without very good reasons. If you do, I think you not only need to have a trained nurse for the child, but a very good one, one who would be really patient and understanding about him and would know how to win his love. And she would have to give him the comfort in the nights that he needs, not to treat him sternly and strictly. I certainly would not want to put on a little girl of fifteen the enormous responsibility of managing the child satisfactorily without you. It is one thing for her to look after him when you are there, and another for her to have to deal with every emergency when you are not there to take the responsibility.

NERVOUS STRAIN

The problem of two children who have had to meet unusually trying circumstances are the subject of two letters this week

5 FEBRUARY 1936

I have this week two letters to answer which, although they describe very different problems, serve to illustrate the psychological strain that little children can be put under either by physical illness or by lack of understanding on the part of responsible grown-ups. It is fortunate that neither of these children are typical in their circumstances or their problems. The first one is an illustration of the difficulties that may arise out of what is the genuine spoiling of a child, namely, alternate indulgence and scolding, in a way that is quite outside the child's comprehension.

"Dickie's Mummy" writes: *"I am writing to ask your advice about my little boy, aged three years two months. He has had a very upsetting time during the last year. Till the age of two, he was very delicate and as my husband's work is in the tropics, Dickie and I lived at home with my mother. A year ago, however, as he had quite outgrown his delicacy, we joined my husband abroad. At first Dickie missed his Grannie very much, but he soon grew very fond of his Daddy. He was ill a great deal, however, and never seemed to really settle down. He is a sensitive, highly strung child and a very bad sleeper. His Daddy was very devoted and liked to have Dickie with him as much as possible, and they have all the same mechanical interests. But my husband is not used to children, and would alternately spoil Dickie and be unduly strict with him, scolding or smacking him for something he had encouraged before. Dickie is quite devoted to him, but would often ask me. 'Am I being good or naughty?' Then I was very ill, and as a second baby is expected in the spring, Dickie and I have had to come home. Since then, he has been a great problem. He screams for nothing, and seems to take a delight in doing just the opposite when I tell him to do a thing, even though I*

explain the reason. He will not listen to explanations, or reasons, but just screams. If people come in, he immediately pretends to be a dog and barks or tries to bite. His table manners have got terrible, and he throws his spoon and fork and food about. It is all such a change, and his relations are always talking to me about it and comparing him with his very good little cousin. Dickie is a very intelligent little boy and thinks things out in the way of a boy two years older than himself. He can read a little, and I wonder if I ought to give him an hour's simple lessons a day to keep him occupied – there is no nursery school near. He scorns educational toys, but will make most complicated stations, trains, etc., with bricks, and if clockwork toys go wrong, can nearly always mend them himself, but things must have some mechanical interest for him. He also draws and paints very well. We have a large garden in which he plays and takes a lot of exercise. He wakes two or three times a night, and at 5.30 a.m. always wants to come in my bed, as he says he is afraid he will lose me. He knows there is another baby coming and is very pleased. He calls it his 'very own baby'. There are no children near. I wonder if it would help to get a mother's help with a child of her own as company. But though he loves other children, he gets so excited that he is rough, and there is always trouble when he is with his little cousin, so I am rather afraid of it. I hope this letter is not too long, but I wanted to explain everything, as I am really worried about his behaviour, which I feel is not just naughtiness."

I am sure the majority of my readers will agree that it is not at all surprising, in view of the history of this little boy's experience, that he has become so contrary and neurotic. First of all, there was the physical delicacy, then the tremendous experience for a child of two of the journey to a tropical country, the loss of the loved grandmother, and the totally different environment in which he found himself. Added to these experiences was the father's unfortunate way of handling the child, the alternate indulgence and strictness, and inconsistency of behaviour. One can hear the bewilderment which the child felt in his pathetic question, "Am I being good or naughty?" I have known other instances of children who had to do with contrary and incomprehensible adults, who showed this same complete insecurity of feeling and inability to judge their own behaviour. How can the child come to any consistency in himself if the people around him are inconsistent; or even if one of the important figures in his environment, such as his father, is himself, so completely contrary? "Dickie's Mummy" cannot be surprised if the child now delights in doing the opposite, and does not know where he is. Within a year of the first journey the child has had another, and his desperate psychological situation is shown by his falling back on the pretence of being an animal. He does not know how to be a pleasant and sensible human being, and if relations add to all these difficulties by severe criticism in his presence and comparing him with a good little cousin, who has probably had a straightforward course of life, then it is not to be wondered at that the child is so distressed that he feels he would rather be a dog than a little boy. I feel I must apologise to "Dickie's Mummy" for the very long time she has had to wait for a reply to what was clearly a most urgent and difficult problem. I have, however, had so many letters that I have not been able to deal with them more expeditiously in the limited space of my article. It certainly would help the boy if he were to have an hour's definite teaching, not along rigid and formal lines, but simply in order to give him the sense that he is being helped to learn to understand. I would suggest that "Dickie's Mummy" should write to Paul and Marjorie Abbatt, Ltd., 29, Tavistock Square, W.C.1. for their catalogue of educational material. She might find Nancy Catty's book, "The Child at Home: His Occupations and First Lessons", published by Sidgwick & Jackson, useful with regard to the method of helping him to learn to read. It is possible that a mother's help with a child of her own would be an advantage, but I do not feel I can answer this categorically, since everything would depend on the age and nature of the child. A slightly younger child would probably be of more value to Dickie than an older one, unless the stranger were a good deal older. Sometimes a boy of this type is helped by having an eight- or ten-year-old boy as friend, again provided – and this is a very important point – that the latter did not tease or torment. If hers were friendly and helpful, then he would make a great deal of difference to the small boy. Dickie would get less excited with a child living in the house than he does with an occasional visitor, and he is bound to get rough and excited with his little cousin, if he has heard himself being compared unfavourably to the latter. But the boy will need time, and extra time as compared with the ordinary child, to grow out of his difficulties, and it is very important that he should have the support of sensible, consistent treatment, that whilst firm, also enables him to respect himself as a human being. I should certainly encourage him in the things that he can do well and not criticise him for the things in which he fails.

WHEN A CHILD ASKS ABOUT DEATH

The best way of dealing with this problem is to answer questions frankly and simply, not trying to evade or wrap things up too much

3 OCTOBER 1934

The first two letters this week raise the same problem in different forms: the question of the child's feelings about death.

"Anthony" writes: "I should be so glad if you could help me with this problem. My little daughter, aged five and a half years, has for the last six months been curious about dying. She seems very frightened of death and the other night ran into the day nursery where nurse was sitting after she had tucked her up in bed saying, 'Is there a last day before we all die? Do we get put under the road? Do we come alive again after we are dead?' Nurse did her best to comfort her and as far as we can tell she had not been frightened by any foolish talk, nor does she know anyone who had died. Is this a usual problem for a five-year-old child? I should be glad to know how to deal with it – nothing we can say seems to allay her fear about dying. Once when out for a walk with the housemaid on nurse's day off she watched a funeral going on in the distance over the churchyard wall. The housemaid told her that a man had died and that seems to have started the trouble. I feel sure she did not say anything else to frighten her as I asked her everything most carefully. She could not see the coffin lowered into the grave or anything, but only people in black and the flowers. But the impression remains with her. She is a healthy, happy child, and has a little sister of nearly two years. Otherwise she has no fears at all. Is this likely to be a lasting fear for the whole of her life?"

It is not very unusual for little children to develop a temporary phase in which they show conscious preoccupation with the problem of death, and considerable fear about it. As a rule, there has been some particular stimulus to the onset of this preoccupation. With "Anthony's" little girl there has been the sight of the funeral, but I wonder very much whether there has not been something more immediate and direct, for example, the sight of an animal dying. When such fears develop acutely, it is not easy to know how best to deal with them. As a rule, the excessive preoccupation with the problem passes away after a time, especially when the child develops satisfactory friendships and interests in school life. She then finds so much satisfaction in her daily life that the problem of death falls away into the background. It does not in the least follow that she will go on to fearing death in this acute persistent way all her life, especially as she is otherwise happy and jolly. The best way of dealing with this problem is to answer questions frankly and simply, not trying to evade or wrap things up too much. The child always knows when we are evading difficulties, and that makes her all the more frightened, because she thinks that we are frightened, too, and hiding things from her. It is better to say simply and frankly that death comes to all of us in the end, but that it doesn't usually come until we are old and tired and glad to lie down and go to sleep. The best comfort to her is to see that we ourselves are not preoccupied with this problem, but remain cheerfully interested in life, and happy in our relationships with other people, in spite of the inescapable fact of ultimate death. But it is very important that the child should feel able to talk about it and ask questions, since there is always the possibility that the child has had something frightening or threatening said to her which, if she had to keep to herself, would be extremely disturbing.

"Frances" writes: "I should be so grateful if you would give me your advice as to the best way of approaching the subject of death with a small child. My little boy's father died when he was only a year old and he is now nearly three. Since then we have been living right in the country, and so far no explanation has been necessary, but I am shortly moving into the neighbouring town in order to get more companionship for him, and send him to a small school as soon as he seems ready for it. He is already beginning to ask

a good many questions, and I feel that when he sees more children and takes in their family life he is sure to ask why he has no
Daddy, and I do not want to give a hasty, ill-considered answer. I
want, of course, to be truthful, and yet not to frighten him, and it
seems to me extraordinarily difficult to try to explain something
which is beyond one's own comprehension. As far as I can judge he
is developing quite normally, both mentally and physically, and is
a happy, healthy and active child and does not appear to be unduly
sensitive, but at the same time he does seem rather to cling to me.
This may be simply natural affection, and the result of my having looked him entirely for the past two years, but I have thought
that the changes during his first year may have something to do
with it. (He was born abroad, but came home for the summer at
six months old. Then he lost his Daddy only two months after we
returned to our station and had to do the long and complicated
journey once more, leaving behind his native nanny, to whom he
had become much attached.) He is quite good if I have to leave him
for a day, or even for a night (with his aunt whose house we share),
but I am always careful to explain where I am going and when I
expect to be back and to leave with as little fuss as possible. You will
understand from all this that I do not want to say anything which
could increase any feeling of uncertainty that may be present in
his mind, and yet I feel that some sort of explanation will soon be
necessary, and I shall be most grateful if you can help me from
your experience."

The problem for this little boy's mother is, of course, a different one
from that which "Anthony" has to face, since there is, on the one
hand, no acute fear in the child himself, but on the other, there is
the sad reality of the loss of his father. Doubtless the boy will begin
to ask questions before very long, and it is certainly no easy matter
to explain so profound and disturbing a reality to a little child in
an intelligible and comforting way. Again, I would suggest that the
only solution is frankness, telling the boy that unfortunately it does
sometimes happen that people become ill and die, and that happened
to his Daddy, so that you and the boy lost him. The greatest support
that the child could possibly get against the feelings of bewilderment
and distress which this must arouse is actual experience of your own
ability to bear up against such a loss, and remain equal to life in

spite of it. Doubtless his extra clinging to you is due both to the fact that you have been thrown together rather more than happens when there is a father as well as a mother, and also, too, the series of actual changes the boy experienced at the end of his first year. I would not offer any explanation about there being no Daddy unless the boy asks. He is sure to do this sooner or later, and if you anticipated the question you might be raising an unnecessary uncertainty. But if the uncertainty is there, then simple frankness can only help him, because it will give him at least the certainty of knowing that you will do your best to answer even the difficult questions, on the one hand, and on the other, that you are cheerful and sensible and able to help him in spite of his having no Daddy. It would seem a very wise decision to move into surroundings where he will be able to get more companionship, both from other children and from grown-up men friends, who can give him at least some approximation towards the companionship of a father.

INSTANT OBEDIENCE

11 SEPTEMBER 1935

"Well-meaning" writes: *"Having frequently admired the wisdom of your published replies to readers I venture to ask your opinion on the question whether it is desirable, and if so by what methods, to aim at being able to secure 'instant obedience' before a child is old enough to understand the principle underlying its necessity. My little girl, not quite two, is as obedient as a strong-willed child who is keenly interested in what she is doing at the moment can be expected to be, but she is quite capable of assuming complete deafness, or reiterating a determined 'No', or just running away if told to come here, or to put something down. Relatives tell me that she is too young to be expected to obey, and advocate the – to my mind - lazy and useless method of distracting her attention. My own view is that while obtaining her obedience by distracting her attention is a useful resource when she is tired, or when there are special reasons for avoiding a scene, it does not teach her anything, and that suitable opportunities should be frequently taken for training her to obey as a conscious act. Surely life is too dangerous for a child who will not*

obey a sudden order without first having some distraction provided. She might be electrocuted in the interval. I should be most interested to hear your views as to whether one should wait until a child is old enough for argument before attempting to teach it obedience. If you agree that the process can be begun as soon as the child unmistakably understands what is said to it (my child talks fluently and has a good memory), what steps do you recommend for securing obedience, in addition to the obvious one of limiting the frequency of one's 'do's' and 'don'ts'? Is a mild slap on the hand that persists in touching the forbidden object a very mistaken method? Sometimes I can see no other way of preventing the child from thinking; 'Mother goes on saying "Don't touch," but nothing seems to happen if I do." Is it a psychological fact that at barely two a child may forget a repeated command within a few seconds? My little girl's persistence in picking flowers in the garden (though I always give her some for herself whenever she shows the slightest sign of wanting them) suggests that it must be so. Sometimes I wonder if it is just that the fascination is so great that she simply cannot desist, though she knows must not pick. If that is so, how can I deal with it? Picking flowers for her and allowing her to pick for herself in certain places do not meet the case. It is not that I attach such importance to the devastation of my garden, but that I feel the problem is probably typical of others that we shall have to face. In case it is relevant, I had better mention that the child has the very hopeful characteristic of being more obedient if I leave her for a moment or two rather than if I am present. She will remain glued to a chair if I tell her not to get down til I come back, though, of course, I never strain this virtue too far. Another small point: I have always been lavish with praise when it has been earned, and now K. is beginning to pat herself on the back in a way that is amusing, but might become intolerable in time. 'Kitty's a kind girl to bring that flower to show Mother.' 'Good girl not to drop that parcel.' 'Brave Kitty not to cry.' Such phrases as these are sometimes reiterated in tones of indescribable smugness, but provided it passes off, don't you think it is preferable to the sullen defensiveness of the child who imagines that people only comment on its behaviour in order to condemn? If you think I have been overdoing encouragement, I should like to be told. I shall await your views on the subject of obedience with great interest."

Instant obedience is only given by a child to a parent on the basis of trust and confidence, built up by experience. One can, of course, enforce it by fear. That is to say, one can stir up so much fear in many children that they will obey as long as the feared grown-up is present, although this has very little bearing upon what they will do when there is no risk of being found out. That, however, is not the situation which you desire. The instant obedience which is based upon love and trust cannot be secured by our merely willing it to happen, nor is it possible for many children to give during the first two or three years. It can be given by a child of four or five, who has learnt that his parents will not demand it without good reason. Two years of age is very rarely a period when a child can obey. Occasionally a child has such a naturally docile temperament that she will obey at any age, but this is not very usual, and not necessarily the most desirable attitude of mind. Any child who is going to be independent and forceful and resourceful in later life is certain to show a phase of obstinacy and contrariness in the second and third years, and your little girl is behaving quite typically when she resists your demands if you interfere with her pursuits of the moment. We cannot hope to train tiny children to the virtues of later childhood, and we shall only waste our time and exasperate ourselves and them if we try to do so. It needs real supervision by the adult and appropriate planning of the environment to keep the child of two years, or even three or four, safe. And it is quite useless to imagine that one can ensure this safety by mechanical obedience from the child. But surely you are exaggerating the dangers? In ordinary circumstances, how is a child of two to get electrocuted? If you are taking her by tube, for example, you are not going to rely upon any habit of instant obedience to keep her from running on the line. You will surely rely upon your own arms and watchfulness to safeguard her, without putting upon her the tremendous burden of her own safety? The same applies to crossing the road, and to any of the risks that carelessness might bring in the way of little child in the ordinary house; for example, dangerous knives, matches etc. These are not the grounds for training obedience. The value of obedience is surely a social one, and the type of obedience that is socially valuable is one that rests upon experienced confidence and trust and love of the authority that demands obedience. As regards touching the ordinary objects, we have no right to have things about within reach of the child that are really dangerous to her. I would not take a two year old into a room where there were precious objects that I did not want broken. One can expect a child of four or five not to touch other people's belongings but not a two year old. I would certainly never expect a child of two or under to be able to resist the charm and attraction of flowers in a garden. By the time she is three and a half or four, she can understand clearly enough that some things are not for her and others for other people, although even then one should not expect too much in the way of being able to resist temptation. But at two years, it is really asking the impossible to expect the child not to do what she sees her mother doing – reaching out for the lovely flowers and picking them. She cannot understand, and there is nothing in the child to enable her to check the impulse. Such a power is a matter of slow growth, and there is no use expecting it before time to ripen.

It certainly sounds to me as if you had been overdoing the giving of praise. It is far better to take good behaviour for granted as the ordinary stuff of life – at any rate to a greater extent than you seem to be doing. However, you need not worry about her comments upon herself. They are natural enough, too, and are only part of the child's attempt to articulate the whole of her experience. However, I should be a little more sparing of the praise. A smile and a "Thank you" are usually enough reward for the child.

FATHER CHRISTMAS

What shall the children be told?

30 NOVEMBER 1932

"Christmas" writes: "I have found your answers to other people in THE NURSERY WORLD so very helpful and of great interest. I should be very glad if you could give me your advice on one small point. My little boy is six years old and goes to a small kindergarten. This is his second term. As we are now thinking of Christmas I am wondering what I shall say to Peter if he finds out from some child at school that that there really is no Father Christmas. He has always been told there is, and enjoys it all very much indeed. So, I shall be very sorry if he is told, but what bothers me is how to explain to

him the reason for our telling him what was not true. He is very advanced, and I know it will be difficult to avoid hurting him over this, as in all other things he has been told 'it is only pretending'. But it seemed to me such a pity to deprive him of the thrill of Father Christmas's visit. I should be so glad of your help."

It seems you have created rather a difficult problem for yourself and your boy by getting him to believe that there really is a Father Christmas. It is, I feel, a pity to do this, because it does not detract in the least from the child's enjoyment to know that it is "only pretending", any more than it detracts from our enjoyment of drama because we know that it's "only" acting. The thrill is not any the less when the child knows that Father Christmas is really his own father. I should always allow the child to understand this as soon as he begins to make any distinction between fact and fancy. I would not say to a child of two or three, "Daddy is going to pretend to be Father Christmas", but if he asked at any stage whether there was a real Father Christmas I should certainly not tell him that there was, since this creates a confusion as to the truth and untruth in the child's mind. It is very puzzling to him. I wonder very much whether an intelligent boy of six does, in fact, believe in a real Father Christmas of the legendary type, even though he appears to believe? Children often reflect more upon these things and see through our subterfuges more clearly than we like to believe, and it seems to me perfectly possible that your boy knows that it is only pretending, but is too loving and polite to let you know that he is aware of the distinction between reality and the pleasant little pretence.

At any rate, he is quite certain to hear other children say that Father Christmas is not real, or to gather from their references that this is so. I should be inclined definitely to forestall such a situation by telling him within the next two or three weeks, when some suitable moment in conversation occurs, that Father Christmas is not a real person in the same sense in which you and he are real. He is an imaginary figure, used to express the real goodwill of fathers to their children at Christmas time. What he represents is real, although he himself is not. And I should tell your boy quite frankly that you had not tried to make this plain to him before, but had spoken as if Father Christmas was literally real, in order that he should enjoy it more. I should say you knew that he would come to understand the difference later on, but that you had felt that he might enjoy all the pleasures of Christmas time more keenly. It cannot do any harm to let your boy know the real reason in this way. This will be much better than letting him find himself in a position of contradiction with other children and puzzlement as to why you told him what will then appear to be a downright lie. You could tell the boy what is also true, that the simpler peoples[5] of the world do still believe that Santa Claus and fairies and gnomes are quite real, although we understand them simply to be an imaginary way of expressing our own feelings and wishes. I think this should carry you through the difficulty successfully.

5 As Graham (2009, p. 317) explains, Isaacs believed in the "importance of heredity in determining the level of intelligence" – in common with the large majority of thinkers and writers of her era. So she would have taken it as read that some peoples and races were "simple". I have left the text in its original form and not edited it in any way for inherent offensiveness in the terminology used.

REFERENCES

Dweck, C. (2007) The Perils and Promises of Praise. *Educational Leadership*, 65(2): 34–39.

Freud, S. (1905) *Three Essays on the Theory of Sexuality*, Standard Edition VII. London: Hogarth.

Gardner, D.E.M. (1969) *Susan Isaacs: The First Biography*. London: Methuen Education Ltd.

Graham, P. (2009) *Susan Isaacs: A Life Freeing the Minds of Children*. London: Karnac Books.

Grosz, S. (2013) *The Examined Life: How We Lose and Find Ourselves*. London: Vintage Books.

Hardyment, C. (1984) *Dream Babies – Child Care from Locke to Spock*. Oxford: Oxford University Press.

Her Majesty's Stationery Office (HMSO) (1967) *Children and their Primary Schools: A Report of the Central Advisory Council for Education (England)* ("The Plowden Report"). Available online at: www.educationengland.org.uk/documents/plowden/plowden1967-1.html [19 June 2017].

Hinchelwood, R.D. (1989) *A Dictionary of Kleinian Thought*. London: Free Association Books.

Isaacs, S. (1930) *Intellectual Growth of Young Children*. London: Routledge and Kegan Paul.

Isaacs, S. (ed.) (1941) *The Cambridge Evacuation Survey: A Wartime Study in Social Welfare and Education. Contributions to modern education* (General editor – Susan Isaacs). London: Methuen and Co. Ltd.

Isaacs, S. (1948a) *Troubles of Children and Parents*. London: Methuen and Co. Ltd.

Isaacs, S. (1948b) On the Nature and Function of Phantasy. *International Journal of Psychoanalysis* 29: 73–97; republished (1952) in Melanie Klein, Paula Heimann, Susan Isaacs and Joan Riviere (eds) *Developments in Psychoanalysis*. London: Hogarth.

King. F.T. (1913) *The Feeding and Care of Baby*. London: Macmillan.

King, F.T. (1924) *The Expectant Mother, and Baby's First Months*. London: Macmillan.

Liebschner, J. (1992) *A Child's Work: Freedom and Play in Froebel's Educational Theory and Practice*. Cambridge: The Lutterworth Press.

March, N.H. (1915) *Towards Racial Health*. London: Routledge.

Pines, M. (2004) Isaacs, Susan Sutherland (1885–1948). *Dictionary of National Biography*. Oxford: Oxford University Press.

Whorton, James C. (2000) *Inner Hygiene: Constipation and the Pursuit of Health in Modern Society*. Oxford: Oxford University Press.

INDEX

 Taylor & Francis eBooks

Helping you to choose the right eBooks for your Library

Add Routledge titles to your library's digital collection today. Taylor and Francis ebooks contains over 50,000 titles in the Humanities, Social Sciences, Behavioural Sciences, Built Environment and Law.

Choose from a range of subject packages or create your own!

Benefits for you

» Free MARC records
» COUNTER-compliant usage statistics
» Flexible purchase and pricing options
» All titles DRM-free.

Benefits for your user

» Off-site, anytime access via Athens or referring URL
» Print or copy pages or chapters
» Full content search
» Bookmark, highlight and annotate text
» Access to thousands of pages of quality research at the click of a button.

REQUEST YOUR **FREE** INSTITUTIONAL TRIAL TODAY

Free Trials Available
We offer free trials to qualifying academic, corporate and government customers.

eCollections – Choose from over 30 subject eCollections, including:

Archaeology	Language Learning
Architecture	Law
Asian Studies	Literature
Business & Management	Media & Communication
Classical Studies	Middle East Studies
Construction	Music
Creative & Media Arts	Philosophy
Criminology & Criminal Justice	Planning
Economics	Politics
Education	Psychology & Mental Health
Energy	Religion
Engineering	Security
English Language & Linguistics	Social Work
Environment & Sustainability	Sociology
Geography	Sport
Health Studies	Theatre & Performance
History	Tourism, Hospitality & Events

For more information, pricing enquiries or to order a free trial, please contact your local sales team:
www.tandfebooks.com/page/sales

Routledge
Taylor & Francis Group

The home of Routledge books

www.tandfebooks.com